U·N·I·T·Y
IN THE WORK OF SERVICE

John Paul II

On the Occasion
of His Second Pastoral Visit
to the United States

National Conference of Catholic Bishops
United States Catholic Conference

Introduction

"Unity in the Work of Service" was the theme proposed by the National Conference of Catholic Bishops for the second pastoral visit of Pope John Paul II to the United States. From his arrival in Miami on September 10 to his departure from Detroit on September 19, the Holy Father exemplified its meaning in an extraordinary, edifying manner.

The presence of the Vicar of Christ not only expressed but also built up the unity in faith and charity—with him and with one another—of the Catholics of our land, while recalling the universality of the Church and the spiritual bonds linking American Catholics with their brothers and sisters in the faith everywhere. Moreover, Pope John Paul's pastoral visit was a great work of service to the Church and its people and was rendered with unstinting generosity and pastoral solicitude.

The papal visit was many things. Partly it was a kaleidoscopic series of moving events captured by the media in images which touched the hearts of millions. But it was also the occasion for homilies and addresses by the pope in which he presented Catholic doctrine and applied it memorably to contemporary circumstances, as well as an occasion for a number of thought-provoking presentations by women and men speaking on behalf of the ministries and apostolates sponsored by the Church in the United States. These structured dialogues contributed greatly to the success of the visit and the realization of its theme.

This volume contains the written record of the papal visit. Its contents deserve close and prayerful study. In this way the substantial achievements of those exciting ten days will not only be remembered, but also continued long into the future. Pope John Paul II's pastoral visit now is history, but "Unity in the Work of Service" remains the Church's mission and its mandate.

Most Reverend John L. May
Archbishop of St. Louis
President
National Conference of Catholic Bishops
United States Catholic Conference

CONTENTS

Miami, Florida

Columbia, South Carolina

New Orleans, Louisiana

Los Angeles, California

Tuesday, September 15, 1987

Wednesday, September 16, 1987

Monterey, California

Thursday, September 17, 1987

Homily at Monterey Eucharist / 175
Laguna Seca

Address at Carmel Mission Basilica / 179

San Francisco, California

Thursday, September 17, 1987

Address at Mission Dolores Basilica / 183

Meeting with Men and Women Religious
Saint Mary's Cathedral
    Presentation by Sister Helen Garvey / 185
    Presentation by Reverend Stephen Tutas / 190
    John Paul II's Response / 193

Friday, September 18, 1987

Meeting with the Laity from throughout the United States
Saint Mary's Cathedral
    Presentation by Mrs. Donna Hanson / 200
    Presentation by Dr. Patrick S. Hughes / 202
    John Paul II's Response / 207

Homily at San Francisco Eucharist / 213
Candlestick Park

Detroit, Michigan

Saturday, September 19, 1987

Meeting with Polish Americans / 219
Hamtramck

Meeting with Permanent Deacons and Their Wives
Ford Auditorium
    Welcome by Deacon Samuel M. Taub / 226
    John Paul II's Response / 227

Address on Social Justice Issues / 232
Hart Plaza

Homily at Detroit Eucharist / 240
Pontiac Silverdome

Departure from Detroit Metropolitan Airport / 244

MIAMI, FLORIDA

Thursday, September 10, 1987

Arrival at Miami International Airport

Welcome by President Ronald Reagan

Your Holiness, after an audience with you five years ago in Vatican City, I met a group of American priests and seminarians who were studying in Rome. And when I happened to mention my hope that one day you would return to the United States, and that perhaps this time your visit would extend to the South and the West—when I mentioned this—those seminarians broke into applause. Today, Your Holiness, you begin just such a return visit. And today, all America applauds.

In a document of the Second Vatican Council, which you helped to draft, it is written: "In language intelligible to every generation, the Church should be able to answer the ever-recurring questions which men ask about the meaning of this present life and of the life to come."

"In language intelligible to every generation"—certainly, no one can speak with greater force to our own generation than you. In Poland, you experienced Nazism and Communism. As pope, you suffered a terrorist attack that nearly claimed your life. Still you proclaim that the central message of our own time—that the central message of all time—is not hatred, but love.

During your papacy, you have taken this message to some 68 countries. You have celebrated Mass in the ancient capitals of Europe. You have spoken words of truth and comfort on the African savannah. You have visited new churches on the islands of the Pacific. You have addressed vast gatherings throughout South America and the Far East. Now you have come back to the United States, the nation of citizens from all nations.

If I might just interject something, Your Holiness, I know that in your travels you have made it a point to speak to people in their own language. Well, here in Miami, I have a suspicion that you will find many in your audience eager to hear you speak the beautiful language of Spain.

1

But in this, the very month of your visit, we in the United States will be celebrating the 200th anniversary of our Constitution. That document says a great deal about the fundamental values in which we Americans believe. In the words of the distinguished Catholic philosopher, Jacques Maritain: "The founding fathers were neither metaphysicians nor theologians, but their philosophy of life and their political philosophy, their notion of natural law and of human rights, were permeated with concepts worked out by Christian reason and backed up by an unshakeable religious feeling."

From the first, then, our nation embraced the belief that the individual is sacred and that God respects human liberty, so too must the State. In freedom, we Americans have in these 200 years built a great country—a country of goodness and abundance. Indeed, Your Holiness, it is precisely because we believe in freedom, because we respect the liberty of the individual in the economic as well as the political sphere, that we have achieved such prosperity.

We are justly proud of the Marshall Plan, whose 40th anniversary was celebrated in Europe earlier this year. In Europe and elsewhere, we continue to place our might on the side of human dignity. In Latin America and Asia, we are supporting the expansion of human freedom, in particular, the powerful movement toward democracy.

And yet, we Americans admit freely to our shortcomings. As you exhort us, we will listen. With all our hearts, we yearn to make this good land better still.

In Florida and South Carolina; in Louisiana and Texas; in Arizona, California, and Michigan; tens of thousands of Americans—more than 50 million Catholics—will greet you. They do great works, America's Catholics, in the name of their Church.

Here in the United States, American Catholics put their faith into action in countless ways: maintaining parochial schools that give underprivileged children in our inner cities the chance to receive a good education; supporting the AIDS hospices established by Mother Teresa's Missionaries of Charity; and, perhaps simply putting, helping to put on a fund-raising dinner for the local parish. Abroad, American Catholics likewise seek to translate their faith into deeds, whether supporting missionaries in distant lands or helping America's Knights of Columbus restore the facade of Saint Peter's in Rome.

But it will not be Catholics alone who greet you. Protestants of every denomination, Jews, Muslims, even many with no defined faith at all—Americans of every kind and degree of belief—will wish Your Holiness well, responding to your moral leadership. Today's Florida sunshine is no warmer than the affection that you will meet.

I began a moment ago by quoting from one document of the Second Vatican Council. Permit me to close by quoting from a second.

"By the hidden and kindly mystery of God's will, a supernatural solidarity reigns among men. A consequence of this is that—one person's holiness helps others." Today, Americans feel this solidarity. And we thank you for the courage and sanctity, the kindness and wisdom with which you have done so much to help our troubled world.

On behalf of all Americans, Your Holiness, welcome back.

John Paul II's Response

Mr. President, Dear Friends, Dear People of America,

It is a great joy for me once again to be in your country, and I thank you for your warm welcome. I am deeply grateful to you all. I express my special thanks to the President of the United States, who honors me by his presence here today. I thank the bishops' conference and all the individual bishops who have invited me to their dioceses, and who have done so much to prepare for my visit.

My cordial greetings and good wishes go to all the people of this land. I thank you for opening your hearts to me and for supporting me by your prayers. I assure you of my own prayers.

To everyone, I repeat on this occasion what I said on that memorable day in 1979 when I arrived in Boston: "On my part I come to you, America, with sentiments of friendship, reverence, and esteem. I come as one who already knows you and loves you, as one who wishes you to fulfill completely your noble destiny of service to the world" (October 1, 1979).

Today, like then, I come to proclaim the gospel of Jesus Christ to all those who freely choose to listen to me; to tell again the story of God's love in the world; to spell out once more the message of human dignity, with its inalienable human rights and its inevitable human duties.

Like so many before me coming to America and to this very city of Miami, I come as a pilgrim: a pilgrim in the cause of justice and peace and human solidarity, striving to build up the one human family.

I come here as a pastor, the pastor of the Catholic Church, to speak and pray with the Catholic people. The theme of my visit, "Unity in the Work of Service," affords me the welcome opportunity to enter into ever deeper communion with them in our common service to the Lord. It also enables me to experience ever more keenly with them their hopes and joys, their anxieties and griefs.

I come as a friend, a friend of America and of all Americans: Catholics, Orthodox, Protestants and Jews, people of every religion, and all men and women of good will. I come as a friend of the poor and the sick and the dying; those who are struggling with the problems of each day; those who are rising and falling and stumbling on the

3

journey of life; those who are seeking and discovering, and those not yet finding the deep meaning of "life, liberty, and the pursuit of happiness."

And finally, I come to join you as you celebrate the Bicentennial of that great document, the Constitution of the United States of America. I willingly join you in your prayer of thanksgiving to God for the providential way in which the Constitution has served the people of this nation for two centuries; for the union it has formed; the justice it has established; the tranquillity and peace it has ensured; the general welfare it has promoted; and the blessings of liberty it has secured.

I join you also in asking God to inspire you—as Americans who have received so much in freedom and prosperity and human enrichment—to continue to share all this with so many brothers and sisters throughout the other countries of the world who are still waiting and hoping to live according to standards worthy of the children of God.

With great enthusiasm I look forward to being with you in the days ahead. Meanwhile, my prayer for all of you, dear people of America, is this:

> The Lord bless you and keep you!
> The Lord let his face shine upon you,
>   and be gracious to you!
> The Lord look upon you kindly
>   and give you peace! (Nm 6:24-26).

God bless America!

Address at Saint Mary's Cathedral

Dear Archbishop McCarthy and My Other Brother Bishops,
Dear Brothers and Sisters, Dear Friends,

It is a great joy for me to begin my pastoral visit here in Miami, in this Cathedral of Saint Mary's. This church represents a long history of faith and dedicated Christian life and witness on the part of countless clergy, religious, and laity in this city and in the State of Florida.

In coming among you, I wish to commend you for the "Jubilee Year of Reconciliation" that you have observed in preparation for my visit, and for the Archdiocesan Synod that you are holding. These events are meant to be of lasting spiritual value for all of you of the archdiocese, so that your Christian witness in everyday life may be ever more fruitful in the society of which you are a part. I also commend you for meeting the challenges of a rapidly expanding local Church. Over the years, you have welcomed hundreds of thousands of refugees of different languages and cultures, fleeing religious or political oppression. You have struggled along with them and for them to build a united community in Christ. I urge all of you—the clergy, religious, and laity of Miami, in communion with your archbishop and with me—to continue seeking ways to deepen our ecclesial unity in the one Body of Christ.

This unity is expressed in many ways. It is unity in preaching the gospel, professing the creed, celebrating the liturgy, and participating in the sacraments, especially the Holy Eucharist. It is unity in going forward as a missionary Church to evangelize the world. But our very presence in this house of God reminds us of another source of unity. I am referring to the personal prayer of each and every one of us, whether offered here in a moment of silence or amid the many settings in which our daily life unfolds. "The spiritual life," as the Second Vatican Council reminds us, "is not confined to participation in the liturgy. The Christian is certainly called to pray with others, but he must also enter into his room to pray to the Father in secret; indeed, according to the teaching of the Apostle Paul, he should pray without ceasing" (*Sacrosanctum Concilium*, 12).

People always have a great interest in prayer. Like the apostles, they want to know how to pray. The response that Jesus gives is one known to all of us: it is the "Our Father," in which he reveals in a few simple words all the essentials of prayer. The focus is not primarily on ourselves, but on the heavenly Father to whom we commit our lives in faith and trust. Our first concern must be his name, his Kingdom, his will. Only then do we ask for our daily bread, for forgiveness, and for deliverance from trials yet to come.

The "Our Father" teaches us that our relationship to God is one of dependence. We are his adopted sons and daughters through Christ. All that we are and all that we have comes from him and is destined to return to him. The "Our Father" also presents prayer to us as an expression of our desires. Beset as we are by human weakness, we naturally ask God for many things. Many times we may be tempted to think that he does not hear or answer us. But as Saint Augustine wisely reminds us, God already knows what we desire even before we ask. He says that prayer is for our benefit, because in praying we "exercise" our desires so that we will grasp what God is preparing to give us. It is an opportunity for us to "widen our hearts" (cf. *Letter to Proba*, Epistle 30).

In other words, God is always listening to us and answering us—but from the perspective of a love far greater and a knowledge far deeper than our own. When it appears that he is not fulfilling our desires by granting the things we ask, however unselfish and noble they may be, in reality he is purifying those desires of ours for the sake of a higher good that often surpasses our understanding in this life. The challenge is to "widen our hearts" by hallowing his name, by seeking his Kingdom, and by accepting his will. Like Christ in the

Garden of Gethsemane, we may sometimes pray either for ourselves or others, "Father, you have the power to do all things. Take this cup away!" But also like Christ we must add, "Not my will but your will be done" (cf. Mt 26:39,42; Mk 14:36; Lk 22:42).

The act of praying is also meant to open us up to God and our neighbor, not only in words but also in action. That is why Christian spirituality, following Jesus himself (cf. Mt 6), associates prayer with fasting and almsgiving. A life of self-denial and charity is a sign of conversion to God's way of thinking, to his way of love. By humbling ourselves through penance, we open ourselves to God. By giving in charity, over and above the demands of justice, we open ourselves to our neighbor. Saint Peter Chrysologus gives witness to this tradition when he says: "Prayer, fasting, and mercy . . . give life to one another. What prayer knocks for upon a door, fasting successfully begs and mercy receives. For, fasting is the soul of prayer; and mercy is the life of fasting. . . . Fasting does not germinate unless watered by mercy" (Sermon 43).

Dear brothers and sisters, we must never underestimate the power of prayer to further the Church's redemptive mission and to bring good where there is evil. As I mentioned earlier, we must be united in prayer. We pray not just for ourselves and our loved ones, but also for the needs of the universal Church and of all mankind—for the missions and for priestly and religious vocations, for the conversion of sinners and the salvation of all, for the sick and the dying. As members of the Communion of Saints, our prayer also embraces the souls of those in purgatory who, in the loving mercy of God, can still find after death the purification they need to enter into the happiness of heaven. Prayer also makes us realize that sometimes our own troubles and desires are small compared to the needs and to the sufferings of so many of our brothers and sisters throughout the world. There is the spiritual suffering of those who have lost their way in life because of sin or a lack of faith in God. There is the material suffering of millions of people who lack food, clothing, shelter, medicine, and education; of those who are deprived of the most fundamental human rights; of those who are exiles or refugees because of war and oppression. I know that Miami is no stranger to this kind of suffering. We must act to alleviate it, but we must also pray not only for those who suffer, but also for those who inflict suffering.

Dear bothers and sisters, as pastor of the whole Church, I have benefited from the prayers of millions of the faithful throughout the world, and today I express my gratitude to you for the prayers you offer for me, and I ask you to continue. Indeed, with Saint Paul I say, "Pray for me that God may put his word on my lips, that I may have courage to proclaim it as I ought" (Eph 6:19). And at this moment, I am praying in a special way for all of you who make up the household of the faith in this archdiocese. We are called today and always to remain united in prayer for the glory of the Father, and of the Son, and of the Holy Spirit. Amen.

Meeting with Priests from throughout the United States
Saint Martha's Church

Presentation by Reverend Frank J. McNulty

Your Holiness, welcome! Those of us here this afternoon represent a group of men far too large for this church, the priests of the United States. We come from every diocese in our country, and we bring the love, affection, esteem, and loyalty of all our brothers at home. We come with enthusiasm and with happy hearts because we have been chosen to spend this time with you. Your Holiness, the priests of this country are glad you have returned to us once again—a warm, joyful welcome from all of us.

I have entitled my presentation "If Priests Could Open Up Their Hearts" and begin with a story.

After a large dinner at one of England's stately mansions, a famous actor entertained the guests with stunning Shakespearean readings. Then, as an encore, he offered to accept a request. A shy, gray-haired priest asked if he knew the Twenty-Third Psalm. The actor said, "Yes, I do, and I will give it on one condition: that when I am finished you recite the very same psalm." The priest was a little embarrassed, but consented. The actor did a beautiful rendition: "My Shepherd is the Lord, there is nothing I shall want," and on and on. The guests applauded loudly when the actor was done, and then it was the priest's turn. The man got up and said the same words but this time there was no applause, just a hushed silence and the beginning of a tear in some eyes. The actor savored the silence for a few moments and then stood up. He said, "Ladies and Gentlemen, I hope you realize what happened here tonight. I knew the psalm, but this man knows the Shepherd."

All of us gathered here are dedicated to knowing the Shepherd. The men here tonight and their brothers back home have gotten to know him even better by walking the valleys of darkness with him. These recent years have not been easy for priests. But where there are valleys, there are also mountains, and if priests could open up their hearts and tell you of their priesthood, you would hear of "top of the mountain" moments—moments of joy, peace, and satisfaction. They would speak of ministry, and if you looked into their eyes, you would see a spark, a rejoicing in the Lord as their Shepherd, a rejoicing in their love of ministry.

Ministry is the center of our lives. Baptism and confirmation called us to that ministry, but ordination added a special dimension. On

7

that day, we became co-workers with the bishop, collaborators in his mission and yours to continue the work of Jesus Christ. Thus our loyalty has a solid base and so does our desire for unity with you, our bishops, and with each other. Bonding among priests and bishops has increased in our country through support groups, presbyterial councils, retreats, continuing education, convocations, and the like. There is communion. We treasure it; we yearn for more.

Priests value diversity too. Ours is a pluralistic society, and we have learned how to hold fast to our Catholic value system while respecting the convictions of other people. Our backgrounds are diverse, and we minister to multicultural, multiracial groups. Here in Miami, the priests serve at least 28 nationalities. In your letter to our bishops before their last meeting, you spoke of "Petrine Service," which among other things guarantees the Church her Catholic unity and protects our legitimate variety. We welcome all your efforts to do that. We share a dream with you and each other, to proclaim Jesus and his gospel, even if, at times, there are differences among us on just how to make that dream a reality. Because of this dream, the current emphasis on evangelization has captured our imagination.

If priests could open up their hearts and tell you of their priesthood, they would speak of joy and consolations. At times, the responsibility to minister in the name of Jesus is awesome, but what a source of happiness. The longer we are priests, the more convinced we are that our lives make a difference. Through our ministry of word and sacrament we are the instruments Jesus uses to nourish his people spiritually and to build them up as a community of faith and love.

This awesome responsibility is not without concerns. Today's world does not always appreciate the values which give our lives meaning. In such a climate, we must struggle to model our lives after that of Jesus, as we promised we would do when we were ordained. Those of us who give retreats to priests are edified to find in them such a deep longing, thirst, and hunger for a life of prayer. But we ask how we can develop that inner life when daily pressures and demands claim so much of our time and energy. Priests identify easily with the scene in Mark when the Lord goes off by himself to pray and his disciples find him to say, "Everyone is looking for you." We also ask how we can maintain our identity and spirituality, precisely as priests, while walking the journey with our people and sharing life's challenges with them.

If priests could open their hearts and tell you of their priesthood, they would speak of Vatican II. Bishops and theologians may have been the architects of that Council, but your priests are the ones who struggle to enflesh it every day in varied ministerial settings. Priests continue to bring the Council documents to life, especially the vision of Church in *Lumen Gentium* and *Gaudium et Spes*. They try hard to make their service collaborative and collegial; they try hard to make their decisions consultative and their responsibilities shared. They keep getting better at it. As they orchestrate the scene, they call the

8

laity to their rightful roles and walk the journey with them as fellow pilgrims. The renewed Church in this country is alive and well.

If priests could open up their hearts and tell you of their priesthood, they would speak of social justice. As we try to take courageous and prophetic stands, it helps us to know how close these questions are to your own heart and to hear your strong words. In a climate where we must at times be countercultural, we are heartened and strengthened by the episcopal conference of this country. Our bishops have not backed away from the complex and controversial issues of social justice.

If priests could open up their hearts and tell you of their priesthood, they would speak of God's people. We are eyewitnesses to wonderful things which do not get officially recorded: their enthusiasm, their spirit, their remarkable generosity, and especially their genuine love for priests. They understand our humanness; they forgive our failings; and they are a constant source of joy. And, with all this, they constantly challenge us to be holy.

On our part, we identify readily with the words of Ambrose to another bishop that "the most important thing is the people entrusted to our care." We recall our ordination day when we were urged to "always remember the example of the Good Shepherd who came not to be served but to serve and to seek out and rescue those who were lost." Because priests take that charge so seriously, there are some serious concerns about our ministry.

As we proclaim the moral message and help our people live out our value system, we sometimes find ourselves in tension. Our God is a God who calls us to be the best we can be, and a God rich in mercy, tenderness, and forgiveness. Our Church and we, as a part of it, are committed to a bold proclamation of the truth, even when it weighs heavy or is countercultural. Yet we are also a forgiving Church, ready to reflect the merciful Lord whose ambassadors we are. It troubles us that people often do not perceive the Church as proclaiming integral truth and divine mercy, but rather as sounding harsh, demanding. Sometimes it may be a question of style, for example, the technical approach of some of our ecclesial documents. Or it may be an altogether false perception, with no foundation in fact. But whatever the reason, as we meet the brokenhearted, wipe away tears, and seek out the lost sheep, we want them to hear the full truth and the full-hearted mercy of the gospel.

When Pope John XXIII opened the Vatican Council, he said, "Nowadays, the spouse of Christ prefers to make use of the medicine of mercy rather than that of severity. She considers that she meets the needs of the present day by demonstrating the validity of her teaching rather than by condemnation." As we go about trying to heal the wounded, it saddens us that many have a different image of the Church we love and serve. It saddens us that the Church is not as credible to those within it and to those outside of it, as we would like it to be.

9

If priests could open up their hearts and tell you of their priesthood, they would speak of worries. There is a real and dramatic shortage of priests, a situation critical enough to make us worry about the future. In some areas, each passing day finds the priest less able to meet needs and fulfill expectations. Age and ministerial fatigue are harsh realities. Morale suffers when we see so few young men follow in our footsteps. Morale suffers when we see parishes without priests and prayer services taking the place of Sunday Mass. We worry that we might become only a Church of the word and lose our sacramental tradition. The suffering intensifies when we realize that in ten years we could have half the present number of priests.

Yes, we must surely work and pray for vocations. Despite the many possibilities which compete for their attention, there are many generous young men who are willing to give their lives in service of the Lord as priests. We must personally invite them. Perhaps the greatest motivation of all for them is the joy we project in our own lives and ministry.

But even as we promote vocations, the celibacy question—as you so well know—continues to surface. Its value has eroded and continues to erode in the minds of many. This is of great concern to us because it has serious implications for the Church. We know, Holy Father, that you have been unequivocal in your support for the celibate commitment which thousands of priests in the United States have made and intend to keep. For your support, we are grateful because it is not easy to strive to be warm, loving, and affective men and yet remain faithful to that commitment. We can only ask you to continue along paths of support and exploration. Support for those who want to persevere; exploration of the gift of celibacy which has such a long tradition; exploration of how the discipline of celibacy can be most effectively implemented today; exploration of how priests can help each other make it a transparent sign of pastoral charity and the coming of the Kingdom in the pattern of Jesus Christ, our High Priest.

If priests could open up their hearts and tell you of their priesthood, they would speak of hopes. They hope that all charisms will be fully recognized, celebrated, and utilized in the Church. The charisms mentioned by Saint Paul in his letters provide a striking theme for your visit. Priests see the charism of pope and bishops as integral, necessary, and irrevocable. You are the authoritative teachers. As pastors, we share in this teaching function.

Theologians have a charism too, and we are grateful for their gift. They draw the traditions of faith into a fruitful encounter with contemporary realities and concerns. Our hope for them is for a free sense of inquiry and a loving fidelity to the wider mission of the Church. When they function with freedom and fidelity, we priests are supported in our pastoral efforts.

Those of us in pastoral work have a charism too. There is a collective wisdom that should be heard by the rest of the Church. Priests help people live and die; they baptize and bury; they celebrate sacraments; they lead the worship. They listen in every season and in every setting

10

to the tearing complexities and the wrenching ambiguities that the love and pain of human life create. Vatican II encourages people to speak their minds humbly and courageously about those matters in which they enjoy competence.

Priests enjoy competence in pastoral practices, the serving of that human life. We hope that real, effective, and felt participation from those engaged in pastoral work will always be the prelude to definitive decisions relating to pastoral practices. The point is not democratic consensus. Rather, priests hope that their collective wisdom will be heard as part of a process. This is why priests applaud the selection of a bishop who shares their competence. This is why they hope to continue to have a consultative voice in the selection of their bishops.

Although I am speaking today for the priests of the country and not for women in ministry, still the bonds of close collaboration between priests and women in ministry prompt me to offer some words about them. Priests are encouraged by Your Holiness' words of support to women whose service—as you have amply indicated—is essential for the life of the Church. We would also be greatly encouraged if the Holy See, together with the local churches, would continue to explore the range of service that women might appropriately offer the Church. Their collaboration with priests has been generous and effective. Our ministry tells us that they are gifted, willing, and needed. The movement of women toward practical equality is a major dynamic of our time. Because of the complexity and urgency of this movement, especially as it relates to the Church, there is need for study, reflection, and, above all, more dialogue with women.

If priests could open up their hearts and tell you of their priesthood, they could not do so without some controversial questions surfacing. In our country there is an attitude toward questions; it comes from our heritage, those historical events which help make us the way we are. We treasure freedom—freedom of conscience, freedom of religion, freedom of expression. Questions brought our nation into being. In such settings, people do not run from questions about what they believe and how they live out those beliefs. Priests know well that there are no easy answers but want to face the questions with honesty.

Last year, the priests of one diocese asked me to speak at their convocation about the state of the priesthood and gave simple instructions. "Be honest," they said, "but also be encouraging." I have tried this afternoon to be both. To be dishonest would be a terrible disservice to you and my brother priests.

And we do need encouragement—from you, from your Roman Congregations, from our bishops, from each other. It has been encouraging for all of us to look into the hearts of priests. How wonderful it is that priests care enough to have concerns, worries, fears, hopes, and questions about the Church and how she prospers. What an encouraging sign that they care so deeply about their people, particularly the alienated.

It has been encouraging to look into the hearts of priests, but not easy to articulate what is found there. A poet once said it this way:

Sometimes it happens in conversation: we stand
facing truth and lack the words,
have no gesture, no sign;
and yet—we feel—no word, no gesture
or sign would convey the whole image . . .

This is part of a poem called *Thought's Resistance to Words* by Karol Wojtyla. And this, too, is an encouraging note: that we have a pope who is also a poet, because poets know the human heart.

But most encouraging of all, Your Holiness, is this moment, this event. We and our priest brothers throughout our country are touched that you care enough to ask us how it has been for us. You have listened; we will do the same. Tell us what we can do to help build up the Body of Christ.

Your Holiness, our prayer is that today's words will be the deepening of an honest, ongoing, heart-to-heart dialogue.

John Paul II's Response

Dear Brother Priests,

Coming here today, I wish to open my heart to you and to celebrate with you the priesthood that we all share. I am convinced that there is no better way to start than to direct our thoughts to that Shepherd whom we all know, the Good Shepherd, the one High Priest, our Lord and Savior Jesus Christ.

My heart is full of gratitude and praise as I express my love for the priesthood, the vocation in which we participate not because we are worthy, but because Christ loves us and has entrusted to us this particular ministry of service. And I thank God for you, my brother priests. In the words of Saint Paul: "I thank God . . . whenever I remember you in my prayers . . . as indeed I do constantly, night and day" (2 Tm 1:3).

I am also grateful to you my brother priests for your welcome of fraternal love, expressed personally and through Father McNulty as your representative. I address my words to all of you present here and to all the priests in the United States. To all of you, I express my gratitude for your ministry, for your perseverance, for your faith and love, for the fact that you are striving to live the priesthood, close to the people, in truth—the truth of being ministers of Christ the Good Shepherd.

As priests, we all hold a "treasure in earthen vessels" (2 Cor 4:7). Through no merit of our own, and with all our human weaknesses, we have been called to proclaim God's word, to celebrate the sacred mysteries, especially the Eucharist, to care for the People of God, and to continue the Lord's ministry of reconciliation. In this way, we are servants both of the Lord and of his people, being ourselves constantly called to conversion, constantly invited to "walk in newness of life" (Rom 6:4).

I have come to the United States, my brother priests, in order to confirm you in your faith, according to the will of Christ (cf. Lk 22:32). I have come to you because I want all distances to be bridged, so that, together, we may grow and become ever more truly a communion of faith, hope and love. I affirm you in the good gifts you have received and in the generous response you have made to the Lord and his people, and I encourage you to become more and more like Jesus Christ, the Eternal High Priest, the Good Shepherd.

Saint Paul reminds us, as he reminded Timothy, to be fearless in serving Christ: "The Spirit God has given us is no cowardly spirit, but rather one that makes us strong, loving and wise. Therefore, never be ashamed of your testimony to our Lord . . . but with the strength which comes from God bear your share of the hardship which the gospel entails" (2 Tm 1:7-8). We know that proclaiming the gospel and living out our ministry very definitely entail hardship. It would be wrong to reduce priestly life to this one dimension of suffering, but it would also be wrong not to recognize this dimension or to resent it when we encounter it. We are not exempt from the human condition, nor can we ever escape that emptying of self, after the example of Jesus, who "was himself tested through what he suffered" (Heb 2:18).

It is important that we find satisfaction in our ministry, and that we be clear about the nature of the satisfaction which we can expect. The physical and emotional health of priests is an important factor in their overall human and priestly well-being, and it is necessary to provide for these. I commend your bishops and you yourselves for giving particular attention to these matters in recent years. Yet, the fulfillment that comes from our ministry does not, in the final analysis, consist in physical or psychological well-being; nor can it ever consist in material comfort and security. Our fulfillment depends on our relationship with Christ and on the service that we offer to his body, the Church. Each of us is most truly himself when he is "for others."

And just here, of course, arises a problem for us in our ministry. So much is asked of us by so many different people, and so often it seems that our response is inadequate to their needs. Sometimes this is due to our own human limitations. We can then be tempted to indulge in excessive self-criticism, forgetting that God can use our weakness as easily as our strength in order to accomplish will.

It is a great credit to you, my brothers, that you are striving to be merciful and gentle and forgiving like the Good Shepherd whom you know and imitate and love, and to whom you have pledged your fidelity. No other path is possible. Sometimes, however, what is asked of you in the name of compassion may not be in accord with the full truth of God, whose eternal law of love can never contradict the fact

13

that he is always "rich in mercy" (Eph 2:4). True mercy takes into account God's plan for humanity, and this plan, marked by the sign of the cross, was revealed by a merciful High Priest, who is able "to sympathize with our weakness, . . . one who was tempted every way that we are, yet never sinned" (Heb 4:15). If on the other hand, what is claimed to be a gesture of mercy goes contrary to the demands of God's word, it can never be truly compassionate or beneficial to our brothers and sisters in need. Jesus, who was himself the perfect expression of the Father's mercy, was also conscious of being "a sign of contradiction" (Lk 2:34). The apostle John tells us that, at a certain point in the Lord's ministry, "many of his disciples broke away and would not remain in his company any longer" (Jn 6:66).

And today there are indeed many sensitive issues which priests must deal with in their daily ministry. I know from listening to many priests and many bishops that there are different approaches to such issues. What is seen in one way by some of our brothers is evaluated differently by others. Yes, we all have questions that arise from the exercise of our priesthood, questions that require us to seek continually the light and wisdom that come only from the Holy Spirit.

In this regard, however, it is important for us to realize that the same Holy Spirit from whom come all the different and wonderful charisms, and who dwells in the hearts of all the faithful, has placed in the Church the specific charism of the Magisterium, through which he guides the whole community to the fullness of truth. Through the action of the Holy Spirit the promise of Christ is constantly being fulfilled: "Know that I am with you always, until the end of the world" (Mt 25:20). We know that through the Second Vatican Council the Church has clearly and collegially expressed her teaching on many of the sensitive issues and that much of this teaching has subsequently been reiterated in the different sessions of the Synod of Bishops. By its nature, therefore, this teaching of the Church is normative for the life of the Church and for all pastoral service. The forthcoming synod, after extensive consultation and fervent prayer, will consider at length and take a pastoral position on other important issues in the life of the Church.

I am very much aware that your fidelity to Christ's will for his Church and your pastoral sensitivity demand great sacrifice and generosity of spirit. As I told the bishops of the United States, just a few weeks after I was elected pope: "Like yourselves, I learned as a bishop to understand firsthand the ministry of priests, the problems affecting their lives, the splendid efforts they are making, the sacrifices that are an integral part of their service to God's people. Like yourselves, I am fully aware of how much Christ depends on his priests in order to fulfill in time his mission of redemption" (November 9, 1978).

In expressing the conviction that Christ needs his priests and wills to associate them with himself in his mission of salvation, we must also emphasize the consequence of this: the need for new vocations to the priesthood. It is truly necessary for the whole Church to work and pray for this intention. As Father McNulty stated so well, we

14

priests must personally invite generous young men to give their lives in the service of the Lord; they must truly be attracted by the joy that we project in our own lives and ministry.

There is still one more factor to be considered in evaluating the future of vocations, and it is the power of Christ's Paschal Mystery. As the Church of Christ, we are all called to profess his power before the world; to proclaim that he is able, in virtue of his death and resurrection, to draw young people to himself, in this generation as in the past; to declare that he is strong enough to attract young men even today to a life of self-sacrifice, pure love, and total dedication to the priesthood. As we profess this truth, as we proclaim with faith the power of the Lord of the harvest, we have a right to expect that he will grant the prayers that he himself has commanded to be offered. The present hour calls for great trust in him who has overcome the world.

The authentic renewal of the Church initiated by the Second Vatican Council has been a great gift of God to his people. Through the action of the Holy Spirit, an immense amount of good has been done. We must continue to pray and work that the Holy Spirit will bring his design to fulfillment in us. In this regard, priests have an indispensable role to play in the renewed life of the Church.

Each day the Church is being renewed by grace as she seeks a deeper and more penetrating understanding of the word of God, as she strives to worship more authentically in spirit and in truth, and as she recognizes and develops the gifts of all her members. These dimensions of renewal require those enduring tasks of priests which give their ministry its unique character, namely, the ministry of word and sacrament, the tending of the flock of Christ.

True renewal presupposes the clear, faithful, and effective proclamation of the word of God. The Second Vatican Council indicated that this is the priest's first task (*Presbyterorum Ordinis*, 4). Those who preach must do so with dynamic fidelity. This means being ever faithful to what has been handed on in Tradition and Scripture, as taught by the living pastoral authority of the Church, and making every effort to present the gospel as effectively as possible in its application to new circumstances of life. As often as the word is truly proclaimed, Christ's work of redemption continues. But what is proclaimed must first be lived.

Renewal in Christ greatly depends on the development of the Church's life of worship. Because we priests preside at the liturgy, we must come to know and appreciate the rites of the Church through study and prayer. We are called to lead celebrations which are both faithful to the Church's discipline and legitimately adapted, according to her norms for the good of our people.

Genuine renewal also depends upon the way in which priests exercise their task of tending the flock of Christ, especially as they encourage the faithful to use their gifts in the apostolate and in various special forms of service. The Church's commitment to evangelization, to proclaiming the word of God, to calling people to holiness of life, cannot be sustained without the tireless efforts and selfless support of priests. In the matter of inviting people, as Jesus did, to conversion—the total conversion of the gospel—the example of priests is extremely important for the authenticity of the Church's life.

This is particularly true in our own use of the Sacrament of Penance, through which we are repeatedly converted to the Lord. On this condition rests the full supernatural effectiveness of our "ministry of reconciliation" (2 Cor 5:18) and of our whole priestly lives. The experience of the Church teaches us that "the priest's celebration of the Eucharist and administration of the other sacraments, his pastoral zeal, his relationship with the faithful, his communion with his brother priests, his collaboration with his bishop, his life of prayer, in a word, the whole of his priestly existence, suffers an inexorable decline if by negligence or for some other reason he fails to receive the Sacrament of Penance at regular intervals and in a spirit of genuine faith and devotion. If a priest were no longer to go to confession or properly confess his sins, his priestly being and his priestly action would feel its effects very soon, and this would also be noticed by the community of which he was the pastor" (*Reconciliatio et Paenitentia*, 31).

People expect us to be men of faith and prayer. People look to us for Christ's truth and the teaching of his Church. They ask to see Christ's love incarnate in our lives. All this reminds us of a very basic truth, that the priest is "another Christ." In a sense, we priests are Christ to all those to whom we minister. This is true of all aspects of our priestly work. But it is particularly true in the Eucharistic Sacrifice from which our priestly identity flows and in which it is expressed most clearly and effectively. This truth has special relevance also for our service as ministers of the Sacrament of Reconciliation, through which we render a unique service to the cause of conversion and peace and to the advancement of God's Kingdom on earth. At this point, I would like to repeat those words which I have already addressed to the priests of the Church: "Praise then to this silent army of our brothers who have served well and serve each day the cause of reconciliation through the ministry of sacramental penance" (*Reconciliatio et Paenitentia*, 29).

In her mission to the world, the Church is renewed as she calls humanity to respond to God's commandment of love, and as she upholds and promotes the values of the gospel as they affect public life. In doing this, she becomes a prophetic voice on matters of truth and justice, mercy and peace. In these tasks involving the world, the leadership of priestly ministry has been and continues to be decisive. Priests who encourage and support the laity help them to exercise their own mission to bring the values of the gospel into public life. Thus, priests and lay people working together can challenge society itself to defend life and all human rights, to protect family life, to work for greater social justice, to promote peace.

One of the notable experiences of priests in the United States in the years since the Council has been a renewal of their spiritual lives.

Many priests have sought this renewal in groups of fraternal support, through spiritual direction, retreats, and other commendable endeavors. These priests have found their ministry revitalized by a rediscovery of the importance of personal prayer. As you continue to discover Christ both in your prayer and in your ministry, you will experience more deeply that he, the Good Shepherd, is the very center of your life, the very meaning of your priesthood.

My brothers, in speaking to you about prayer, I am not telling you what you do not know or urging you to do something that you do not practice. Prayer has been part of your daily lives since your seminary years and even earlier. But perseverance in prayer, as you know, is difficult. Dryness of spirit, external distractions, the tempting rationalization that we could be spending our time more usefully, these things are familiar to anyone who is trying to pray. Inevitably, at one time or another, these elements assail the prayer life of a priest.

For us priests, prayer is neither a luxury nor an option to be taken up or put aside as seems convenient. Prayer is essential to the pastoral life. Through prayer we grow in sensitivity to the Spirit of God at work in the Church and in ourselves. And we are made more aware of others, becoming more "attentive to their needs, to their lives and destiny." (Holy Thursday Letter to Priests, 1987, no. 11). Indeed, through prayer we come to love deeply those whom Jesus has entrusted to our ministry. Of special importance for our lives and our ministry is the great prayer of praise, the Liturgy of the Hours, which the Church enjoins on us and which we pray in her name and in the name of our Lord Jesus Christ.

In recent years, priests have often told me of the need they feel for support in their ministry. The challenges of priestly service today are indeed great, and the demands on our time and energy seem to increase every day. In such circumstances how easily we can give in to temptations to discouragement. But, dear brothers, at these times it is more important than ever that we heed the advice of the Letter to the Hebrews: "Let us keep our eyes fixed on Jesus, who inspires and perfects our faith. For the sake of the joy which lay before him he endured the cross, heedless of its shame. . . . Remember how he endured the opposition of sinners; hence do not grow despondent or abandon the struggle." (Heb 12:2-4).

The encouragement and support that we find in one another is a great gift of God's love, a characteristic of Christ's priesthood. The increase of mutual support among brother priests through prayer and sharing is a most encouraging sign. The same can be said, on a different level, for the development of presbyteral councils committed to the solidarity of priests with one another and with their bishop in the mission of the universal Church.

As priests we also need examples of priestly ministry, "artists" of pastoral work who both inspire us and intercede for us—priests like Philip Neri, Vincent de Paul, John Vianney, John Bosco, and Maximilian Kolbe. And we can also reflect upon the priestly lives of men

17

whom we have known personally, exemplary priests who inspire us because they have lived the one priestly ministry of Jesus Christ with deep generosity and love.

To persevere in our pastoral ministry we need above all that "one thing only" which Jesus tells us is "required" (cf. Lk 10:42). We need to know the Shepherd very well. We need a deep personal relationship with Christ—the source and supreme model of our priesthood—a relationship that requires union in prayer. Our love for Christ, rekindled frequently in prayer, especially prayer before the Blessed Sacrament, is at the foundation of our commitment to celibacy. This love also makes it possible for us, as servants of God's Kingdom, to love our people freely and chastely and deeply.

My brothers, sharing in the one priesthood of Christ, we share the same joys and sorrows. What a joy it is for me to be with you today. I thank you again for the gift of yourselves to Christ and his Church, and I want you to know that I am close to you in your efforts to serve the Lord and his people. You have my gratitude, my prayers, my support, and my love. And as I conclude, I express the hope that each of us will always experience the joy of which the psalmist speaks: "Behold, how good it is, and how pleasant, where brethren dwell at one!" (Ps 133:1).

Dear brother priests, Catholic unity is our vocation. As priests in America you are called to live this Catholic unity in the particular churches—the dioceses—to which you belong. But all these particular churches are never more completely themselves, never more faithful to their identity, than when they are living to the full the communion of faith and love of the universal Church. At the summit of your priestly ministry is this mystery of ecclesial unity, and you are called to live it in sacrifice and love, in union with Mary, the Mother of Jesus.

The protection and tender human love of our Blessed Mother is a great support to all of us priests. Her prayers assist us, her example challenges us, her closeness consoles us. In her presence we experience the joy and hope that we need so much. Is this not the day and the hour, dear brother priests, to turn to her as we must have done on our ordination day and to entrust to her anew ourselves, our people, and our sacred ministry. Why? For the glory of the Father, and of the Son, and of the Holy Spirit.

Dear priests of America, dear brothers, "My love to all of you in Christ Jesus" (1 Cor 16:24).

Meeting with President and Mrs. Reagan
Vizcaya

Mr. President,

I am grateful for the great courtesy that you extend to me by coming personally to meet me in this city of Miami. Thank you for this gesture of kindness and respect.

On my part, I cordially greet you as the elected Chief Executive of the United States of America. In addressing you, I express my own deep respect for the constitutional structure of this democracy which you are called to "preserve, protect, and defend." In addressing you, Mr. President, I greet once again all the American people with their history, their achievements, and their great possibilities of serving humanity.

I willingly pay honor to the United States for what she has accomplished for her own people, for all those whom she has embraced in a cultural creativity and welcomed into an indivisible national unity, according to her own motto: *E pluribus unum.* I thank America and all Americans—those of past generations and those of the present—for their generosity to millions of their fellow human beings throughout the world. Also today, I wish to extol the blessings and gifts that America has received from God and cultivated, and which have become the true values of the whole American Experiment in the past two centuries.

For all of you, this is a special hour in your history: the celebration of the Bicentennial of your Constitution. It is a time to recognize the meaning of that document and to reflect on important aspects of the constitutionalism that produced it. It is a time to recall the original American political faith, with its appeal to the sovereignty of God. To celebrate the origin of the United States is to stress those moral and spiritual principles, those ethical concerns that influenced your founding fathers and have been incorporated into the experience of America.

Eleven years ago, when your country was celebrating another great document, the Declaration of Independence, my predecessor Paul VI spoke to American congressmen in Rome. His statement is still pertinent today: "At every turn," he said, "your Bicentennial speaks to you of moral principles, religious convictions, inalienable rights given by the Creator." And he added: "We earnestly hope that . . . this commemoration of your Bicentennial will constitute a rededication to those sound moral principles formulated by your Founding Fathers and enshrined forever in your history" (*Address,* April 26, 1976).

Among the many admirable values of this nation, there is one that stands out in particular. It is freedom. The concept of freedom is part of the very fabric of this nation as a political community of free people. Freedom is a great gift, a great blessing of God.

From the beginning of America, freedom was directed to forming a well-ordered society and to promoting its peaceful life. Freedom was channeled to the fullness of human life, to the preservation of human dignity, and to the safeguarding of all human rights. An experience in ordered freedom is truly a cherished part of the history of this land.

This is the freedom that America is called to live and guard and to transmit. She is called to exercise it in such a way that it will also benefit the cause of freedom in other nations and among other peoples. The only true freedom, the only freedom that can truly satisfy is the freedom to do what we ought as human beings created by God according to his plan. It is the freedom to live the truth of what we are and who we are before God, the truth of our identity as children of God, as brothers and sisters in a common humanity. That is why Jesus Christ linked truth and freedom together, stating solemnly: "You will know the truth and the truth will set you free" (Jn 8:32). All people are called to recognize the liberating truth of the sovereignty of God over them, both as individuals and as nations.

The effort to guard and perfect the gift of freedom must also include the relentless pursuit of truth. In speaking to Americans on another occasion about the relationship between freedom and truth, I said that "as a people you have a shared responsibility for preserving freedom and for purifying it. Like so many other things of great value, freedom is fragile. Saint Peter recognized this when he told the Christians never to use their freedom 'as a pretext for evil' (1 Pt 2:16). Any distortion of truth or dissemination of nontruth is an offense against freedom; any manipulation of public opinion, any abuse of authority or power, or, on the other hand, just the omission of vigilance, endangers the heritage of a free people. But even more important, every contribution to promoting truth in charity consolidates freedom and builds up peace. When shared responsibility for freedom is truly accepted by all, a great new force is set at work for the service of humanity" (*Address*, June 21, 1980).

Service to humanity has always been a special part of the vocation of America and is still relevant today. In continuity with what I said to the President of the United States in 1979, I would now repeat: "Attachment to human values and to ethical concerns, which have been a hallmark of the American people, must be situated, especially in the present context of the growing interdependence of peoples across the globe, within the framework of the view that the common good of society embraces not just the individual nation to which one belongs but the citizens of the whole world. . . . The present-day relationships between peoples and between nations demand the establishment of greater international cooperation also in the economic field. The more powerful a nation is, the greater becomes its international responsibility, the greater also must be its commitment to the betterment of the lot of those whose very humanity is constantly

20

being threatened by want and need. . . . America, which in the past decades has demonstrated goodness and generosity in providing food for the hungry of the world, will, I am sure, be able to match this generosity with an equally convincing contribution to the establishing of a world order that will create the necessary economic and trade conditions for a more just relationship between all the nations of the world, in respect for their dignity and their own personality" (*Address at the White House*, October 6, 1979).

Linked to service, freedom is indeed a great gift of God to this nation. America needs freedom to be herself and to fulfill her mission in the world. At a difficult moment in the history of this country, a great American, Abraham Lincoln, spoke of a special need at that time: "that this nation under God shall have a new birth of freedom." A new birth of freedom is repeatedly necessary: freedom to exercise responsibility and generosity; freedom to meet the challenge of serving humanity; the freedom necessary to fulfill human destiny; the freedom to live by truth, to defend it against whatever distorts and manipulates it; the freedom to observe God's law—which is the supreme standard of all human liberty—the freedom to live as children of God, secure and happy; the freedom to be America in that constitutional democracy which was conceived to be "one nation under God, indivisible, with liberty and justice for all."

Friday, September 11, 1987

Meeting with Jewish Leadership
Metro-Dade Cultural Center

Presentation by Rabbi Mordecai Waxman

It is our honor and pleasure to welcome you to the United States. We do so in behalf of the Jewish organizations who are represented here today—organizations that have been in fruitful conversations with the Roman Catholic Church through the years. They include representatives of the American Jewish Committee; the American Jewish Congress; the Anti-Defamation League of B'nai Brith; and the Synagogue Council of America, which is here representing the Union of American Hebrew Congregations, United Synagogue of America, Central Conference of American Rabbis, and Rabbinical Assembly. Also present with us this morning are the leaders of other major organizations in American Jewish life, as well as members of the Greater-Miami Jewish community.

The men and women assembled here reflect the rich diversity of American Jewish life; we constitute a variety of religious and communal affiliations; American born and immigrant; some are survivors of the Shoah, the Nazi Holocaust, while others have never experienced the dark shadow of anti-Semitism in their own lives. We come from all sections of the United States, and we come as full participants in the pluralistic and democratic society that has encouraged us to be proudly American and fully Jewish at the same time. Your visit to this country happily coincides with the 200th anniversary of the U.S. Constitution, a document that guarantees religious liberty for all American citizens, which has enabled all faith communities to flourish in an atmosphere of religious pluralism. This has made possible a free and flourishing religious life for all.

It has been 22 years since the conclusion of the Second Vatican Council and the promulgation of *Nostra Aetate*. The broad teachings that emerged in 1965 have been further enriched and strengthened by a series of formal Catholic documents and pronouncements, some of them your own. These statements have transformed Catholic-Jewish relationships throughout the world, and this positive change is especially evident here in the United States.

As the largest Jewish community in the world, we have developed close and respectful ties with many Roman Catholics, both lay and clergy, and we value these warm relationships and treasure these friendships. We particularly cherish our relationship with the National Conference of Catholic Bishops and its Secretariat for Catholic-Jewish

Relations. In almost every place where Catholics and Jews live in the United States, we relate to each other in some organized fashion. We constantly exchange views and opinions, and as Jews and Catholics we often share our positions, sometimes agreeing, sometimes disagreeing, but always striving for a spirit of mutual respect and understanding.

Throughout the United States, American Jews and Catholics work in concert with one another on a wide range of social justice issues and fight for global human rights and against all forms of racism and bigotry. Our common agenda has always embraced, and our future agenda will continue to embrace, the many crucial problems of the human family as a whole.

One of the major achievements of our joint encounters is the shared recognition that each community must be understood in its own terms, as it understands itself. It is particularly gratifying that our Catholic-Jewish meetings are conducted in a spirit of candor and mutual respect.

Such meetings took place last week at the Vatican and at Castel Gondolfo. These conversations, although quickly arranged, were highly significant. You and high church leaders listened to the deeply felt concerns of the Jewish community that were raised following last June's state visit to the Vatican by Austrian President Kurt Waldheim, who has never expressed regrets for his Nazi past.

Obviously, the differences expressed at last week's meetings have not been resolved. However, this opportunity for us to express the pain and anger of the Jewish community in face-to-face meetings and for you and leaders of your church to listen with respect and openness, represents an important confirmation of the progress our communities have made in recent decades. One of the results of those meetings will be an instrumentality to develop closer communication and contact between our communities.

A basic belief of our Jewish faith is the need "to mend the world under the sovereignty of God"—"L'takken olam b'malkhut Shaddai." To mend the world means to do God's work in the world. It is in this spirit that Catholics and Jews should continue to address the social, moral, economic, and political problems of the world. Your presence here in the United States affords us the opportunity to reaffirm our commitment to the sacred imperative of "tikkun olam,"—"the mending of the world."

But before we can mend the world, we must first mend ourselves. A meeting such as this is part of the healing process that is now visibly underway between our two communities. It is clear that the teachings proclaimed in Nostra Aetate are becoming major concerns of the Catholic Church and, under your leadership, are being implemented in the teachings of the Church and in the life of Catholics everywhere.

Catholics and Jews have begun the long overdue process of reconciliation. We still have some way to go because Catholic-Jewish relations are often filled with ambivalences, ambiguities, and a painful history which must be confronted. Yet in a world of increasing in-

23

terreligious, interracial, and interethnic strife, the progress in Catholic-Jewish relations is one of this century's most positive developments.

We remain concerned with the persistence of anti-Semitism—the hatred of Jews and Judaism, which is on the rise in some parts of the world. We are encouraged by your vigorous leadership in denouncing all forms of anti-Semitism, and by the Church's recent teachings. The Church's repudiation of anti-Semitism is of critical importance in the struggle to eradicate this virulent plague from the entire human family. Anti-Semitism may affect the body of the Jew, but history has tragically shown that it assaults the soul of the Christian world and all others who succumb to this ancient, but persistent, pathology.

We hope that your strong condemnations of anti-Semitism will continue to be implemented in the schools, the parishes, teaching materials, and the liturgy and reflected in the attitudes and behavior of Catholics throughout the world. Greater attention needs to be paid to the Christian roots of anti-Semitism. The "teaching of contempt" for the Jews and Judaism must be ended once and for all.

The "teaching of contempt" reaped a demonic harvest during the Shoah, in which one-third of the Jewish people were murdered as a central component of a nation's policy. The Nazi Holocaust-Shoah brought together two very different forms of evil: on the one hand, it represented the triumph of an ideology of nationalism and racism, the suppression of human conscience, and the deification of the state—concepts that are profoundly anti-Christian as well as anti-Jewish. On the other hand, the Shoah was the culmination of centuries of anti-Semitism in European culture for which Christian teachings bear a heavy responsibility.

While your sensitive concerns and your noteworthy pronouncements about the Shoah have been heartening, we have observed recent tendencies to obscure the fact that Jews were the major target of Nazi genocidal policies. It is possible to visit Nazi death camps today and not be informed that the majority of its victims were Jews. Your letter about Shoah, sent last month to Archbishop John May, the President of the National Conference of Catholic Bishops, represented a deep level of understanding of that terrible period.

We look forward to the forthcoming Vatican document on the Shoah, the historical background of anti-Semitism, and its contemporary manifestations.

Many Catholic schools in the U.S. are already teaching about the Holocaust, and efforts are underway to develop a specific curriculum about the Shoah for Catholic students. This material is being jointly developed by Catholic and Jewish educators.

Even though many of the great centers of Jewish learning were destroyed during the Shoah, there has been a remarkable renewal of Jewish religious life throughout the world. This renaissance of the spirit is taking place not only in the United States, in the State of Israel, and in other lands of freedom, but in the Soviet Union as well. Many Soviet Jews are discovering that the covenant between God and the people of Israel is indeed "irrevocable" as you declared last year at the Grand Synagogue in Rome. The struggle of Soviet Jews to achieve freedom is a major concern of the Jewish community, and we appreciate the support American Catholics have given to this cause.

The return to Zion and the reestablishment of Jewish sovereignty in the land of Israel, play a paramount role in Jewish self-understanding today. Because of the importance that the State of Israel occupies in the mind, spirit, and heart of Jews, whenever Christians and Jews meet in a serious conversation, Israel is at the center of that encounter. The reemergence of an independent Jewish State onto the world stage in 1948 has compelled Christians and Jews to examine themselves and each other in a new light.

We must express our concern at the absence of full diplomatic relations between the Holy See and the State of Israel. We welcome the recent statements from Vatican leaders declaring that no theological reasons exist in Catholic doctrine to inhibit such relations. We strongly urge once again that full and formal diplomatic relations be established soon between the Vatican and the State of Israel. Such a step would be a positive and constructive contribution by the Vatican to the peace process, and it would send a strong signal to the international community that the Holy See recognizes Israel as a permanent and legitimate member of the family of nations.

One of the most welcome results of the recent Catholic-Jewish encounter has been the recognition by Catholics that Judaism has continued and deepened its unique spiritual development after the separation of the Christian Church from the Jewish people some nineteen hundred years ago.

A meeting such as today's is a vivid reminder that we live in an historic moment. Clearly, as two great communities of faith, repositories of moral and spiritual values, Catholics and Jews need to move together in this new moment. The last quarter-century has irreversibly changed the way we perceive and act toward each other.

In an age of great challenges and great possibilities, there is a compelling need for a "vision for the times,"—"*Chazon L'moed*" (Hb 2:3). Our vision for Catholics and Jews is a prayer of the Synagogue.

At the end of the Torah reading, the Scroll is held high so the entire congregation may see the words of God, and together the congregation prays, "*Hazak, Hazak, v'nithazek*,"—"Be strong, be very strong, and let us strengthen one another."

John Paul II's Response

Dear Friends, Representatives of So Many Jewish Organizations Assembled Here from across the United States, My Dear Jewish Brothers and Sisters,

I am grateful to you for your kind words of greeting. I am indeed pleased to be with you, especially at this time when the United States tour of the Vatican Judaica Collection begins. The wonderful material, including illuminated bibles and prayerbooks, demonstrates but a small part of the immense spiritual resources of Jewish tradition across the centuries and up to the present time, spiritual resources often used in fruitful cooperation with Christian artists.

It is fitting, at the beginning of our meeting to emphasize our faith in the one God, who chose Abraham, Isaac, and Jacob, and made with them a covenant of eternal love, which was never revoked (cf. Gn 27:13; Rom 11:29). It was rather confirmed by the gift of the Torah to Moses, opened by the prophets to the hope of eternal redemption and to the universal commitment for justice and peace. The Jewish people, the Church, and all believers in the merciful God, who is invoked in the Jewish prayers as 'Av Ha-Rakhamîm, can find in this fundamental covenant with the patriarchs a very substantial starting point for our dialogue and our common witness in the world.

It is also fitting to recall God's promise to Abraham and the spiritual fraternity which it established: "In your descendants all the nations shall find blessing, all this because you obeyed my command" (Gn 22:18). This spiritual fraternity, linked to obedience to God, requires a great mutual respect in humility and confidence. An objective consideration of our relations during the centuries must take into account this great need.

It is indeed worthy of note that the United States was founded by people who came to these shores, often as religious refugees. They aspired to being treated justly and to being accorded hospitality according to the word of God, as we read in Leviticus: "You shall treat the alien who resides with you no differently than the natives born among you; have the same love for him as for yourself; for you too were once aliens in the land of Egypt. I, the Lord, am your God" (Lv 19:34). Among these millions of immigrants there was a large number of Catholics and Jews. The same basic religious principles of freedom and justice, of equality and moral solidarity, affirmed in the Torah as well as in the Gospel, were in fact reflected in the high human ideals and in the protection of universal rights found in the United States. These in turn exercised a strong positive influence on the history of Europe and other parts of the world. But the paths of the immigrants in their new land were not always easy. Sadly enough, prejudice and discrimination were also known in the New World as well as in the

Old. Nevertheless, together, Jews and Catholics have contributed to the success of the American experiment in religious freedom, and, in this unique context, have given to the world a vigorous form of interreligious dialogue between our two ancient traditions. For those engaged in this dialogue, so important to the Church and to the Jewish people, I pray: May God bless you and make you strong for his service.

At the same time, our common heritage, task and hope do not eliminate our distinctive identities. Because of her specific Christian witness, "The Church must preach Jesus Christ to the world" (*1974 Guidelines*, I). In so doing we proclaim that "Christ is our peace" (Eph 2:14). As the apostle Paul said: "All this is from God, who through Christ reconciled us to himself and gave us the ministry of reconciliation" (2 Cor 5:18). At the same time, we recognize and appreciate the spiritual treasures of the Jewish people and their religious witness to God. A fraternal theological dialogue will try to understand, in the light of the mystery of redemption, how differences in faith should not cause enmity but open up the way of "reconciliation," so that in the end "God may be all in all" (1 Cor 15:28).

In this regard, I am pleased that the National Conference of Catholic Bishops and the Synagogue Council of America are initiating a consultation between Jewish leaders and bishops which should carry forward a dialogue on issues of the greatest interest to the two faith communities.

Considering history in the light of the principles of faith in God, we must also reflect on the catastrophic event of the Shoah, that ruthless and inhuman attempt to exterminate the Jewish people in Europe, an attempt that resulted in millions of victims including women and children, the elderly and the sick, exterminated only because they were Jews.

Considering this mystery of the suffering of Israel's children, their witness of hope, of faith, and of humanity under dehumanizing outrages, the Church experiences ever more deeply her common bond with the Jewish people and with their treasure of spiritual riches in the past and in the present.

It is also fitting to recall the strong, unequivocal efforts of the popes against anti-Semitism and Nazism at the height of the persecution against the Jews. Back in 1935, Pius XI declared that "anti-Semitism cannot be admitted" (September 6, 1935), and he declared the total opposition between Christianity and Nazism by stating that the Nazi cross is an "enemy of the Cross of Christ" (*Christmas Allocution*, 1938). And I am convinced that history will reveal ever more clearly and convincingly how deeply Pius XII felt the tragedy of the Jewish people, and how hard and effectively he worked to assist them during the Second World War.

Speaking in the name of humanity and Christian principles, the Bishops' Conference of the United States denounced the atrocities with a clear statement: "Since the murderous assault on Poland, utterly devoid of every semblance of humanity, there has been a premeditated and systematic extermination of the people of this nation. The same

27

satanic technique is being applied to many other peoples. We feel a deep sense of revulsion against the cruel indignities heaped upon the Jews in conquered countries and upon defenseless peoples not of our faith" (November 14, 1942).

We also remember many others, who, at risk of their own lives, helped persecuted Jews, and are honored by the Jews with the title of *Tzaddigê 'ummôt ha-'olâm* (Righteous of the Nations).

The terrible tragedy of your people has led many Jewish thinkers to reflect on the human condition with acute insights. Their vision of man and the roots of this vision in the teachings of the Bible, which we share in our common heritage of the Hebrew Scriptures, offer Jewish and Catholic scholars much useful material for reflection and dialogue.

In order to understand even more deeply the meaning of the Shoah and the historical roots of anti-Semitism that are related to it, joint collaboration and studies by Catholics and Jews on the Shoah should be continued. Such studies have already taken place through many conferences in your country, such as the national workshops on Christian-Jewish relations. The religious and historical implications of the Shoah for Christians and Jews will now be taken up formally by the International Catholic-Jewish Liaison Committee, meeting later this year in the United States for the first time. And as was affirmed in the important and very cordial meeting I had with Jewish leaders in Castelgandolfo on September 1, a Catholic document on the Shoah and anti-Semitism will be forthcoming, resulting from such serious studies.

Similarly, it is to be hoped that common educational programs on our historical and religious relations, which are well developed in your country, will truly promote mutual respect and teach future generations about the Holocaust so that never again will such a horror be possible. Never again.

When meeting the leaders of the Polish-Jewish community, in Warsaw, in June of this year, I underscored the fact that through the terrible experience of the Shoah, your people have become "a loud warning voice for all of humanity, for all nations, for all the powers of this world, for every system and every individual . . . a saving warning" (*Address of June 14, 1987*).

It is also desirable that in every diocese Catholics should implement, under the direction of the bishops, the statement of the Second Vatican Council and the subsequent instructions issued by the Holy See regarding the correct way to preach and teach about Jews and Judaism. I know that a great many efforts in this direction have already been made by Catholics, and I wish to express my gratitude to all those who have worked so diligently for this aim.

Necessary for any sincere dialogue is the intention of each partner to allow others to define themselves "in the light of their own religious experience" (*1970 Guidelines*, Introduction). In fidelity to this affirmation, Catholics recognize among the elements of the Jewish experience that Jews have a religious attachment to the land, which finds its roots in biblical tradition.

After the tragic extermination of the Shoah, the Jewish people began a new period in their history. They have a right to a homeland, as does any civil nation, according to international law. "For the Jewish people who live in the State of Israel and who preserve in that land such precious testimonies to their history and their faith, we must ask for the desired security and the due tranquillity that is the prerogative of every nation and condition of life and of progress for every society" (*Redemptionis Anno*, April 20, 1954).

What has been said about the right to a homeland also applies to the Palestinian people, so many of whom remain homeless and refugees. While all concerned must honestly reflect on the past—Muslims no less than Jews and Christians—it is time to forge those solutions which will lead to a just, complete, and lasting peace in that area. For this peace, I earnestly pray.

Finally, as I thank you once again for the warmth of your greeting to me, I give praise and thanks to the Lord for this fraternal meeting, for the gift of dialogue between our peoples, and for the new and deeper understanding between us. As our long relationship moves toward its third millennium, it is our great privilege in this generation to be witnesses to this progress.

It is my sincere hope that, as partners in dialogue, as fellow believers in the God who revealed himself, as children of Abraham, He will strive to render a common service to humanity, which is so much needed in this our day. We are called to collaborate in service and to unite in a common cause wherever a brother or sister is unattended, forgotten, neglected, or suffering in any way; wherever human rights are endangered or human dignity offended; wherever the rights of God are violated or ignored.

With the psalmist, I now repeat:

> I will hear what God proclaims;
>   the Lord—for he proclaims peace
> To his people, and to his faithful ones,
>   and to those who put in him their hope (Ps 85:9).

To all of you, dear friends, dear brothers and sisters; to all of you dear Jewish people of America, with great hope I wish you the peace of the Lord: *Shalom! Shalom!* God bless you on this Sabbath and in this year: *Shabbath Shalom! Shanah Tovah we-Hatimah Tovah!*

Homily at Miami Eucharist
Tamiani Park

Let the peoples praise you, O God;
let all the peoples praise you.
"Que todos los pueblos te alaben" (Ps 67:6).

Dear Brothers and Sisters in Christ,

The psalm of today's liturgy urges all the peoples and nations of the earth to give glory to God. In the exultant spirit of this exhortation I find myself on American soil, joined with all of you here in Miami, to express and praise the glory of God through the sacrifice of Jesus Christ, in the Eucharist. There is no better way to express God's glory than this sacrament. There is no other prayer which more profoundly unites earth with heaven, or the creature with the Creator, than the Eucharist. There is no other sacrifice in which everything that exists, and particularly man, is able to become a gift for the one who has so generously lavished him with gifts.

Dear brothers and sisters in Christ, all of you assembled here today in southern Florida and all the people of this land, you the great nation of the United States give glory to God together with me, the Bishop of Rome, the successor of Saint Peter, who is beginning here in Miami his act of papal service. May God's blessing be upon us. May the holy fear of God reach the ends of the earth (cf. Ps 67:8).

I am very pleased to be with you in Florida, this beautiful land of the sun. I warmly greet you, my brothers and sisters of the Catholic faith, and I extend cordial greetings to those of you who are not members of the Church but are here as welcome friends. I thank you all for coming. I also acknowledge among you the presence of so many ethnic groups, including Cubans, Haitians, Nicaraguans, others from Central America and the Caribbean, together with all the rest who make up the community of the Church. I embrace you all in the love of Christ.

The Church in Florida has a rich and varied history, extending back more than four and a half centuries. Ponce de Leon discovered this land at Easter time in 1513 and gave it the Spanish name for Easter, *Pascua Florida*. Hence the very name of your state recalls the central mystery of our Christian faith, the resurrection of our Lord and Savior Jesus Christ. The first settlement and the first parish of North America were established here in the early 1560s, more than 50 years before the Pilgrim Fathers landed at Plymouth Rock.

While Floridians can rightly be proud of their illustrious history, they can also boast of contemporary dynamism and expansion. Today, Miami is emerging as an international city of ever-increasing influence. It is a gateway, a crossroads of diverse cultures and languages, a center of communication, travel, and commerce, a bridge connecting early and modern American history.

This land of fascinating nature, this home of so many different peoples, this place of tourists and haven of senior citizens, this center of the scientific achievements of Cape Canaveral, this state which is Florida, has also been a land of rapid growth in building up the Body of Christ. An indication of this remarkable recent growth is the fact that within just 29 years the Catholic Church in Florida has grown from one diocese to seven. It is indeed a joy for me to be in the midst of this dynamic Church in Florida, a Church which proclaims by word and deed the Good News of the Easter mystery.

Who is the God whose glory we desire to proclaim by means of the Eucharist?

He is the God who shows us the way of salvation. Thus the psalmist, who urges all the nations of the earth to praise the glory of God, at the same time exclaims: "May your ways be known upon earth; among all nations your salvation" (Ps 67:3). Our God shows us the way. He is not the God of intellectual abstraction, but the God of the covenant, the God of salvation, the Good Shepherd.

Christ, the Son of the living God, speaks to us this very day in the gospel, using this word, so simple yet so eloquent and rich: *Shepherd!* "I am the Good Shepherd," he says. "I know my sheep and my sheep know me in the same way that the Father knows me and I know the Father" (Jn 10:14-15). In another passage of the gospel, Christ says to us: "No one knows the Son but the Father, and no one knows the Father but the Son—and anyone to whom the Son wishes to reveal him" (Mt 11:27). The Son, Jesus Christ, is the shepherd precisely because he reveals the Father to us. He is the Good Shepherd. And the Father is our shepherd through the Son, through Christ. And in his Son the Father wants us to have eternal life.

Jesus goes on to tell us, in words that speak eloquently of his deep love for us: "The Good Shepherd lays down his life for the sheep" (Jn 10:11). Who is this God whose truth we desire to confess by means of the Eucharist? He is the Father who in Christ gives life to us whom he created in his own image and likeness. This life in God is salvation. It is liberation from death. It is redemption from our sins. And this God is Christ, the Son who is of one substance with the Father, who became man for us and for our salvation, Christ the Good Shepherd who has given his very own life for the sheep.

The Eucharist proclaims this truth about God. The Sacrament of the Body and Blood of Christ is offered as a redemptive sacrifice for the sins of the world. It is the sacrament of the death and resurrection of Christ, in which our new life in God begins.

This God is Love. The Good Shepherd expresses this truth about God. More than the truth, he expresses the very reality of God as Love. Love desires what is good. It desires salvation. It is "gentle and patient," and it "will have no end" (cf. 1 Cor 13:4-8). It will not rest before it has nourished and given life to all in the great sheepfold, before it has embraced all. For this reason Jesus says: "I have other

31

sheep that do not belong to this fold. I must lead them, too, and they shall hear my voice. There shall be one flock then, one shepherd" (Jn 10:16).

We draw the image of the flock and the sheepfold from the text of John's gospel. At the same time, the reading from the Letter to the Ephesians that we have heard in today's liturgy enables us to see this image with the eyes of Paul the apostle. For him the flock is "the body" of which the head is Christ. And thus it is the Body of Christ. In this context, it is not difficult to find the likeness between the head and the shepherd.

At the same time, however, the entire image acquires a new meaning and a new expression. The shepherd leads the flock to the springs of life. As head, Christ is the source of life for all those who make up his body. Thus all of us, who as one single flock follow Christ the Good Shepherd, are at the same time called "to build up the body of Christ" (Eph 4:12).

According to the Letter to the Ephesians, this "building up" has two dimensions: a personal dimension and a community dimension. Each person must attain that form of perfection which is Christ come to full stature (cf. Eph 4:13). At the same time, we must all come to maturity "together" in the community of the Church. As the whole People of God, we move toward this fullness in Christ.

Christ gives the Church a rich variety of charisms for the purpose of deepening our communion as his Body. He bestows on the Church a great diversity of vocations, not just for the well-being of each person but for the good of all. As Saint Paul says of Jesus: "It is he who gave apostles, prophets, evangelists, pastors and teachers in roles of service for the faithful to build up the body of Christ till we become one in faith and in the knowledge of God's Son" (Eph 4:11-13).

The Church in the United States, and in a particular way the Church in Miami, experiences this mystery of unity in diversity in a very real sense. Yours is a community of compassion, which over and over again has echoed the message inscribed on the Statue of Liberty: "Give me your tired, your poor, your huddled masses yearning to breathe free." The civic community and the Church in southern Florida have time after time opened their arms to immigrants and refugees. These people were strangers and you welcomed them. And be sure that as often as you did it for them, you did it for Christ (cf. Mt 25:31-46).

I take this occasion to assure you of the Church's particular concern for those who leave their native countries in suffering and desperation. The frequent repetition of this experience is one of the saddest phenomena of our century. Yet it has often been accompanied by hope and heroism and new life. Here in Miami, I know, there are many who in the face of distress have been faithful to the gospel and the law of God. Like others who have remained faithful to Christ and his Church in time of oppression, you must guard and protect your Catholic faith as you now live your lives in freedom.

Fidelity to religious practice requires great personal effort in a complex and industrialized society. It takes maturity of faith and strong conviction to take up the cross each day and follow in the footsteps of Christ. In today's second reading we hear Saint Paul's encouragement: "Let us, then, be children no longer, tossed here and there, carried about by every wind of doctrine that originates in human trickery and skill in proposing error. Rather, let us profess the truth in love and grow to the full maturity of Christ the head" (Eph 4:14-15).

As I gaze at this great city with its many peoples and cultures, I pray that you will all help one another with your gifts. Stay in touch with your own roots, your cultures, and your traditions; pass on your heritage to your children; and at the same time, place all these gifts at the service of the whole community. Above all, "Make every effort to preserve the unity which has the Spirit as its origin and peace as its binding force" (Eph 4:3).

The work of building up the Body of Christ rests upon all of us in the Church. Certainly, there is a vital need today for evangelization. And it takes a variety of forms. There are many ways to serve the gospel. Despite scientific and technological progress, which truly reflects a form of human cooperation in the creative work of God, faith is challenged and even directly opposed by ideologies and life styles which acknowledge neither God nor the moral law.

Basic human and Christian values are challenged by crime, violence, and terrorism. Honesty and justice in business and public life are often violated. Throughout the world great sums are spent on armaments while millions of poor people struggle for the basic necessities of life. Alcohol and drug abuse take a heavy toll on individuals and on society. The commercial exploitation of sex through pornography offends human dignity and endangers the future of young people. Family life is subjected to powerful pressures as fornication, adultery, divorce, and contraception are wrongly regarded as acceptable by many. The unborn are cruelly killed and the lives of the elderly are in serious danger from a mentality that would open the door wide to euthanasia.

In the face of all this, however, faithful Christians must not be discouraged, nor can they conform to the spirit of the world. Instead, they are called upon to acknowledge the supremacy of God and his law, to raise their voices and join their efforts on behalf of moral values, to offer society the example of their own upright conduct, and to help those in need. Christians are called to act with the serene conviction that grace is more powerful than sin because of the victory of Christ's cross.

An important part of the mission of evangelization is the task of reconciliation. God "has reconciled us to himself through Christ and has given us the ministry of reconciliation" (2 Cor 5:1S). For this reason, I am happy that in preparation for my visit to the United States you have made special efforts to promote reconciliation, reconciliation with God, among yourselves and between different races

33

and cultures. In this context, too, I remind you of Christ's promise in today's gospel, namely, that when all of us truly listen to his voice, "there shall be one flock then, one shepherd" (Jn 10:16).

Deeply conscious of the truth as it is presented to us in this liturgy by the word of God, let us exclaim once again with the psalmist: "God be gracious to us and bless us, may the light of your face shine upon us" (Ps 67:2).

Who is this God to whom our prayer is addressed? Who is this God whom our community proclaims and to whom our hearts speak? Let us listen once again to the words of the prophet Zephaniah: "Fear not, O Zion, be not discouraged. The Lord, your God, is in your midst: a mighty savior" (Zep 3:16-17).

The Mighty One!

It is he whom we invoke here, in this land, which in so many ways manifests the strengths and achievements of humanity, of human genius, of intellect, of knowledge and science, of technology and progress.

> Who is this God? Once again let us repeat: the Mighty One!
> He alone is the Mighty One!
> He who is! (cf. Ex 3:14).
> He in whom "we live and move and have our being!" (Acts 17:28).
> "The Alpha and the Omega!"(Rv 1:8).
> He alone is the Mighty One! Because he alone is Love.

Here in this land, in this culture of the most advanced progress and affluence, is not the human person at times insecure and confused about the ultimate meaning of existence, the ultimate meaning of life? Is not the human person at times very far from Love?

> Yet only Love saves, and God is Love!
> O God of love, O God who saves,
>   "may the light of your face shine upon us" (Ps 67:2).
> Amen.

34

COLUMBIA, SOUTH CAROLINA

Friday, September 11, 1987

Address at Saint Peter's Church

You are the Messiah, the Son of the living God (Mt 16:16).

Dear Bishop Unterkoefler, Dear Brothers and Sisters in Christ,

These words, which are recorded in the gospel of Saint Matthew, were spoken by Simon Peter, the first bishop of Rome. They are full of meaning for everyone who believes in Christ, but they have special meaning for us who are gathered here today in this Church of Saint Peter in Columbia, which the successor of Peter is privileged to visit.

It is a great joy for me to come to the Diocese of Charleston. I thank you for receiving me with such warmth and fraternal love. Your famous "southern hospitality" makes me feel at home.

As you know, I have come to Columbia to take part in ecumenical dialogue with national leaders of other Christian churches and ecclesial communities and to join with a large gathering of our brothers and sisters in an ecumenical prayer service. Our Lord prayed "that all may be one" (Jn 17:21). We all want to do our part to make this unity come about.

You are the Messiah, the Son of the living God.

These words of Peter express the heart of our faith, for they reveal the mystery of Christ; they reveal Christ as the Son of the living God, the eternal Word who became man and was born of the Virgin Mary.

Peter was the first of the apostles, the first disciple to make a public declaration of his faith in Jesus the Messiah. The words of Peter's profession of faith were words spoken with real personal conviction; and yet, these words did not find their ultimate origin in him. As Jesus told him: "Blest are you, Simon son of Jonah. No mere man has revealed this to you, but my heavenly Father" (Mt 16:17). Faith in Christ is a gift. It is not a human achievement. Only God the Father can draw us to Jesus; only he can give us the grace to know Jesus, to accept him as the eternal Son of God, and to profess our faith in him.

35

From that day in the neighborhood of Caesarea Philippi, Peter's life was radically changed. And not only his life. The other apostles, the other disciples as well, were granted the gift of faith, and they too became witnesses of the words and deeds of Jesus. A whole new era began in the history of the world, in the history of salvation. And so it has continued down through the ages. People of all centuries, people from all countries have, like Peter, come to know Jesus, to accept him as God's Son—one in being with the Father—to profess their faith in him and to make his holy gospel the basis of their Christian lives. The person of Jesus Christ and his word are forever the center of the Church's life.

But the wonderful gift of faith is not separate from the cross. Belief in Christ is not free from difficulties. It is not without cost. In fact, our faith in Jesus Christ is often put to the test. Peter came to know this only too well. And therefore he writes: "You may for a time have to suffer the distress of many trials; but this is so that your faith, which is more precious than the passing splendor of fire-tried gold, may by its genuineness lead to praise, glory, and honor when Jesus Christ appears" (1 Pt 1:6-7).

We recall too the time, after our divine Master spoke of the mystery of the Eucharist, when "many of his disciples broke away and would not remain in his company any longer. Jesus then said to the Twelve, "Do you want to leave me too?' Simon Peter answered him, 'Lord: to whom shall we go? You have the words of eternal life. We have come to believe; we are convinced that you are God's holy one' " (Jn 6:66-69).

When our faith is tested, when we are tempted to doubt and turn away, we can find courage and renewed hope in these words of Peter: "Lord, to whom shall we go? You have the words of eternal life." Christ gives us the strength to live according to our faith and to meet all the challenges against it. From Christ, we must learn the way to overcome those sad divisions that still exist today among Christians. We must be eager to be fully one in faith and love.

I know that you share this ecumenical conviction with me. Indeed, Catholics in South Carolina have long felt the need for ecumenical dialogue and collaboration. First of all, because you are a distinct minority, less than three percent of the population. Moreover, the Catholic Church here has a long tradition of ecumenical initiative. Your first bishop, John England, accepted the invitations of other Christians to preach in their churches and to explain the teachings of our faith. And, with the passage of the years, you have never lost this ecumenical spirit.

In more recent times, in particular, you have joined with other Christian believers to promote justice and truth, to further mutual understanding and collaboration. This cooperation has been particularly striking in regard to efforts to improve racial relations among citizens of your state. I commend you in these deserving endeavors, so worthwhile and so important.

At the same time, you must never cease to strive for personal

36

holiness and conversion of heart. For, as the Second Vatican Council has said: "This change of heart and holiness of life, along with public and private prayer for the unity of Christians, should be regarded as the soul of the whole ecumenical movement" (*Unitatis Redintegratio*, 8).

Dear friends in Christ, representatives of all the Catholics of the Diocese of Charleston, I thank you for coming to greet me. I wish to assure you of my esteem for all of you who make up this local Church, spread out across this entire State of South Carolina. Know that the pope admires all the efforts you and your forebears have made to preserve your faith in Jesus Christ, to live this faith, and to transmit it to your children.

And now I ask you to take home with you those other words ascribed to Peter—words that explain so well what it means to believe in Christ, the Son of the living God. He wrote: "Although, you have never seen him, you love him, and without seeing you now believe in him and rejoice with inexpressible joy touched with glory because you are achieving faith's goal: your salvation" (1 Pt 1:8-9).

Dear Catholic people of this Diocese of Charleston, never forget that faith in Jesus Christ brings you to salvation and eternal life.

Meeting with Ecumenical Leaders
President's House, University of South Carolina

Statement of the Christian Leadership
Read by Bishop Philip R. Cousin

As representatives of Christian people in the United States of America, we welcome you, Pope John Paul II, in our country and in this city on this occasion. We greatly appreciate that you have made this visit to our country, for we believe that it is important that you become better acquainted with Christianity in America and with our nation, and that we as Christians and citizens here increase our understanding of you and your ministry.

We wish to express our gratitude and joy for this occasion, which has been initiated at your request and occurs as a result of your own ecumenical commitment. We view this meeting as one of historic significance. The prayers and the hopes of many American Christians uphold us in this meeting, that it may represent another step in the journey of reconciling the divided People of God.

The Churches in America

As Bishop of Rome and chief pastor of your Church, you have come here today as an ecumenical pilgrim. By this very action, you symbolize much of what is the United States. Most of the people of our land, either personally or in their family histories, share the immigrant experience. Some found their place here by forced slavery or impressment. But, with the exception of Native Americans, citizens of this country keep in their memory a journey and a heritage from other places and cultures. South Carolina is an illustration of this characteristic. In this place are Native American, black, and white persons, most of whom are Christians. Early in the history of this state, Anglicans, Baptists, Lutherans, Methodists, Roman Catholics, and other Christians settled here. In its diversity, South Carolina is typical of the American scene.

You will again notice, as you no doubt did during other visits to the United States, that this nation is like no other you have encountered during your extensive travels. This is true culturally and socially, and it is also true of our religious life. Many of our earliest immigrants from Europe—Jew and Christian alike—came here seeking religious freedom. From the beginning of our constitutional life, we have had a commitment to freedom of religious expression, though sometimes unrealized. We have neither ancient sees nor state churches. We do have a multiplicity of churches of diverse politics and histories, a gathering of Christian traditions. American Christians have been shaped by this pluralism, which includes freedom of religious expression, and have helped, in turn, to influence the nature of this pluralism. The variety of church life almost exceeds imagination. It includes the Roman Catholic Church, the black churches, the Orthodox churches; churches whose identities are influenced by the sixteenth-century Reformation; churches, movements, and organizations with American origins; and a variety of forms of witness.

In the course of American history, religious identities and divisions have been questioned and tested. Some Christians are challenged in their identity in America. Some are seeking an overarching and basic Christian identity and unity that are beyond and behind the present identities and divisions. The encounter of living communities representing Western Christianity and Eastern Christianity, for example, gives the opportunity for mutual discovery of the Christian tradition, including life, faith, and spirituality.

In our time, pressures of secularism and materialism are great throughout the world as they are here. Excessive individualism and consumerism are particularly evident in the United States. Nevertheless, church attendance here is comparatively high. The vast majority of Americans report in annual surveys that they believe in God. This reflects the paradox of being a most religious and secular people simultaneously. A sense of religious strength is present among us, which may offer the possibility of unique evangelical expression and ecumenical advance.

Trends and Issues

Today, moral and ethical values are being questioned, reflecting change in the diverse and complex American scene. Inadequacies of the past and present are being acknowledged. For example, we experience changes in relationships between women and men, the role of state and church in various aspects of family life, and the relationships between the poor and those who establish structures that either perpetuate or seek to ameliorate these conditions. While current trends can be threatening, they can also be liberating. The present situation is not only a social challenge and source of personal pain, but a theological challenge to Christianity in America to respond with integrity.

There is among us in the United States a heightened consciousness of the profound problems of the world and our nation. These include the issues of hunger, injustice, poverty, sexism, racism, and militarism. There is particular concern about the oppression of blacks, Hispanics, Native Americans, Asians, and women, and the needs of those who have disabilities. This oppression exists in both society and the churches. New ways must be developed to address it wherever it is found.

Such concerns necessarily involve the themes of justice, authority, and the movement of the Holy Spirit in society and Church. These concerns in the Church relate to personal freedoms, freedom of inquiry, the authority of bishops and other church leaders, and even the authority of Scripture and traditions. The Spirit is the source of a liberty that permits us faithfully to renew traditions and to be open to new occasions which call for new duties.

There is also among us in the United States a continuing deep interest in the Bible and its application to life and society. This has taken various directions among Christians, with a resulting spectrum of understandings and applications. In all of this, we sense a spiritual yearning that cannot be satisfied by secularism or materialism.

There is as well among us an increasing interest in spirituality. In the midst of our materialism, bible study, retreats, meditation, and prayer are in the ascendancy.

A continuing interest in ecumenism is also present among us. The councils and associations of churches across this country, the dialogues, and continuing relationships among churches all keep the vision of ecumenism alive. The dialogues among some of us have produced a movement of convergence indicated in such a landmark document as *Baptism, Eucharist, and Ministry*. There is interest in the official response of your own Church to this document.

There is also in our nation a renewed attention to Christian witness and evangelism. This is widespread, involving both the traditional churches and parachurch organizations in a wide variety of contexts and methods. There is continuing debate about the manner of responsible and effective witness.

Points of Conversation

Christians share a concern for moral values because of their common desire to witness to faith in Jesus Christ. Issues such as social justice, family life, the impact of technologies, stewardship of creation, and global peace remain urgent for us. In what concrete ways is collaboration possible with the Roman Catholic Church to promote justice, to exercise compassion, and to search for the peace of the resurrection?

Christians share a concern for the evangelical mission of the Church. Does our commitment to the proclamation of the gospel to the world bring us together or keep us apart? With growing insights into the principles of common witness resulting from closer contact and dialogue, how can we work with the Roman Catholic Church in concrete ways to bring the witness of the gospel to unbelievers?

Christians recall with humility the prayer of our Lord, Jesus Christ, for the unity of the Church. Since the Second Vatican Council, much has happened through theological dialogues and various contacts among churches, resulting in an increased awareness of Christian community (*koinonia*). Based on the considerable and careful work since the Council, how can we work with the Roman Catholic Church in concrete ways to take practical and responsible steps now to manifest this *koinonia*?

We thank you for this opportunity to initiate these conversations and pray that they will be a significant moment in our pilgrimage toward reconciliation. As we witness to the present and coming reign of God, let us work together to make the dawn of the third millennium since the advent of Christ a special time for deepening signs of unity, mission, and common witness in the world on behalf of the gospel of Jesus Christ.

John Paul II's Response

Dear Friends, Dear Brothers and Sisters,

I praise "the God and Father of our Lord Jesus Christ who has bestowed on us in Christ every spiritual blessing in the heavens" (Eph 1:3). In particular, I give thanks to him today for granting me the opportunity of this meeting with you, representatives of Christian churches and ecclesial communities in the United States. I believe that our meeting is important not only in itself, for the reflections and Christian experience that we share with each other, but also as an outspoken testimony on our part that we are definitively committed to treading the path which the Holy Spirit has opened before us: the path of repentance for our divisions and of working and praying for that perfect unity which the Lord himself wishes for his followers.

I am grateful to you for your presence, and for the statement with which you have wished to open this meeting. And in the wider perspective, I wish to thank you for the ecumenical contacts and collaboration in which you so willingly engage here in the United States with the National Conference of Bishops and the Catholic dioceses. Indeed, I am grateful for all the earnest ecumenical activity carried out in this country.

In recent decades, especially under the impulse of the Second Vatican Council, the Catholic Church has placed renewed emphasis on the term "communion" (*koinonia*) as an especially appropriate way of describing the profound divine and human reality of the Church, the Body of Christ, the unity of the baptized in the Father, the Son, and the Holy Spirit. Our communion is primarily with the Triune God, but it intimately unites us among ourselves.

This communion is increased in us as we share in the gifts with which Christ has endowed his Church. Some of these are eminently spiritual in nature, such as the life of grace; faith, hope, and charity; and other interior gifts of the Holy Spirit (cf. *Unitatis Redintegratio*, 3). In addition, there are exterior gifts, which include the word of God in Sacred Scripture, baptism, and the other sacraments, as well as the ministries and charisms which serve ecclesial life. Although we are not yet in agreement as to how each of our churches and ecclesial communities relates to the fullness of life and mission which flow from God's redemptive act through the cross and resurrection of Jesus Christ, it is no small achievement of the ecumenical movement that after centuries of mistrust, we humbly and sincerely recognize in each other's communities the presence and fruitfulness of Christ's gifts at work. For this divine action in the lives of all of us, we offer thanks to God.

I wish to note in particular the reference made in the opening statement to the sense of spiritual yearning among Christians in this country, a yearning which, in part, manifests itself in an increasing interest in the life of prayer, in spirituality, and in ecumenism. In a word, it is a yearning for deeper insights into our Christian identity and, consequently, for a renewal of our ecclesial life. This important phenomenon can be found to a greater or lesser degree in all ecclesial communities, not only in the United States but throughout the world. Surely it is a sign of the action of the Holy Spirit in the People of God. As leaders in our respective communions, we have the awesome task and privilege of collaborating to ensure that this grace will not be received by us in vain (cf. 2 Cor 6:1).

From the Catholic perspective, a primary factor relating to ecumenical involvement with other Christian bodies has been, from the outset, the purification and renewal of Catholic life itself. The Second Vatican Council's *Decree on Ecumenism* indicated: "In ecumenical work,

41

Catholics must assuredly be concerned for their separated brethren, praying for them, keeping them informed about the Church, making the first approaches toward them. But their primary duty is to make an honest and careful appraisal of whatever needs to be renewed and achieved in the Catholic household itself . . ." (*Unitatis Redintegratio,* 4).

It is not difficult to see how the internal renewal and purification of the ecclesial life of all of us is essential to any progress we may make toward unity. For Christ's call to unity is at the same time a call to holiness and a call to greater love. It is a call for us to render our witness more authentic. Only by becoming more faithful disciples of Jesus Christ can we hope to travel the path of unity under the guidance of the Holy Spirit and in the strength of his grace. Only by fully accepting Jesus Christ as the Lord of our lives can we empty ourselves of any negative thinking about each other.

It is important for all of us to realize how much conversion of heart depends on prayer, and how much prayer contributes to unity. The Second Vatican Council spoke about a "spiritual ecumenism" which it described as "the soul of the whole ecumenical movement," and which it identified as "a change of heart and holiness of life, coupled with public and private prayer for the unity of Christians" (*Unitatis Redintegratio,* 8).

In speaking of the priority of internal renewal and prayer in the ecumenical task, I do not intend in any way to minimize other important factors such as our common Christian service to those in need or our common study carried out in theological dialogues.

In the case of dialogues, the results reached in them thus far merit the most serious consideration and gratitude from all of us. They tend to increase mutual understanding in ways that have already greatly changed our relationship for the better. Our meeting here today is itself a testimony of this.

Further, these dialogues continue to uncover the deep sources of our common faith and the extent to which that faith, even while we remain apart, is truly shared by our churches and ecclesial communities. In doing so, such exchanges help us to face our remaining differences in a more intelligible context. It is the task of dialogue to face these differences and to work toward the time when it will be possible for Christians to confess together the one faith and to celebrate together the one Eucharist.

On the international level, the response of the Catholic Church to the document *Baptism, Eucharist, and Ministry,* which has now been sent to the Commission on Faith and Order, is an effort to contribute to this process directed toward confessing the one faith together. I am convinced that the Lord will give us the light and strength to pursue this course together for the glory of his name.

Indispensable as the work of dialogue is, and even though the act of dialogue itself begins to improve relations between us, our ultimate purpose goes beyond the statements and reports of ecumenical commissions. Those statements must be properly evaluated by our respective churches and ecclesial communities in order to determine the level of ecclesial communion that actually exists, so that it may be properly reflected in the "lifestream" of ecclesial life. We must greatly rejoice in discovering the extent to which we are already united, while we respectfully and serenely acknowledge the factors that still divide us.

In regard to our common service and collaboration, the statement you have presented puts before all of us important questions: How may we collaborate to promote justice? exercise compassion? search for peace? bring the witness of the gospel to unbelievers? manifest our *koinonia?* These issues challenge all of us. Together we must seek to discover the concrete ways in which we may respond in common.

You rightly designate these questions as "points of conversation" among us. As an initial approach, an introduction to our conversation, I would like to make the following brief remarks. First, we are all convinced that the deepest lessons a Christian can learn in this life are learned at the foot of the cross. When our churches and ecclesial communities address one another and the whole human family, we must do so from the foot of the cross of Jesus Christ, the wellspring of wisdom and the source of our witness. From the cross, we learn the qualities required in our ecumenical search for unity. "For it is from newness of attitudes (cf. Eph 4:23), from self-denial and un-stinted love that yearnings for unity take their rise and grow toward maturity" (*Unitatis Redintegratio*, 7). Ecumenism is not a matter of power and human "tactics." It is a service of truth in love and humble submission to God.

Similarly, our collaboration in the important areas you list is not a matter of measured calculation. We do not collaborate simply for the sake of efficiency, or for reasons of mere strategy, or for advantage and influence. We collaborate for the sake of Christ, who urges us to be one in him and in the Father, so that the world may believe (cf. Jn 17:21).

The ecumenical community has now welcomed me twice to this country. I, in turn, have had the joyful opportunity of welcoming many of you to Rome, the City of the Apostles and Martyrs, Peter and Paul. I believe that these and other cordial meetings have the effect, with God's grace, of breaking down the barriers of misunder-standing that have plagued us for centuries. How often we read in the Scriptures of encounters being occasions of grace, either encoun-ters of the Lord with his disciples or encounters of the disciples with others to whom they are bringing the word. I believe that in meetings such as these, where two or three or more of us are gathered in his name, Christ is here in our midst, asking from each of us a greater depth of commitment to service in his name, and, therefore, a greater degree of unity among ourselves.

I join my prayer to yours that the Christian communities of the United States may continue to meet with each other, to work with each other, and to pray with each other, so that the Father will be glorified in the fulfillment of Christ's prayer:

That their unity may be complete.
So shall the world know that you sent me,
    and that you loved them as you loved me (Jn 17:23).

So be it.

Address at the Ecumenical Prayer Service
Williams-Brice Stadium

Praised be Jesus Christ!

Dear Brothers and Sisters,

I greet each one of you in our Lord and Savior Jesus Christ. It is indeed the "Lord of both the dead and the living" (Rom 14:9) who has brought us together in this holy assembly of Christian people, a joy-filled gathering of different ecclesial communions: Orthodox, Anglicans, Methodists, Baptists, Lutherans, Presbyterians, members of the United Church of Christ and of other Reformed Churches, Disciples of Christ, members of the Peace Churches, Pentecostals, members of the Polish National Catholic Church, and Catholics.

We stand, side by side, to confess Jesus Christ, "the one mediator between God and man" (1 Tm 2:5), for "at Jesus' name every knee must bend in the heavens, on the earth and under the earth, and every tongue proclaim to the glory of God the Father: Jesus Christ is Lord!" (Phil 2:10).

We have come here to pray, and in doing so we are following the example of all the saints from the beginning, especially the apostles, who in awaiting the Holy Spirit "devoted themselves to prayer, together with the women and Mary the Mother of Jesus, and with his brethren" (Acts 1:14). Together we are renewing our common faith in the eternal redemption which we have obtained through the cross of Jesus Christ (cf. Heb 9:12), and our hope that, just as Jesus rose from the dead, so too we shall rise to eternal life (cf. Phil 3:11). In fact, through our baptism in the name of the Father and of the Son and of the Holy Spirit, we have been buried with Christ "so that, just as Christ was raised from the dead by the glory of the Father, we too might live a new life" (Rom 6:4). Living a new life in the Spirit, we are a pilgrim people, pressing forward amid the persecutions of the world and the consolations of God, announcing the death of the Lord until he comes (cf. 1 Cor 11:26; *Lumen Gentium*, 8).

Brothers and sisters, we are divided in many ways in our faith and discipleship. But we are here together today as sons and daughters of the one Father, calling upon the one Lord Jesus Christ, in the love which the same Holy Spirit pours forth into our hearts. Let us give thanks to God and let us rejoice in this fellowship. And let us commit ourselves further to the great task which Jesus himself urges upon us: to go forward along the path of Christian reconciliation and unity "without obstructing the ways of divine Providence and without pre-judging the future inspiration of the Holy Spirit" (*Unitatis Redintegratio*, 24).

In this service of Christian witness, we have listened together to the word of God given to us in the Holy Scriptures. The Scriptures are dear to all of us. They are one of the greatest treasures we share. In the Sacred Scriptures and in the deeds of divine mercy which they narrate, God our Father, out of the abundance of his love, speaks to us as his children and lives among us. The Bible is holy because in its inspired and unalterable words the voice of the Holy Spirit lives and is heard among us, sounding again and again in the Church from age to age and from generation to generation (cf. *Dei Verbum*, 21).

Today, this stadium has resounded with passages from Holy Scripture bearing on the reality of the family. We have heard the plea and promise made by the young widow, Ruth: "wherever you go I will go, wherever you lodge I will lodge, your people shall be my people, and your God my God. Wherever you die I will die and there be buried" (Ru 1:16-17). To hear these words is to be moved with a deep feeling for the strength of family ties—stronger than the fear of hardships to be faced; stronger than the fear of exile in an unfamiliar land; stronger than the fear of possible rejection. The bond that unites a family is not only a matter of natural kinship or of shared life and experience. It is essentially a holy and religious bond. Marriage and the family are sacred realities.

The sacredness of Christian marriage consists in the fact that in God's plan the marriage covenant between a man and a woman becomes the image and symbol of the Covenant which unites God and his people (cf. Hos 2:21; Jer 3:6-13; Is 54:5-10). It is the sign of Christ's love for his Church (cf. Eph 5:32). Because God's love is faithful and irrevocable, so those who have been married "in Christ" are called to remain faithful to each other forever. Did not Jesus himself say to us: "What therefore God has joined together, let no man put asunder" (cf. Mt 19:6)?

Contemporary society has a special need of the witness of couples who persevere in their union, as an eloquent, even if sometimes suffering, "sign" in our human condition of the steadfastness of God's love. Day after day, Christian married couples are called to open their hearts ever more to the Holy Spirit, whose power never fails, and who enables them to love each other as Christ has loved us. And, as Saint Paul writes to the Galatians, "the fruit of the Spirit is love, joy, peace, patient endurance, kindness, generosity, faith, mildness, and chastity" (Gal 5:22-23). All of this constitutes the rule of life and the program of personal development of Christian couples. And each

45

Christian community has a great responsibility to sustain couples in their love.

From such love, Christian families are born. In them children are welcomed as a splendid gift of God's goodness, and they are educated in the essential values of human life, learning above all that "man is more precious for what he is than for what he has" (cf. *Gaudium et Spes*, 35). The entire family endeavors to practice respect for the dignity of every individual and to offer disinterested service to those in need (cf. *Familiaris Consortio*, 37).

Christian families exist to form a communion of persons in love. As such, the Church and the family are, each in its own way, living representations in human history of the eternal loving communion of the Three Persons of the Most Holy Trinity. In fact, the family is called the "Church in miniature," "the domestic Church," a particular expression of the Church through the human experience of love and common life (cf. *Familiaris Consortio*, 49). Like the Church, the family ought to be a place where the gospel is transmitted and from which the gospel radiates to other families and to the whole of society.

In America and throughout the world, the family is being shaken to its roots. The consequences for individuals and society in personal and collective instability and unhappiness are incalculable. Yet, it is heartening to know that in the face of this extraordinary challenge many Christians are committing themselves to the defense and support of family life. In recent years, the Catholic Church, especially on the occasion of the 1980 Synod of Bishops, has been involved in an extensive reflection on the role of the Christian family in the modern world. This is a field in which there must be the maximum collaboration among all who confess Jesus Christ.

So often the pressures of modern living separate husbands and wives from one another, threatening their lifelong interdependence in love and fidelity. Can we also not be concerned about the impact of cultural pressures upon relations between the generations? upon parental authority and the transmission of sacred values? Our Christian conscience should be deeply concerned about the way in which sins against love and against life are often presented as examples of "progress" and emancipation. Most often, are they not but the age-old forms of selfishness dressed up in a new language and presented in a new cultural framework?

Many of these problems are the result of a false notion of individual freedom at work in our culture, as if one could be free only when rejecting every objective norm of conduct, refusing to assume responsibility, or even refusing to put curbs on instincts and passions! Instead, true freedom implies that we are capable of choosing a good, without constraint. This is the truly human way of proceeding in the choices—big and small—which life puts before us. The fact that we are also able to choose not to act as we see we should is a necessary condition of our moral freedom. But in that case, we must account for the good that we fail to do and for the evil that we commit. This sense of moral accountability needs to be reawakened if society is to survive as a civilization of justice and solidarity.

It is true that our freedom is weakened and conditioned in many ways, not least as a consequence of the mysterious and dramatic history of mankind's original rebellion against the Creator's will, as indicated in the opening pages of the Book of Genesis. But we remain free and responsible beings who have been redeemed by Jesus Christ, and we must educate our freedom to recognize and choose what is right and good and to reject what does not conform to the original truth concerning our nature and our destiny as God's creatures. Truth—beginning with the truth of our redemption through the cross and resurrection of Jesus Christ—is the root and rule of freedom, the foundation and measure of all liberating action (cf. *Instruction on Christian Freedom and Liberation,* 3).

It would be a great tragedy for the entire human family if the United States, which prides itself on its consecration to freedom, were to lose sight of the true meaning of that noble word. America: You cannot insist on the right to choose, without also insisting on the duty to choose well, the duty to choose the truth. Already there is much breakdown and pain in your own society because fundamental values, essential to the well-being of individuals, families, and the entire nation, are being emptied of their real content.

And yet, at the same time, throughout this land there is a great stirring, an awareness of the urgent need to recapture the ultimate meaning of life and its fundamental values. Surely by now we must be convinced that only by recognizing the primacy of moral values can we use the immense possibilities offered by science and material progress to bring about the true advancement of the human person in truth, freedom, and dignity. As Christians, our specific contribution is to bring the wisdom of God's word to bear on the problems of modern living, in such a way that modern culture will be led to a more profoundly restored covenant with divine wisdom itself (cf. *Familiaris Consortio,* 8). As we heard proclaimed in the gospel reading, Jesus indicates that the supreme norm of our behavior and our relationships, including our relationship with him, is always obedience to the will of the Creator: "Whoever does the will of my heavenly Father is brother and sister and mother to me" (Mt 12:50).

Brothers and sisters, to the extent that God grants us to grow in Christian unity, let us work together to offer strength and support to families, on whom the well-being of society depends, and on whom our churches and ecclesial communities depend. May the families of America live with grateful hearts, giving thanks to the Lord for his blessings, praying for one another, bearing one another's burdens, welcoming one another as Christ has welcomed them.

My prayer for all of you at the end of this second day of my visit echoes the words of Paul to the Thessalonians: "May the God of peace make you perfect in holiness. . . . May the grace of our Lord Jesus Christ be with you" (1 Thes 5:23,28).

NEW ORLEANS, LOUISIANA

Address at Saint Louis Cathedral

*The grace of the Lord Jesus Christ,
and the love of God, and the fellowship
of the Holy Spirit be with you all!* (2 Cor 13:14).

Dear Archbishop Hannan, Dear Brothers and Sisters,

From this cathedral of Saint Louis I am happy to greet, in the name of the Most Holy Trinity, the whole Church in New Orleans, all those who make up her membership, all those who work together to fulfill her mission. In particular today I greet all of you, dear priests and religious of Louisiana. Here in this mother church of the archdiocese, I give thanks and praise to the living God for your lives of dedicated service to Christ and his Church.

This temple of God, this house of prayer and gate of heaven stands as the central point of the city of New Orleans, and from this place all distances are measured. Here Christ dwells in your midst, present in word and sacrament, making this a place of grace and blessing for all the People of God. Here God the Father is adored in spirit and truth (cf. Jn 4:23); and here the Holy Spirit is always at work in the hearts of the faithful, preparing them for the glory of the heavenly Jerusalem.

And just as this cathedral of Saint Louis is the focal point of the city of New Orleans, so too Christ is the very center of your lives. Christ is for you "the beginning and the end" (Rv 21:6); he is for you "the way, and the truth, and the life" (Jn 14:6). So closely are you identified with Christ that each of you can say, as did Saint Paul: "The life I live now is not my own; Christ is living in me. I still live my human life, but it is a life of faith in the Son of God, who loved me and gave himself for me" (Gal 2:20). And together with Saint Paul you must proclaim: "Nothing will be able to separate us from the love of God that comes to us in Christ Jesus, our Lord" (Rom 8:39).

The Church in Louisiana owes a great debt of gratitude to the many priests and religious who have labored here from the beginning. That tradition of heroic dedication in proclaiming the gospel of Christ by

49

word and deed continues today in the service that you render to the People of God. Always remember that the supernatural effectiveness of your service within the Church is linked to the witness of your life lived in union with Christ. You are therefore called to conform your lives more and more to the person and message of Jesus Christ. And never forget that the precise goal of all apostolic service is to lead all people to communion with the Most Holy Trinity.

Our lives as Christians find their origin and destiny in the mystery of the Most Holy Trinity, the fundamental mystery of our Christian faith. The one God whom we worship is a unity of Three Divine Persons, "equal in majesty, undivided in splendor, yet one Lord, one God, ever to be adored" (*Preface of the Most Holy Trinity*). The Father and the Son and the Holy Spirit exist in an eternal communion of life and love with one another. In the Church we are privileged to participate now and forever in the communion of life and love, which is the mystery of God, One in Three.

The Second Vatican Council teaches that "it is from the mission of the Son and the mission of the Holy Spirit that the Church takes her origin, in accordance with the decree of God the Father" (*Ad Gentes*, 2). Thus as members of the Church we benefit from the mission of the Son and the mission of the Holy Spirit which flow from "'that fountain of love' or charity within God the Father" (ibid., 2). It is from the Father, "who is 'origin without origin,' that the Son is begotten and the Holy Spirit proceeds through the Son" (ibid., 2).

In revealing to us the mystery of the Father, the Son carries out the Father's will and brings about our salvation. And in describing the mission of the Holy Spirit, the Council says: "When the work which the Father had given the Son to do on earth (cf. Jn 17:4) was accomplished, the Holy Spirit was sent on the day of Pentecost in order that he might forever sanctify the Church, and thus all believers would have access to the Father through Christ in the one Spirit (cf. Eph 2:15)" (*Lumen Gentium*, 4).

In Saint John's gospel we read: "No one has ever seen God. It is God the only Son, ever at the Father's side who revealed him" (Jn 1:18). Although the Old Testament contained elements that prepared us for the revelation of Jesus, it did not unveil this profound mystery of God: the mystery of the Father, the intimate life of God, the communion of the Three Divine Persons. Only the Son of God made man bears witness to the truth about the Trinity; only he reveals it.

The truth about the divine Sonship of Jesus and the Trinitarian mystery of the Father and the Son and the Holy Spirit are alluded to at the time of the Annunciation, as well as during the baptism of Jesus in the Jordan. Moreover, during his public ministry Jesus speaks about his Father and the Holy Spirit. In the gospel of John we find many affirmations by Jesus about the intimate union that he shares with the Father. But it is during his discourse at the Last Supper that Jesus discloses in a definitive way the truth about the Holy Spirit and the relationship which the Spirit has with the Father and the Son.

We can say that throughout his teaching Jesus "has opened up vistas closed to human reason" (*Gaudium et Spes*, 24) concerning the life of the One God in the Trinity of Divine Persons. When he had completed his Messianic mission and he was taking leave of his apostles on the day of his Ascension, Jesus announced to them: "Go, therefore, and make disciples of all nations. Baptize them, in the name of the Father, and of the Son, and of the Holy Spirit" (Mt 25:19). Thus with these last words Jesus solemnly entrusts to them the supreme truth of the undivided unity of the Most Holy Trinity.

Dear brothers and sisters, your life of service dedicated to Christ and his Church bears witness to the reality of God's love for his people. You joyfully proclaim the Good News of faith, that "God is love" (1 Jn 4:5). In Jesus' conversation with Nicodemus we hear those words: "Yes, God so loved the world that he gave his only Son, that whoever believes in him may not die but may have eternal life" (Jn 3:16). The Father so loved the world that he sent us his only Son, and through his Son he sent the Holy Spirit. Today and each day of our lives we celebrate the love of God the Father for each of us, the love revealed in the Word made flesh and in the gift of the Holy Spirit. Moreover, we proclaim that God sent his only Son into the world not to condemn the world, but that the world might be saved through him. Yes, we proclaim to the world God's everlasting love.

May the prayers of the Blessed Virgin Mary, Our Lady of Prompt Succor and Mother of Divine Love, help you and the whole Church in New Orleans and throughout Louisiana to bear witness to the merciful love of the Father, and the Son, and the Holy Spirit.

Meeting with Black Catholics
Louisiana Superdome

Dear Brothers and Sisters in Christ,

"Go into the whole world and proclaim the Good News to all creation" (Mk 16:15). With these words, our Lord Jesus Christ directed the Church to speak his own message of life to the whole human family. The apostles first responded to the Savior's call and travelled throughout the known world, sharing with everyone who would listen what they had seen and heard (cf. 1 Jn 1:3), speaking about God's Kingdom and about reconciliation in Christ.

Today, almost two thousand years later, the Church still seeks to respond generously to Christ's command. The world we must serve today is much bigger, and the people who long to hear the word of life are numerous indeed. While the words of the Lord remain true,

51

"The harvest is good but laborers are scarce" (Mt 9:37), still we rejoice that the Holy Spirit has enriched the Church with many hands for the harvest. There are worthy laborers in every corner of the earth, people of every culture, who are eager to live the gospel and to proclaim it by word and example.

I am especially happy to meet with you who make up the black Catholic leadership in the United States. Your great concern, both as blacks and as Catholics, is—and must always be—that all your black brothers and sisters throughout America may hear and embrace the saving and uplifting gospel of Jesus Christ. I willingly join my voice to those of the bishops of your country who are encouraging you to give priority to the great task of evangelization, to be missionaries of Christ's love and truth within your own black community. To all the members of the black community throughout the United States, I send my greetings of respect and esteem.

My dear brother bishops, who share with me the burdens and joys of the episcopacy, I am pleased that the universality of the gospel and the cultural diversity of your nation are increasingly mirrored in the composition of the American hierarchy. While your apostolic ministry draws you to serve all the faithful of your respective dioceses, and in collegial unity the whole Body of Christ, it is fitting for many reasons that your own black brothers and sisters should have a special right to your pastoral love and service. United with the successor of Peter in the College of Bishops, you are a sign of the unity and universality of the Church and of her mission. As bishops, we are entrusted with the task of preserving in its integrity the Good News of salvation and of presenting it as effectively as possible to our people, so that they may all discover in Jesus Christ "the way, and the truth, and the life" (Jn 14:6).

Our brothers in the priesthood, ministering in the person of Christ and in union with us, transmit the teaching of the faith and celebrate the sacred mysteries of salvation. How fruitful it is for the mission of the Church in America when so many priests from different racial and ethnic groups proclaim together Christ's liberating gospel and thus bear witness to the fact that it rightfully belongs to everyone.

The Church in the United States is distinguished by its large number of deacons, among whom are several hundred from the black Catholic community. As heralds of the gospel and servant ministers of Christ, dear brothers, you complete the threefold ministry of the Sacrament of Orders. In the Church you are called to the service of the word, of the Eucharist, and of charity. Your generous response is a clear indication of the growing maturity of the black Catholic community, a maturity emphasized by the black bishops of your country in their pastoral letter *What We Have Seen and Heard*.

Even in those days, by the grace of God now long past, when your people struggled under the terrible burden of slavery, brave spirits within the community embraced the evangelical counsels and dedicated themselves to the religious life. Thus they bore eloquent witness to the power of the Holy Spirit accomplishing the work of spiritual freedom even in the moment of physical oppression. Black religious today offer a comparable witness to the Church and society, proclaiming God's Kingdom to a world shackled by consumerism, mindless pleasure-seeking, and irresponsible individualism—shackles of the spirit which are even more destructive than the chains of physical slavery.

I am close to the whole black community in the great mission and responsibility of encouraging more and more young Americans of their race to respond to the Lord's invitation to religious life and the priesthood. I urge you to be faithful to prayer and to do all you can to ensure that those who are called will find the support and the assistance which they need in order to pursue these vocations and to persevere in them.

The Church's work of evangelization finds entry into the human community in a special way through the lives of lay people. As my predecessor Paul VI pointed out, the laity's "own field of evangelizing activity is the vast and complicated world of politics, society, and economics, but also the world of culture, of the sciences and the arts, of international life, of the mass media" (*Evangelii Nuntiandi*, 70). By fulfilling worthily the broad range of their temporal involvement, lay men and women bear witness in a unique way to the universal call to holiness. The witness of their faithful lives speaks an uplifting message to the world.

I express my deep love and esteem for the black Catholic community in the United States. Its vitality is a sign of hope for society. Composed as you are of many lifelong Catholics, and many who have more recently embraced the faith, together with a growing immigrant community, you reflect the Church's ability to bring together a diversity of people united in faith, hope, and love, sharing a communion with Christ in the Holy Spirit. I urge you to keep alive and active your rich cultural gifts. Always profess proudly before the whole Church and the whole world your love for God's word; it is a special blessing which you must forever treasure as a part of your heritage. Help us all to remember that authentic freedom comes from accepting the truth and from living one's life in accordance with it, and the full truth is found only in Christ Jesus. Continue to inspire us by your desire to forgive, as Jesus forgave, and by your desire to be reconciled with all the people of this nation, even those who would unjustly deny you the full exercise of your human rights.

I am sure that you share with me a special concern for that most basic human community, the family. Your faithful Christian families are a source of comfort in the face of the extraordinary pressures affecting society. Today, you must rediscover the spirit of family life which refuses to be destroyed in the face of even the most oppressive forces. Surely that spirit can be found in exploring your spiritual and cultural heritage. The inspiration you draw from the great men and women of your past will then allow your young people to see the value of a strong family life. Know that the pope stands united with the black community as it rises to embrace its full dignity and lofty destiny.

The family is the first setting of evangelization, the place where the Good News of Christ is first received, and then, in simple yet profound ways, handed on from generation to generation. At the same time, families in our time vitally depend upon the Church to defend their rights and to teach the obligations and responsibilities which lead to the fullness of joy and life. Thus, I urge all of you, especially the clergy and religious, to work for the promotion of family values within the local community. And I remind those responsible for making and administering laws and public policies that social problems are never solved, but only worsened, by positions which weaken or destroy the family.

Even in this wealthy nation, committed by its founding fathers to the dignity and equality of all persons, the black community suffers a disproportionate share of economic deprivation. Far too many of your young people receive less than an equal opportunity for a quality education and for gainful employment. The Church must continue to join her efforts with the efforts of others who are working to correct all imbalances and disorders of a social nature. Indeed, the Church can never remain silent in the face of injustice, wherever it is clearly present.

In the most difficult hours of your struggle for civil rights amidst discrimination and oppression, God himself guided your steps along the way of peace. Before the witness of history the response of non-violence stands, in the memory of this nation, as a monument of honor to the black community of the United States. Today as we recall those who with Christian vision opted for nonviolence as the only truly effective approach for ensuring and safeguarding human dignity, we cannot but think of the Reverend Dr. Martin Luther King, Jr. and of the providential role he played in contributing to the rightful human betterment of black Americans and therefore to the improvement of American society itself.

My dear brothers and sisters of the black community, it is the hour to give thanks to God for his liberating action in your history and in your lives. This liberating action is a sign and expression of Christ's Paschal Mystery, which in every age is effective in helping God's people to pass from bondage into their glorious vocation of full Christian freedom. And as you offer your prayer of thanksgiving, you must not fail to concern yourselves with the plight of your brothers and sisters in other places throughout the world. Black Americans must offer their own special solidarity of Christian love to all people who bear the heavy burden of oppression, whatever its physical or moral nature.

The Catholic Church has made a profound contribution to the lives of many members of the black community in this land through the splendid commitment of dioceses and parishes, many of you here have joined us at the table of unity and faith as a result of the evangelization carried out in these institutions. Catholic schools have a special place in the work of spreading the gospel of Christ. They are a great gift from God. Keep your Catholic schools strong and active. Their uncompromising Catholic identity and Catholic witness at every level must continue to enrich the black communities of this nation.

In addition to the schools, other means of evangelization should also be given priority. Among these, the means of social communication deserve special attention. The mass media are also a great gift of God's Providence and should be fully utilized in the service of the gospel of our Lord Jesus Christ. They can be of immense service to the millions of black people who long to hear the Good News of salvation proclaimed in ways that speak to their own heritage and traditions.

While remaining faithful to her doctrine and discipline, the Church esteems and honors all cultures; she respects them in all her evangelizing efforts among the various peoples. At the first Pentecost, those present heard the apostles speaking in their own languages (cf. Acts 2:4f). With the guidance of the Holy Spirit, we try in every age to bring the gospel convincingly and understandably to people of all races, languages, and cultures. It is important to realize that there is no black Church, no white Church, no American Church; but there is and must be, in the one Church of Jesus Christ, a home for blacks, whites, Americans, every culture and race. What I said on another occasion, I willingly repeat: "The Church is catholic . . . because she is able to present in every human context the revealed truth, preserved by her intact in its divine content, in such a way as to bring it into contact with the lofty thoughts and most expectations of every individual and every people" (*Slavorum Apostoli*, 18).

Dear brothers and sisters, your black cultural heritage enriches the Church and makes her witness of universality more complete. In a real way the Church needs you just as you need the Church, for you are part of the Church and the Church is part of you. As you continue to place this heritage at the service of the whole Church for the spread of the gospel, the Holy Spirit himself will continue through you his work of evangelization. With a joyful and a hopeful heart, I entrust you and the whole black community to the loving care of Mary, Mother of our Savior. May she, who both listened to the word and believed in it, guide your lives and those of future generations of black Catholics within the one People of God, the one Mystical Body of Christ. Through her intercession, may grace be to all of you "who love our Lord Jesus Christ with unfailing love" (Eph. 6:24).

Meeting with Leadership in Catholic Elementary, Secondary, and Religious Education
Louisiana Superdome

Dear Brothers and Sisters,

I thank all of you for your warm welcome and I praise our Lord and Savior Jesus Christ who gives me this opportunity to meet with you, the representatives of Catholic elementary and secondary schools and leaders in religious education. My first word to you is one of esteem and encouragement. I wish to assure you that I fully appreciate the extraordinary importance of your commitment to Catholic education. I commend you for your concern for the vitality and Catholic identity of the educational centers in which you work, throughout the length and breadth of the United States. I encourage you to continue to fulfill your special role within the Church and within society in a spirit of generous responsibility, intelligent creativity, and the pursuit of excellence.

It is fitting that we should be meeting in this historic city, itself the meeting-point of several rich cultures, where the Capuchin Fathers and the Ursuline Sisters founded schools at the very dawn of your emergence as a nation. You are preparing to observe the 200th anniversary of the signing of the Constitution of the United States. There is no doubt that the guarantee of religious freedom enshrined in the Bill of Rights has helped make possible the marvelous growth of Catholic education in this country.

Over the years much has been attempted and much has been achieved by Catholics in the United States to make available for their children the best education possible. Much has been done in the specific area of bringing the wealth of our Catholic faith to children and adults in the home, in schools, and through religious education programs. The presence of the Church in the field of education is wonderfully manifested in the vast and dynamic network of schools and educational programs extending from the preschool through the adult years. The entire ecclesial community, bishops, priests, religious, the laity, the Church in all her parts, is called to value ever more deeply the importance of this task and mission and to continue to give it full and enthusiastic support.

In the beginning and for a long time afterwards, women and men religious bore the chief organizational and teaching responsibilities in Catholic education in this country. As pioneers they met that challenge splendidly and they continue to meet it today. The Church and, I am certain, the nation will forever feel a debt of gratitude toward them. The importance of the presence of committed religious, and of religious communities, in the educational apostolate has not diminished

56

with time. It is my heartfelt prayer that the Lord will continue to call many young people to the religious life, and that their witness to the gospel will remain a central element in Catholic education.

In recent years, thousands of lay people have come forward as administrators and teachers in the Church's schools and educational programs. By accepting and developing the legacy of Catholic thought and educational experience which they have inherited, they take their place as full partners in the Church's mission of educating the whole person and of transmitting the Good News of salvation in Jesus Christ to successive generations of young Americans. Even if they do not "teach religion," their service in a Catholic school or educational program is part of the Church's unceasing endeavor to lead all to "profess the truth in love and grow to the full maturity of Christ the head" (Eph 4:15).

I am aware that not all questions relating to the organization, financing, and administration of Catholic schools in an increasingly complex society have been resolved to the satisfaction of all. We hope that such matters will be settled with justice and fairness for all. In this regard, it is important to proceed in a proper perspective. For a Catholic educator, the Church should not be looked upon merely as an employer. The Church is the Body of Christ, carrying on the mission of the Redeemer throughout history. It is our privilege to share in that mission, to which we are called by the grace of God and in which we are engaged together.

Permit me, brothers and sisters, to mention briefly something that is of special concern to the Church. I refer to the rights and duties of parents in the education of their children. The Second Vatican Council clearly enunciated the Church's position: "Since parents have conferred life on their children, they have a most solemn obligation to educate their offspring. Hence, parents must be acknowledged as the first and foremost educators of their children" (*Gravissimum Educationis,* 3). In comparison with the educational role of all others, their role is primary; it is also irreplaceable and inalienable. It would be wrong for anyone to attempt to usurp that unique responsibility (cf. *Familiaris Consortio,* 36). Nor should parents in any way be penalized for choosing for their children an education according to their beliefs.

Parents need to ensure that their own homes are places where spiritual and moral values are lived. They are right to insist that their children's faith be respected and fostered. As educators you correctly see your role as cooperating with parents in their primary responsibility. Your efforts to involve them in the whole educational process are commendable. This is an area in which pastors and other priests can be especially supportive. To these I wish to say, "Try to make every effort to ensure that religious education programs and, where possible, parish schools are an important part of your ministry; support and encourage teachers, administrators, and parents in their work." Few efforts are more important for the present and future well-being of the Church and of the nation than efforts expended in the work of education.

Catholic schools in the United States have always enjoyed a reputation for academic excellence and community service. Very often, they serve large numbers of poor children and young people and are attentive to the needs of minority groups. I heartily encourage you to continue to provide quality Catholic education for the poor of all races and national backgrounds, even at the cost of great sacrifice. We cannot doubt that such is part of God's call to the Church in the United States. It is a responsibility that is deeply inscribed in the history of Catholic education in this country.

On another occasion, speaking to the bishops of the United States, I mentioned that the Catholic school "has contributed immensely to the spreading of God's word and has enabled the faithful 'to relate human affairs and activities with religious values in a single living synthesis' (*Sapientia Christiana*, 1). In the community formed by the Catholic school, the power of the gospel has been brought to bear on thought patterns, standards of judgment and norms of behavior. As an institution the Catholic school has to be judged extremely favorably if we apply the sound criterion: 'You will know them by their deeds' (Mt 7:16), and again, 'You can tell a tree by its fruit' (Mt 7:20)" (*Address*, October 25, 1953).

At this point, I cannot fail to praise the financial sacrifices of American Catholics as well as the substantial contributions of individual benefactors, foundations, organizations, and business to Catholic education in the United States. The heroic sacrifices of generations of Catholic parents in building up and supporting parochial and diocesan schools must never be forgotten. Rising costs may call for new approaches, new forms of partnership and sharing, new uses of financial resources. But I am sure that all concerned will face the challenge of Catholic schools with courage and dedication and not doubt the value of the sacrifices to be made.

But there is another challenge facing all those who are concerned with Catholic education. It is the pressing challenge of clearly identifying the aims of Catholic education and applying proper methods in Catholic elementary and secondary education and religious education programs. It is the challenge of fully understanding the educational enterprise, of properly evaluating its content, and of transmitting the full truth concerning the human person, created in God's image and called to life in Christ through the Holy Spirit.

The content of the individual courses in Catholic education is important both in religious teaching and in all the other subjects that go to make up the total instruction of human persons and to prepare them for their life's work and their eternal destiny. It is fitting that teachers should be constantly challenged by high professional standards in preparing and teaching their courses. In regard to the content of religion courses, the essential criterion is fidelity to the teaching of the Church.

Educators are likewise in a splendid position to inculcate into young people right ethical attitudes. These include attitudes toward material things and their proper use. The whole life style of students will reflect the attitudes that they form during their years of formal education.

In these tasks you will find guidance in many documents of the Church. Your own bishops, applying the universal teaching of the Church, have helped point the way for you, notably in their pastoral letter *To Teach As Jesus Did* and in *The National Catechetical Directory*. I would also remind you of the Holy See's documents on *The Catholic School* and *Lay Catholics in Schools: Witnesses to Faith*. There we are reminded that it is the school's task to cultivate in students the intellectual, creative, and esthetic faculties of the individual; to develop in students the ability to make correct use of their judgment, will, and affectivity; to promote in them a sense of values; to encourage just attitudes and prudent behavior; to introduce them to the cultural patrimony handed down from previous generations; to prepare them for their working lives; and to encourage the friendly interchange among students of diverse cultures and backgrounds that will lead to mutual understanding and love.

The ultimate goal of all Catholic education is salvation in Jesus Christ. Catholic educators effectively work for the coming of Christ's Kingdom; this work includes transmitting clearly and in full the message of salvation, which elicits the response of faith. In faith we know God, and the hidden purpose of his will (cf. Eph 1:9). In faith we truly come to know ourselves. By sharing our faith we communicate a complete vision of the whole of reality and a commitment to truth and goodness. This vision and this commitment draw the strands of life into a purposeful pattern. By enriching your students' lives with the fullness of Christ's message and by inviting them to accept with all their hearts Christ's work, which is the Church, you promote most effectively their integral human development, and you help them to build a community of faith, hope, and love.

This Christian message is the more urgent for those young ones who come from broken homes and who, often with only one parent to encourage them, must draw support and direction from their teachers in school.

In your apostolate of helping to bring Christ's message into the lives of your students, the whole Church supports you and stands with you. The Synod of Bishops, in particular, has recognized the importance of your task and the difficulties you face. For these reasons, it has called for concerted efforts to compose a universal catechism. This project will not eliminate the great challenge of a need for creativity in methodology, nor will it minimize the continued need for the inculturation of the Gospel, but it will assist all the local Churches in effectively presenting in its integrity the content of Catholic teaching. In the Church in America, an important part of the truly glorious chapter of Catholic education has been the transmitting of Christ's message through religious education programs designed for children and young people outside Catholic schools. For this too I give thanks to God, recalling all those who throughout the history of this nation have so generously collaborated in this "work of faith and labor of love" (1 Thes 1:3).

Community is at the heart of all Catholic education not simply as a concept to be taught but as a reality to be lived. In its deepest Christian sense, community is a sharing in the life of the Blessed Trinity. Your students will learn to understand and appreciate the value of community as they experience love, trust, and loyalty in your schools and educational programs, and as they learn to treat all persons as brothers and sisters created by God and redeemed by Christ. Help them to grasp this sense of community by active participation in the life of the parish and the diocese and especially by receiving the Sacraments of Penance and the Eucharist. The Second Vatican Council explicitly includes learning to adore God in spirit and in truth among the aims of all Christian education (cf. *Gravissimum Educationis*, 2).

A sense of community implies openness to the wider community. Often, today, Catholic education takes place in changing neighborhoods; it requires respect for cultural diversity, love for those of different ethnic backgrounds, service to those in need, without discrimination. Help your students to see themselves as members of the Universal Church and the world community. Help them to understand the implications of justice and mercy. Foster in your students a social consciousness which will move them to meet the needs of their neighbors and to discern and seek to remove the sources of injustice in society. No human anxiety or sorrow should leave the disciples of Jesus Christ indifferent.

The world needs more than just social reformers. It needs saints. Holiness is not the privilege of a few; it is a gift offered to all. The call to holiness is addressed also to you and to your students. To doubt this is to misjudge Christ's intentions, for "each of us has received God's favor in the measure in which Christ bestowed it" (Eph 4:7).

Brothers and sisters, take Jesus Christ the Teacher as the model of your service, as your guide and source of strength. He himself has told us, "You address me as 'Teacher' and 'Lord,' and fittingly enough, for that is what I am" (Jn 13:13-14). He taught in word and deed, and his teaching cannot be separated from his life and being. In the apostolic exhortation on catechesis I stated: "The whole of Christ's life was a continual teaching: his silences, his miracles, his gestures, his prayer, his love for people, his special affection for the little and the poor, his acceptance of the total sacrifice on the Cross for the redemption of the world, and his Resurrection. . . . Hence for Christians the crucifix is one of the most sublime and popular images of Christ the Teacher" (*Catechesi Tradendae*, 9).

Dear friends, Jesus shares with you his teaching ministry. Only in close communion with him can you respond adequately. This is my hope, this is my prayer: that you will be totally open to Christ. That he will give you an ever greater love for your students and an ever stronger commitment to your vocation as Catholic educators. If you continue to be faithful to this ministry today, as you have been in the past, you will be doing much in shaping a peaceful, just, and hope-filled world for the future. Yours is a great gift to the Church, a great gift to your nation.

Youth Rally
Louisiana Superdome

Dear Young People of New Orleans, Dear Young People of America,

Listening to what you are telling me by your presence and through your representatives, I know that you are very much conscious of having a special mission in this world, of being partners in the mission of the Church.

I also know that in fulfilling your mission you are willing to give, you are willing to share, and you are willing to serve. And you are willing to do all this, together, not alone! In this you are like Jesus: Jesus gave and he served and he was never alone. He tells us: "The one who sent me is with me. He has not left me alone" (Jn 8:29).

Yes, dear young people, I too want to speak about your mission, the reason for your life on earth, the truth of your lives. It is extremely vital for you to have a clear idea of your mission, to avoid being confused or deceived. In speaking to the Christians of his time, Saint Paul explicitly urged them: "Let no one deceive you in any way" (2 Thes 2:3). And today I say the same to you, young people of America: "Let no one deceive you in any way" about your mission, about the truth, about where you are going. Let no one deceive you about the truth of your lives.

But what is the opposite of deception? Where can you turn to find answers that satisfy, answers that will last? The opposite of deception is truth—the person who tells the truth, the person who is truth. Yes, the opposite of deception is Jesus Christ, who tells us: "I am the way, and the truth, and the life" (Jn 14:6). Jesus Christ is the Son of God. He reveals the truth of God. But he is also man. He shares in our humanity and came into the world to teach us about ourselves, to help us discover ourselves.

You young people are proud to live in a free country and you should be grateful to God for your freedom. But even though you can come and go as you like and do what you want, you are not really free if you are living under the power of error or falsehood, or deceit or sin. Only Jesus Christ can make you fully free through his truth. And that is why he said, "You will know the truth, and the truth will set you free." And that is why he added, "If the Son frees you, you will really be free" (Jn 8:32,36). Dear young people, the whole message of Jesus in the gospels and through his Church helps you to discover who you really are, to discover all the dimensions of your lives.

Each of us is an individual, a person, a creature of God, one of his children, someone very special whom God loves and for whom Christ died. This identity of ours determines the way we must live, the way we must act, the way we must view our mission in the world. We come from God, we depend on God, God has a plan for us—a plan for our lives, for our bodies, for our souls, for our future. This plan for us is extremely important, so important that God became man to explain it to us.

In God's plan we are individuals, yes, but we are also part of a community. The Second Vatican Council emphasized the fact that God did not call us to share his life merely as unrelated individuals. Rather, he wanted to mold us into a people as his sons and daughters (cf. *Ad Gentes,* 2). This aspect of our being a community, of our sharing God's life as a people is part of our identity: who we are, what we are, where we are going.

Right away we can see that as persons we have responsibilities and that these responsibilities are part of our freedom. The Vatican Council went so far as to say that "man is defined first of all by his responsibilities toward his brothers and sisters and toward history" (*Gaudium et Spes,* 55).

To understand ourselves as members of a community, as individuals linked together to make up the People of God, as persons with responsibility for others is a great insight, an insight that is necessary for fulfilling our mission properly.

As Christians you have these insights, and Christ today wants to reinforce them in you. You speak about "being partners," of sharing and serving and working together. And all of this is linked to God's plan, according to which we are brothers and sisters in Christ, brothers and sisters who belong to the People of God and who are made to live in community, to think about others, to help others. Dear young people of America, in the Church there are many different gifts. There is room for many different cultures and ways of doing things. But there is no room in the Church for selfishness. There is no room in the world for selfishness. It destroys the meaning of life; it destroys the meaning of love; it reduces the human person to a subhuman level.

When we speak about the need of being open to others, of taking into account the community, of fulfilling our responsibilities to all our brothers and sisters, we are actually talking about the whole world. Your mission as young people today is to the whole world. In what sense? You can never forget the interdependence of human beings wherever they are. When Jesus tells us to love our neighbor, he does not set a geographical limit. What is needed today is a solidarity between all the young people of the world, a solidarity especially with the poor and all those in need. You young people must change society

62

by your lives of justice and fraternal love. It is not just a question of your own country, but of the whole world. This is certainly your mission, dear young people. You are partners with each other, partners with the whole Church, partners with Christ.

In order, however, to accomplish this great work, to be in a condition to change the world in the name of Jesus, you yourselves must actually be living according to your own identity, according to God's plan for your lives. Once again it is the word of Jesus that directs your lives and tells you what that plan is. You remember how much Jesus insisted on the commandment of love, how much he insisted on living according to certain norms called the Beatitudes: "Blessed are the meek. . . . Blessed are the merciful. . . . Blessed are the clean of heart. . . . Blessed are the peacemakers" (Mt 5:3-11). All of this is part of the plan.

When Saint Paul says, "Let no one deceive you," he is in effect saying: do not believe anyone who contradicts Jesus or his message which is transmitted to you by the Church. Jesus speaks to you young people and tells you the value of meekness, mercy, and humility. Other voices in the world will immediately shout out: "Weakness!" In the gospel Jesus emphasizes the value of honesty, uprightness, justice, and fairness. But when you practice these virtues, you are liable to be accused of being naive. Jesus and his Church hold up to you God's plan for human love, telling you that sex is a great gift of God that is reserved for marriage. At this point, the voices of the world will try to deceive you with powerful slogans, claiming that you are unrealistic, out of it, backward, even reactionary. But the message of Jesus is clear: purity means true love and it is the total opposite of selfishness and escape.

Jesus' message applies to all the areas of life. He reveals to us the truth of our lives and all aspects of this truth. Jesus tells us that the purpose of our freedom is to say "yes" to God's plan for our lives. What makes our "yes" so important is that we say it freely; we are able to say "no." Jesus teaches us that we are accountable to God, that we must follow our consciences, but that our consciences must be formed according to God's plan for our lives. In all our relationships to other people and to the world, Jesus teaches us what we must do, how we must live in order not to be deceived, in order to walk in truth. And today, dear young people, I proclaim to you again Jesus Christ: the way, and the truth, and the life—your way, your truth, and your life.

What is in accord with the truth of Jesus is fulfillment, joy, and peace, even if it means effort and discipline. What is not in accord with his truth means disorder, and when done deliberately it means sin. Deliberate or not, it eventually means unhappiness and frustration.

It is with the truth of Jesus, dear young people, that you must face the great questions in your lives, as well as the practical problems. The world will try to deceive you about many things that matter: about your faith, about pleasure, and material things, about the dangers of drugs. And at one stage or another, the false voices of the world will try to exploit your human weakness by telling you that life has no meaning at all for you. The supreme theft in your lives would be if they succeeded in robbing you of hope. They will try, but not succeed if you hold fast to Jesus and his truth.

The truth of Jesus is capable of reinforcing all your energies. It will unify your lives and consolidate your sense of mission. You may still be vulnerable to attack from the pressures of the world, from the forces of evil, from the power of the devil. But you will be invincible in hope: ". . . in Christ Jesus our hope" (1 Tm 1:1).

Dear young people, the word of Jesus and his truth and his promises of fulfillment and life are the Church's response to the culture of death, to the onslaughts of doubt, and to the cancer of despair.

Let me just add two practical thoughts from the Second Vatican Council. The Council tells us that we must avoid thinking that we have at hand the solutions to all the particular problems of life (cf. *Gaudium et Spes*, 33). But at the same time, the Church knows that she possesses the light in which the solutions to the problems of humanity can be discovered (ibid., 12). What is this light? What can it be? Only the truth of Jesus Christ!

Dear young people, I would like to add something else to what I have already said to you. I would like to speak to you briefly about prayer, about communion with God, a communion that is deeply personal between ourselves and God.

In prayer, we express to God our feelings, our thoughts, our sentiments. We wish to love and be loved, to be understood and to understand. Only God loves us perfectly, with an everlasting love. In prayer, we open our hearts and our minds to this God of love. And it is prayer that makes us one with the Lord. Through prayer, we come to share more deeply in God's life and in his love.

One of the most striking things about Jesus was his habit of prayer. In the midst of an active public ministry, we find him going away by himself to be alone in silence and communion with his Father in heaven. On the Sabbath, he made it a practice to go to the synagogue and pray with others in common. When he was together with his disciples, or when he was by himself, he prayed to the Father, whom he dearly loved.

Saint Mark's gospel describes an evening in Capernaum when Jesus cured many who were sick and expelled many demons. After giving us this description of Christ's generous care for others, Saint Mark adds: "Rising early the next morning, he went off to a lonely place in the desert; there he was absorbed in prayer" (Mk 1:35).

And Saint Luke informs us that, before Jesus selected the Twelve to be his apostles, "he went out to the mountain to pray, spending the night in communion with God" (Lk 6:12). In fact, it seems that it was his example of prayer that prompted his disciples to want to pray: "One day he was praying in a certain place," Luke tells us, and "when he had finished, one of his disciples asked him, 'Lord, teach us to pray'" (Lk 11:1). That was the occasion when Jesus taught them the prayer that we call the *Lord's Prayer* or the *Our Father*.

If you really wish to follow Christ, if you want your love for him to grow and last, then you must be faithful to prayer. It is the key to the vitality of your life in Christ. Without prayer, your faith and love and will die. If you are constant in daily prayer and in the Sunday celebration of Mass, your love for Jesus will increase. And your heart will know deep joy and peace, such as the world could never give.

But many young people tell me that they do not know how to pray, or they wonder if they are praying in a way that is correct. Here again, you must look to the example of Christ. How did Jesus himself pray?

First of all, we know that his prayer is marked by a spirit of joy and praise. "Jesus rejoiced in the Holy Spirit and said: 'I offer you praise, O Father, Lord of heaven and earth'" (Lk 10:21). In addition, he entrusted to the Church at the Last Supper the celebration of the Eucharist, which remains for all ages the most perfect means of offering to the Father glory and thanksgiving and praise.

Yet, there were also times of suffering when, in great pain and struggle, Jesus poured out his heart to God, seeking to find in his Father both comfort and support. For example, in the Garden of Gethsemane, when the inner struggle became even more difficult, then "in his anguish he prayed with all the greater intensity, and his sweat became like drops of blood falling to the ground" (Lk 22:44). "He prayed with all the greater intensity"—what an example for us when we find life difficult, when we face a painful decision, or when we struggle with temptation. At times like these, Jesus prayed with all the greater intensity. We must do the same!

When it is difficult therefore to pray, the most important thing is not to stop praying, not to give up the effort. At these times, turn to the Bible and to the Church's liturgy. Meditate on the life and teachings of Jesus as recorded in the gospels. Ponder the wisdom and counsel of the apostles and the challenging messages of the prophets. Try to make your own the beautiful prayers of the Psalms. You will find in the inspired word of God the spiritual food you need. Above all, your soul will be refreshed when you take part wholeheartedly with the community in the celebration of the Eucharist, the Church's greatest prayer.

Do you recall the story of Jesus and his Mother Mary at the wedding feast of Cana? At a certain point in the feast, when they have run out of wine, Mary tells those waiting on table, "Do whatever he tells you" (Jn 2:5). When the waiters follow Mary's advice, Jesus rewards their faith and changes water into wine, a wine that far surpasses the quality of what had been served before. And Mary's advice still holds true today. For the true success of our lives consists in knowing and doing the will of Jesus, in doing whatever Jesus tells us. When you pray, you must realize that prayer is not just asking God for something or seeking special help, even though prayers of petition are true ways of praying. But prayer should also be characterized by thanksgiving and praise, by adoration and attentive listening, by asking God's pardon and forgiveness. If you follow Jesus' advice, and pray to God constantly, then you will learn to pray well. God himself will teach you.

Prayer can truly change your life. For it turns your attention away from yourself and directs your mind and your heart toward the Lord. If we look only at ourselves, with our own limitations and sins, we quickly give way to sadness and discouragement. But if we keep our eyes fixed on the Lord, then our hearts are filled with hope, our minds are washed in the light of truth, and we come to know the fullness of the gospel with all its promise and life.

Prayer also helps us to be open to the Holy Spirit, the Spirit of truth and love, the Spirit who was given to the Church so that she could fulfill her mission in the world. It is the Holy Spirit who gives us the strength to resist evil and do good, to do our part in building up the Kingdom of God.

It is significant that the symbol of the Holy Spirit on Pentecost was tongues of fire. In fact, fire is often the symbol that the Bible uses to speak of the action of God in our lives. For the Holy Spirit truly inflames our hearts, engendering in them enthusiasm for the works of God. And when we pray, the Holy Spirit stirs up within us love of God and love of our neighbor.

The Holy Spirit brings us joy and peace. The modern technological world can offer us many pleasures, many comforts of life. It can even offer us temporary escapes from life. But what the world can never offer is lasting joy and peace. These are the gifts which only the Holy Spirit can give. And these are the gifts that I ask for you, so that you may be strong in hope and persevering in love. But the condition for all of this is prayer, which means contact with Christ, communion with God. Dear young people, my message to you is not new. I have given it before and, with God's grace, I will give it again. And so, as long as the memory of this visit lasts, may it be recorded that I, John Paul II, came to America to call you to Christ; to invite you to pray!

Homily at New Orleans Eucharist
Lakefront Arena

My Lord be patient with me and
I will pay you back in full (Mt 18:26; cf. v. 29).

Dear Brothers and Sisters in Christ,

This plea is heard twice in the gospel parable. The first time it is made by the servant who owes his master ten thousand talents, an astonishingly high sum according to the value of money in New Testament times. Shortly afterwards, the plea is repeated by another servant of the same master. He too is in debt, not to his master, but to his fellow servant. And his debt is only a tiny fraction of the debt that his fellow servant had been forgiven.

The point of the parable is the fact that the servant with the greater debt receives understanding from the master to whom he owes much money. The gospel tells us that "the master let the official go and wrote off the debt" (Mt 15:27). Yet that same servant would not listen to the plea of his fellow servant who owed him money. He had no pity on him, but "had him put in jail until he paid back what he owed" (Mt 18:30).

Jesus often used parables like this one in his teaching; they are a special method of proclaiming the Good News. They enable the listener to grasp more easily the "Divine Reality" which Jesus came to reveal. In today's parable, we sense almost immediately that it is a prelude to the words which Jesus commands us to use when we pray to our heavenly Father: "Forgive us our debts, as we forgive our debtors" (Mt 6:12).

These words from the *Our Father* also have something very important to teach us. If we want God to hear us when we plead like the servant—"Have patience with me"—then we must be equally willing to listen to our neighbor when he pleads: "Give me time and I will pay you back in full." Otherwise, we cannot expect pardon from God, but punishment instead. In the parable, the servant is punished because, though a debtor himself, he is intolerant as a creditor toward his fellow servant.

Christ is very clear: when we ourselves are without sympathy or mercy, when we are guided by "blind" justice alone, then we cannot count on the mercy of that "Great Creditor" who is God, God before whom we are all debtors.

In the parable, we find two different standards or ways of measuring: God's standard and man's standard. The divine standard is one in which justice is totally permeated by merciful love. The human standard is inclined to stop at justice alone, justice which is without mercy, and which in a sense is "blind" with regard to man.

Indeed, human justice is often governed by hatred and revenge, as the first reading from the Book of Sirach reminds us. It reads, and the words of the Old Testament are strong, "Should a man nourish anger against his fellows and expect healing from the Lord? . . . If he who is but flesh cherishes wrath, who will forgive his sins? . . . Remember your last days, set enmity aside. . . . Think of the commandments, hate not your neighbor. . . . Should a man refuse mercy to his fellows, yet seek pardon for his own sins?" (Sir 28:3,5-7,4).

The exhortations in the Book of Sirach and in the gospel both move in the same direction. The human way of measuring, the measure of justice alone, which is often "blind" or "blinded" by hatred, must accept God's standard. Otherwise, justice by itself easily becomes injustice, as we see expressed in the Latin saying: *summum ius, summa iniuria.* The rigorous application of the law can sometimes be the height of injustice.

As I said in my encyclical letter on the mercy of God: "In every sphere of interpersonal relationships justice must, so to speak, be 'corrected' to a considerable extent by that love which, as Saint Paul proclaims, 'is patient and kind' or, in other words, possesses the characteristics of that merciful love which is so much of the essence of the gospel and Christianity" (*Dives in Misericordia*, 14).

Merciful love is also the basis of the Lord's answer to Peter's question: "When my brother wrongs me, how often must I forgive him? Seven times?" "No," Jesus replied, "not seven times; I say, seventy times seven times" (Mt 15:21-22). In the symbolic language of the Bible, this means that we must be able to forgive everyone every time. Surely this is one of the most difficult and radical commands of the gospel. Yet how much suffering and anguish, how much futility, destruction, and violence would be avoided, if only we put into practice in all our human relationships the Lord's answer to Peter.

Merciful love is absolutely necessary, in particular, for people who are close to one another: for husbands and wives, parents and children, and among friends (cf. *Dives in Misericordia*, 14). At a time when family life is under such great stress, when a high number of divorces and broken homes are a sad fact of life, we must ask ourselves whether human relationships are being based, as they should be, on the merciful love and forgiveness revealed by God in Jesus Christ. We must examine our own heart and see how willing we are to forgive and to accept forgiveness in this world as well as in the next.

No relationship as intense and close as marriage and the family can survive without forgiveness "seventy times seven times." If couples cannot forgive with the tenderness and sensitivity that mercy brings, then they will inevitably begin to see their relationship only in terms of justice, of what is mine and what is yours—emotionally, spiritually, and materially—and in terms of real or perceived injustices. This can lead to estrangement and divorce, and often develops into a bitter dispute about property and, more tragically, about children. The plight of the children alone should make us realize that the refusal to forgive is not in keeping with the true nature of marriage as God established it and as he wants it to be lived. No doubt some people will object that Christ's teaching about the indissolubility of marriage, as it is upheld by the Church, is lacking in compassion. But what must be seen is the ineffectiveness of divorce—and its ready availability in modern society—to bring mercy and forgiveness and healing to so many couples and their children, in whose troubled lives there remain a brokenness and a suffering that will not go away. The words of the merciful Christ, who fully understands the human heart, remain forever: "What therefore God has joined together, let no man put asunder" (Mt 19:6).

At the same time, merciful love and forgiveness are never meant to cancel out a person's right to justice, even in marriage. In the encyclical to which I referred a moment ago I said that "properly understood, justice constitutes . . . the goal of forgiveness. In no passage of the gospel message does forgiveness or mercy . . . mean indulgence toward evil, scandals, injury or insult. . . . Reparation for evil and scandal, compensation for injury, and satisfaction for insult are conditions for forgiveness" (*Dives in Misericordia*, 14). All forgiveness requires repentant love.

This also applies in the wider context of social, political, cultural, and economic life within and among nations and peoples. May we not hope for what Pope Paul VI described as the "civilization of love" instead of "an eye for an eye and a tooth for a tooth," the attitude which ravages the face of the earth and scars the family of mankind? As I have said, this love, based on the forgiveness which Jesus described to Peter, does not mean that the objective demands of justice, which people legitimately seek, are thereby canceled out. Sometimes those demands, however, are very complex.

A case with special urgency today is the international debt question. As you know, many developing countries are heavily in debt to industrialized nations, and for a variety of reasons are finding it harder and harder to repay their loans. "Blind" justice alone cannot solve this problem in an ethical way that promotes the human good of all parties. Merciful love calls for mutual understanding and a recognition of human priorities and needs, above and beyond the "blind" justice of financial mechanisms. We must arrive at solutions that truly reflect both complete justice and mercy (cf. *At the Service of the Human Community: An Ethical Approach to the International Debt Question*, Pontifical Commission *Iustitia et Pax*, 1956).

The nature of the Church's concern in these matters is reflected in the pastoral message on the American economy issued by the bishops of the United States. They say: "We write . . . as heirs of the biblical prophets who summon us 'to do justice, to love kindness and to walk humbly with our God' (Mi 6:8). . . . We speak as moral teachers, not economic technicians. We seek . . . to lift up the human and ethical dimensions of economic life . . ." (*Economic Justice for All*, 4, 7). To do justice, yes, but also to love. This is at the heart of Christ's message. It is the only way to reach that "civilization of love" that ensures peace for ourselves and for the world.

Forgive us . . . as we forgive.

The Eucharist which we are celebrating and in which we are taking part is linked to the deepest truth of these words. Each time we participate in the Eucharist, we must translate, as it were, the parable of today's gospel into the reality of that sacrament which is the "great mystery of faith." When we gather together, we must be aware of how much we are debtors to God the Creator, God the Redeemer. Debtors—first for our creation, and then for our redemption. The psalmist exclaims:

Bless the Lord, O my soul;
and all my being, bless his holy name.
Bless . . . and forget not all his benefits (Ps 103:1-2).

This exhortation is directed to each one of us, and at the same time to the whole community of believers. Forget not . . . the gift of God. Forget not . . . that you have received his bounty: in creation—that is to say, in your existence and in all that is in and around you; in redemption—in that grace of adoption as sons and daughters of God in Christ, at the price of his cross.

When we receive a gift we are a debtor. Indeed we are more than a debtor because it is not possible to repay a gift adequately. And yet we must try. We must give a gift in return for a gift. God's generous gift must be repaid by our gift. And our gift, reflecting as it does our great limitations, must aim at imitating the divine generosity, the divine standard of giving. In Christ our gift must be transformed, so as to unite us with God. The Eucharist is the sacrament of such a transformation. Christ himself makes us, "an everlasting gift to the Father." Truly this is the great mystery of faith and love.

Forgive us our debts, as we forgive our debtors.

With these words from the prayer taught to us by the Son of God, I address all those gathered here in New Orleans in the spirit of the gospel, all those who make up the eucharistic assemblies of the local churches of this region. I greet you as the proud heirs of a rich and diverse cultural history, as people who can therefore appreciate the need for merciful love among individuals and groups. Here we have represented the cultures of France and other European nations, of black people, Hispanics, and more recently, Vietnamese. Today this region continues to be the home of various races and cultures now united in one nation, the United States.

All of those races and cultures have enriched the life of your local church within the distinctively French heritage that men like Robert Cavelier, Sieur de la Salle, and Jean Baptiste Le Moyne, Sieur de Bienville conferred upon this land centuries ago. You are also a people who have only to look about you to see the many wonderful gifts conferred by the mighty Mississippi River and its fertile delta, and by the riches of the sea. All this comes to you as a gift from God. By wise stewardship and the responsible use of these resources, you can find dignity in your work as you seek to provide for yourselves and your families. May you continue to work in harmony for the good of the society you belong to, always keeping in mind the words of Christ's prayer: "Forgive us our debts, as we forgive our debtors."

Modern man easily forgets the proportion, or rather, the lack of proportion between what he has received and what he is obliged to give. He has grown so much in his own eyes, and is so sure that everything is the work of his own genius and of his own "industry," that he no longer sees the One who is the Alpha and the Omega, the

Beginning and the End; the One who is the First Source of all that is, as well as its Final End; the One in whom all that exists finds its proper meaning.

Modern man easily forgets that he has received a great gift. Yet, at the base of all that he is and of all that the world is, there is the gift, the free gift of Love. As man loses this awareness, he also forgets the debt and the fact that he is a debtor. He loses his consciousness of sin. Many people today, especially those caught up in a civilization of affluence and pleasure, live as though sin did not exist and as if God did not exist.

For this reason, we need to listen with special attention to the Letter to the Romans: "None of us lives as his own master and none of us dies as his own master. While we live we are responsible to the Lord, and when we die we die as his servants. Both in life and in death we are the Lord's. That is why Christ died and came to life again, that he might be Lord of both the dead and the living" (Rom 14:7-9). We must listen carefully to these words of Saint Paul and remember them well:

My Lord, be patient with me and I will pay you back in full.

Love is patient; love is kind. . . . Love does not rejoice in what is wrong but rejoices with the truth. . . . Love never fails (1 Cor 13:4,6,8). Yes, love is supreme! Amen.

Meeting with Leadership of Catholic Higher Education Xavier University

Dear Friends, Dear Leaders in Catholic Higher Education,

At the end of this day dedicated to the prayerful celebration of Catholic education in the United States, I greet you and all those whom you represent, with esteem and with affection in our Lord Jesus Christ. I thank the Association of Catholic Colleges and Universities for having arranged this meeting. I express my gratitude to Dr. Norman Francis and to all at Xavier University for their hospitality at this institution, which, in so many ways, serves the cause of Catholic higher education.

I will bless the Lord at all times;
his praise shall be ever in my mouth.
Glorify the Lord with me,
let us together extol his name (Ps 34:2,4).

Yes, let us join in thanking God for the many good things that he, the Father of Wisdom, has accomplished through Catholic colleges and universities. In doing so, let us be thankful for the special strengths of your schools, for their Catholic identity, for their service of truth, and for their role in helping to make the Church's presence felt in the world of culture and science. And let us be thankful above all for the men and women committed to this mission, those of the past and those of today, who have made and are making Catholic higher education the great reality that it is.

The United States is unique in its network of more than 235 colleges and universities which identify themselves as Catholic. The number and diversity of your institutions are in fact without parallel; they exercise an influence not only within the United States but also throughout the Universal Church, and they bear a responsibility for her good.

Two years from now you will celebrate the 200th anniversary of the founding by John Carroll of Georgetown University, the first Catholic university in the United States. After Georgetown, through the leadership of religious congregations and farseeing bishops, and with the generous support of the Catholic people, other colleges and universities have been established in different parts of this vast country. For two centuries, these institutions have contributed much to the emergence of a Catholic laity, which today is intimately and extensively involved in industry, government, the professions, arts, and all forms of public and private endeavor, all those activities that constitute the characteristic dynamism and vitality of this land.

Amidst changing circumstances, Catholic universities and colleges are challenged to retain a lively sense of their Catholic identity and to fulfill their specific responsibilities to the Church and to society. It is precisely in doing so that they make their distinctive contribution to the wider field of higher education.

The Catholic identity of your institutions is a complex and vitally important matter. This identity depends upon the explicit profession of Catholicity on the part of the university as an institution, and also upon the personal conviction and sense of mission on the part of its professors and administrators.

During my pastoral visit to this country in 1979, I spoke of various elements that contribute to the mission of Catholic higher education. It is useful once again to stress the importance of research into questions vital for the Church and society—a research carried out "with a just sense of history, together with the concern to show the full meaning of the human person regenerated in Christ"; to emphasize the need for educating men and women of outstanding knowledge who, "having made a personal synthesis between faith and culture,

72

will be both capable and willing to assume tasks in the service of the community and of society in general, and to bear witness to their faith before the world"; and finally, to pursue the establishment of a living community of faith, "where sincere commitment to scientific research and study goes together with a deep commitment to authentic Christian living" (*Address at The Catholic University of America*, Washington, D.C., October 7, 1979, no. 3).

To appreciate fully the value of your heritage, we need to recall the origins of Catholic university life. The university as we know it began in close association with the Church. This was no accident. Faith and love of learning have a close relationship. For the fathers of the Church and the thinkers and academics of the Middle Ages, the search for truth was associated with the search for God. According to Catholic teaching, as expressed also in the First Vatican Council, the mind is capable not only of searching for the truth but also of grasping it, however imperfectly.

Religious faith itself calls for intellectual inquiry; and the confidence that there can be no contradiction between faith and reason is a distinctive feature of the Catholic humanistic tradition, as it existed in the past and as it exists in our own day.

Catholic higher education is called to exercise, through the grace of God, an extraordinary "share in the work of truth" (3 Jn 8). The Catholic university is dedicated to the service of the truth, as is every university. In its research and teaching, however, it proceeds from the vision and perspective of faith and is thus enriched in a specific way.

From this point of view, one sees that there is an intimate relationship between the Catholic university and the teaching office of the Church. The bishops of the Church, as *Doctores et Magistri Fidei*, should be seen not as external agents but as participants in the life of the Catholic university in its privileged role as protagonist in the encounter between faith and science and between revealed truth and culture.

Modern culture reflects many tensions and contradictions. We live in an age of great technological triumphs but also of great human anxieties. Too often, today, the individual's vision of reality is fragmented. At times, experience is mediated by forces over which people have no control; sometimes there is not even an awareness of these forces. The temptation grows to relativize moral principles and to privilege process over truth. This has grave consequences for the moral life as well as for the intellectual life of individuals and of society. The Catholic university must address all these issues from the perspective of faith and out of its rich heritage.

Modern culture is marked by a pluralism of attitudes, points of view, and insights. This situation rightly requires mutual understanding; it means that society and groups within society must respect those who have a different outlook from their own. But pluralism does not exist for its own sake; it is directed to the fullness of truth. In the academic context, the respect for persons which pluralism rightly envisions does not justify the view that ultimate questions about human life and destiny have no final answers or that all beliefs are of equal value, provided that none is asserted as absolutely true and normative. Truth is not served in this way.

It is true, of course, that the culture of every age contains certain ambiguities, which reflect the inner tensions of the human heart, the struggle between good and evil. Hence the gospel, in its continuing encounter with culture, must always challenge the accomplishments and assumptions of the age (cf. Rom 12:2). Since, in our day, the implications of this ambiguity are often so destructive to the community, so hostile to human dignity, it is crucial that the gospel should purify culture, uplift it, and orient it to the service of what is authentically human. Humanity's very survival may depend on it. And here, as leaders in Catholic education in the United States, you have an extremely important contribution to make.

Today there exists an increasingly evident need for philosophical reflection concerning the truth about the human person. A metaphysical approach is needed as an antidote to intellectual and moral relativism. But what is required even more is fidelity to the word of God, to ensure that human progress takes into account the entire revealed truth of the eternal act of love in which the universe and especially the human person acquire ultimate meaning. The more one seeks to unravel the mystery of the human person, the more open one becomes to the mystery of transcendence. The more deeply one penetrates the divine mystery, the more one discovers the true greatness and dignity of human beings.

In your institutions, which are privileged settings for the encounter between faith and culture, theological science has a special role and deserves a prominent place in the curriculum of studies and in the allocation of research resources. But theology, as the Church understands it, is much more than an academic discipline. Its data are the data of God's revelation entrusted to the Church. The deeper understanding of the mystery of Christ, the understanding which theological reflection seeks, is ultimately a gift of the Holy Spirit given for the common good of the whole Church. Theology is truly a search to understand ever more clearly the heritage of faith preserved, transmitted, and made explicit by the Church's teaching office. And theological instruction serves the community of faith by helping new generations to understand and to integrate into their lives the truth of God, which is so vital to the fundamental issues of the modern world.

Theology is at the service of the whole ecclesial community. The work of theology involves an interaction among the various members of the community of faith. The bishops, united with the pope, have the mission of authentically teaching the message of Christ; as pastors, they are called to sustain the unity in faith and Christian living of the entire People of God. In this they need the assistance of Catholic theologians, who perform an inestimable service to the Church. But theologians also need the charism entrusted by Christ to the bishops and, in the first place, to the Bishop of Rome. The fruits of their work, in order to enrich the "lifestream" of the ecclesial community, must ultimately be tested and validated by the Magisterium. In effect, therefore, the ecclesial context of Catholic theology gives it a special character and value, even when theology exists in an academic setting.

Here, the words of Saint Paul concerning the spiritual gifts should be a source of light and harmony for us all: "There are different gifts but the same Spirit; there are different ministries but the same Lord; there are different works but the same God who accomplishes all of them in everyone. To each person the manifestation of the Spirit is given for the common good" (1 Cor 12:4-7). In the different offices and functions in the Church, it is not some power and dominion that is being divided up, but rather the same service of the Body of Christ that is shared according to the vocation of each. It is a question of unity in the work of service. In this spirit, I wish to express cordial support for the humble, generous, and patient work of theological research and education being carried out in your universities and colleges in accordance with the Church's mission to proclaim and teach the saving wisdom of God (cf. 1 Cor 1:21).

My own university experience impels me to mention another related matter of supreme importance in the Catholic college and university, namely, the religious and moral education of students and their pastoral care. I am confident that you too take this special service very seriously, and that you count it among your most pressing and most satisfying responsibilities. One cannot meet with college and university students anywhere in the world without hearing their questions and sensing their anxieties. In their hearts, your students have many questions about faith religious practice and holiness of life. Each one arrives on your campuses with a family background, a personal history, and an acquired culture. They all want to be accepted, loved, and supported by a Christian educational community which shows friendship and authentic spiritual commitment.

It is your privilege to serve your students in faith and love; to help them deepen their friendship with Christ; to make available to them the opportunities for prayer and liturgical celebration, including the possibility to know the forgiveness and love of Jesus Christ in the Sacraments of Penance and the Eucharist. You are able, as Catholic educators, to introduce your students to a powerful experience of community and to a very serious involvement in social concerns that will enlarge their horizons, challenge their life styles, and offer them authentic human fulfillment.

University students, for example, are in a splendid position to take to heart the gospel invitation to go out of themselves, to reject introversion, and to concentrate on the needs of others. Students with the opportunities of higher education can readily grasp the relevance for today of Christ's parable of the rich man and Lazarus (cf. Lk 16:19ff.), with all of its consequences for humanity. What is at stake is not only the rectitude of individual human hearts but also the whole social order as it touches the spheres of economics, politics, and human rights and relations.

Here in the Catholic university centers of this nation, vivified by the inspiration of the gospel, must be drawn up the blueprints for the reform of attitudes and structures that will influence the whole dynamic of peace and justice in the world, as it affects East and West, North and South. It is not enough to offer to the disadvantaged of the world crumbs of freedom, crumbs of truth, and crumbs of bread. The gospel calls for much more. The parable of the rich man and the poor man is directed to the conscience of humanity, and, today in particular, to the conscience of America. But that conscience often passes through the halls of academe, through nights of study and hours of prayer, finally to reach and embrace the whole prophetic message of the gospel. "Keep your attention closely fixed on it," we are told in the Second Letter of Peter, "as you would on a lamp shining in a dark place until the first streaks of dawn appear and the morning star rises in your hearts" (2 Pt 1:19).

Dear brothers and sisters, as leaders in Catholic university and college education, you have inherited a tradition of service and academic excellence, the cumulative effort of so many who have worked so hard and sacrificed so much for Catholic education in this country. Now there lies before you the wide horizon of the third century of the nation's constitutional existence, and the third century of Catholic institutions of higher learning serving the people of this land. The challenges that confront you are just as testing as those your forefathers faced in establishing the network of institutions over which you now preside. Undoubtedly, the greatest challenge is, and will remain, that of preserving and strengthening the Catholic character of your colleges and universities, that institutional commitment to the word of God as proclaimed by the Catholic Church. This commitment is both an expression of spiritual consistency and a specific contribution to the cultural dialogue proper to American life. As you strive to make the presence of the Church in the world of modern culture more luminous, may you listen once again to Christ's prayer to his Father for his disciples: "Consecrate them by means of truth—'Your word is truth' " (Jn 17:17).

May the Holy Spirit, the Counsellor and Spirit of Truth, who has enlivened and enlightened the Church of Christ from the beginning, give you great confidence in the Father's word, and sustain you in the service that you render to the truth through Catholic higher education in the United States of America.

SAN ANTONIO, TEXAS

Sunday, September 13, 1987

Homily at San Antonio Eucharist
Westover Hills

My soul, give thanks to the Lord;
all my being, bless his holy name (Ps 103:1).

Dear Brothers and Sisters, Dear Friends, Citizens of San Antonio and of the State of Texas,

It gives me an immense joy to be with you on this Sunday morning and to invoke God's blessings upon this vast state and upon the whole Church in this region.

Texas! The name immediately brings to mind the rich history and cultural development of this part of the United States. In this marvelous setting, overlooking the city of San Antonio, I cannot but reverently evoke the memory of the Franciscan Father Massanet who, on the feast of Saint Anthony of Padua, June 13, 1691, celebrated Mass along the banks of the San Antonio River for the members of an early Spanish expedition and a group of local Indian people.

Since then, people of many different origins have come here, so that today yours is a multicultural society, striving for the fullness of harmony and collaboration among all. I express my cordial gratitude to the representatives of the State of Texas and the city of San Antonio who have wished to be present at this moment of prayer. I also greet the members of the various Christian communions who join us in praising the name of our Lord Jesus Christ. A special word of thanks to Archbishop Flores and to the bishops, priests, deacons, religious, and all the Catholic faithful of Texas. The peace of Christ be with you all!

Today is Sunday: the Lord's Day. Today is like the "seventh day" about which the Book of Genesis says that "God rested from all the work he had undertaken" (Gn 2:2). Having completed the work of creation, he "rested." God rejoiced in his work; he "looked at everything that he had made, and he found it very good" (Gn 1:31). "So God blessed the seventh day and made it holy" (Gn 2:3).

77

On this day, we are called to reflect more deeply on the mystery of creation, and therefore of our own lives. We are called to ""rest" in God, the Creator of the universe. Our duty is to praise him: "My soul give thanks to the Lord . . . give thanks to the Lord and never forget all his blessings" (Ps 103:1-2). This is a task for each human being. Only the human person, created in the image and likeness of God, is capable of raising a hymn of praise and thanksgiving to the Creator. The earth, with all its creatures, and the entire universe, call on man to be their voice. Only the human person is capable of releasing from the depths of his or her being that hymn of praise, proclaimed without words by all creation: "My soul, give thanks to the Lord; all my being, bless his holy name" (Ps 103:1).

What is the message of today's liturgy? To us gathered here in San Antonio, in the State of Texas, and taking part in the Eucharistic Sacrifice of our Lord and Savior Jesus Christ, Saint Paul addresses these words: ""None of us lives as his own master, and none of us dies as his own master. While we live we are responsible to the Lord and when we die we die as his servants. Both in life and death we are the Lord's" (Rom 14:7-5).

These words are concise, but filled with a moving message. "We live" and "we die." We live in this material world that surrounds us, limited by the horizons of our earthly journey through time. We live in this world, with the inevitable prospect of death, right from the moment of conception and of birth. And yet, we must look beyond the material aspect of our earthly existence. Certainly, bodily death is a necessary passage for us all; but it is also true that what from its very beginning has borne in itself the image and likeness of God cannot be completely given back to the corruptible matter of the universe. This is a fundamental truth and attitude of our Christian faith. In Saint Paul's terms: "While we live we are responsible to the Lord, and when we die we die as his servants." We live for the Lord, and our dying too is life in the Lord.

Today, on this Lord's Day, I wish to invite all those who are listening to my words, not to forget our immortal destiny: life after death— the eternal happiness of heaven, or the awful possibility of eternal punishment, eternal separation from God, in what the Christian tradition has called hell (cf. Mt 22:13; 25:30,41). There can be no truly Christian living without an openness to this transcendent dimension of our lives. "Both in life and death we are the Lord's" (Rom 14:5).

The Eucharist that we celebrate constantly confirms our living and dying "in the Lord": "Dying you destroyed our death, rising you restored our life." In fact, Saint Paul wrote: "we are the Lord's. That is why Christ died and came to life again, that he might be Lord of both the dead and the living" (Rom 14:5-9). Yes, Christ is the Lord!

The Paschal Mystery has transformed our human existence, so that it is no longer under the dominion of death. In Jesus Christ, our Redeemer, "we live for the Lord" and "we die for the Lord." Through him and with him and in him, we belong to God in life and in death. We exist not only "for death" but "for God." For this reason, on this day "made by the Lord" (Ps 118:24), the Church all over the world speaks her blessing from the very depths of the Paschal Mystery of Christ: "My soul, give thanks to the Lord; all my being bless his holy name. Give thanks . . . and never forget all his blessings" (Ps 103:1-2).

"Never forget!" Today's reading from the gospel according to Saint Matthew gives us an example of a man who has forgotten (cf. Mt 15:21-35). He has forgotten the favors given by his lord, and consequently he has shown himself to be cruel and heartless in regard to his fellow human being. In this way, the liturgy introduces us to the experience of sin as it has developed from the beginning of the history of man alongside the experience of death.

We die in the physical body when all the energies of life are extinguished. We die through sin when love dies in us. Outside of love there is no life. If man opposes love and lives without love, death takes root in his soul and grows. For this reason, Christ cries out: "I give you a new commandment: Love one another. Such as my love has been for you, so must your love be for each other" (Jn 13:34). The cry for love is the cry for life, for the victory of the soul over sin and death. The source of this victory is the cross of Jesus Christ: his death and his resurrection.

Again, in the Eucharist, our lives are touched by Christ's own radical victory over sin, sin which is the death of the soul, and ultimately, the reason for bodily death. "That is why Christ died and came to life again, that he might be Lord of the dead" (cf. Rom 14:9), that he might give life again to those who are dead in sin or because of sin.

And so, the Eucharist begins with the penitential rite. We confess our sins in order to obtain forgiveness through the cross of Christ, and so receive a part in his resurrection from the dead. But if our conscience reproaches us with mortal sin, our taking part in the Mass can be fully fruitful only if beforehand we receive absolution in the Sacrament of Penance.

The ministry of reconciliation is a fundamental part of the Church's life and mission. Without overlooking any of the many ways in which Christ's victory over sin becomes a reality in the life of the Church and of the world, it is important for me to emphasize that it is above all in the sacrament of forgiveness and reconciliation that the power of the redeeming blood of Christ is made effective in our personal lives.

In different parts of the world there is a great neglect of the Sacrament of Penance. This is sometimes linked to an obscuring of the religious and moral conscience, a loss of the sense of sin, or a lack of adequate instruction on the importance of this sacrament in the life of Christ's Church. At times the neglect occurs because we fail to take seriously our lack of love and justice, and God's corresponding offer of reconciling mercy. Sometimes there is a hesitation or an unwillingness to accept maturely and responsibly the consequences of the objective truths of faith. For these reasons, it is necessary to emphasize once again that "with regard to the substance of the sacrament there has always remained firm and unchanged in the consciousness of the Church the certainty that, by the will of Christ, forgiveness is offered to each individual by means of sacramental absolution given by the ministers of Penance" (*Reconciliatio et Paenitentia*, 30).

Again I ask all my brother bishops and priests to do everything possible to make the administration of this sacrament a primary aspect of their service to God's people. There can be no substitute for the means of grace which Christ himself has placed in our hands. The Second Vatican Council never intended that this Sacrament of Penance be less practiced; what the Council expressly asked for was that the faithful might more easily understand the sacramental signs and more eagerly and frequently have recourse to the sacraments (cf. *Sacrosanctum Concilium*, 59). And just as sin deeply touches the individual conscience, so we understand why the absolution of sins must be individual and not collective, except in extraordinary circumstances as approved by the Church.

I ask you, dear Catholic brothers and sisters, not to see confession as a mere attempt at psychological liberation, however legitimate this too might be, but as a sacrament, a liturgical act. Confession is an act of honesty and courage; an act of entrusting ourselves, beyond sin, to the mercy of a loving and forgiving God. It is an act of the prodigal son who returns to his Father and is welcomed by him with the kiss of peace. It is easy, therefore, to understand why "every confessional is a special and blessed place from which there is born new and uncontaminated a reconciled individual—a reconciled world" (*Reconciliatio et Paenitentia*, 31, V; cf. III).

The potential for an authentic and vibrant renewal of the whole Catholic Church through the more faithful use of the Sacrament of Penance is immeasurable. It flows directly from the loving heart of God himself! This is a certainty of faith which I offer to each one of you and to the entire Church in the United States. To those who have been far away from the Sacrament of Reconciliation and forgiving love, I make this appeal: Come back to this source of grace; do not be afraid! Christ himself is waiting for you. He will heal you, and you will be at peace with God!

To all the young people of the Church, I extend a special invitation to receive Christ's forgiveness and his strength in the Sacrament of Penance. It is a mark of greatness to be able to say: I have made a mistake; I have sinned, Father; I have offended you, my God; I am sorry; I ask for pardon; I will try again, because I rely on your strength and I believe in your love. And I know that the power of your Son's Paschal Mystery, the death and resurrection of our Lord Jesus Christ, is greater than my weaknesses and all the sins of the world. I will come and confess my sins and be healed, and I will live in your love!

In Jesus Christ the world has truly known the mystery of forgiveness, mercy, and reconciliation, which is proclaimed by God's word this day. At the same time, God's inexhaustible mercy to us obliges us to be reconciled among ourselves. This makes practical demands on the Church in Texas and the Southwest of the United States. It means bringing hope and love wherever there is division and alienation.

Your history registers a meeting of cultures, indigenous and immigrant, sometimes marked by tensions and conflicts, yet constantly moving toward reconciliation and harmony . People of different races and languages, colors and customs, have come to this land to make it their home. Together with the indigenous peoples of these territories, there are the descendants of those who came from almost every country in Europe: from Spain and France; from Germany and Belgium; from Italy, Hungary, and Czechoslovakia; from Ireland, England, and Scotland. And even from my own native Poland, for it was to Texas, and *Panna Maria,* that the first Polish immigrants came to the United States. There are descendants of those who came in chains from Africa; those from Lebanon, the Philippines, and Vietnam; and from every Latin American country, especially from Mexico.

This land is a crossroads, standing at the border of two great nations and experiencing both the enrichment and the complications which arise from this circumstance. You are thus a symbol and a kind of laboratory, testing America's commitment to her founding moral principles and human values. These principles and values are now being reaffirmed by America, as she celebrates the Bicentennial of her Constitution and speaks once more about justice and freedom, and about the acceptance of diversity within a fundamental unity, a unity arising from a shared vision of the dignity of every human person and a shared responsibility for the welfare of all, especially of the needy and the persecuted.

Against this background one may speak of a current phenomenon here and elsewhere, the movement of people northwards, not only from Mexico but from other southern neighbors of the United States. On this matter also there is work of reconciliation to be done. Among you there are people of great courage and generosity who have been doing much on behalf of suffering brothers and sisters arriving from the south. They have sought to show compassion in the face of complex human, social, and political realities. Here human needs, both spiritual and material, continue to call out to the Church with thousands of voices, and the whole Church must respond by the proclamation of God's word and by selfless deeds of service. Here too there is ample space for continuing and growing collaboration among members of the various Christian communions.

In all of this, the Hispanic community itself faces the greatest challenge. Those of you of Hispanic descent—so numerous, so long present in this land, so well equipped to respond—are called to hear the word of Christ and take it to heart: "I give you a new commandment: love one another. Such as my love has been for you, so must your love be for each other" (Jn 13:34). And Jesus specified that this love embraces the entire range of human needs from the least to the greatest: "I promise you that whoever gives a cup of cold water to one of these lowly ones . . . will not want for his reward" (Mt 10:42). The Hispanic community also needs to respond to its own needs and to

81

show generous and effective solidarity among its own members. I urge you to hold fast to your Christian faith and traditions, especially in defense of the family. And I pray that the Lord may provide many more vocations to the priesthood and to the religious life among your young people.

May you who have received so much from God hear the call to a renewal of your Christian life and to fidelity to the faith of your fathers. O may you respond in the spirit of Mary, the Virgin Mother whom the Church sees "maternally present and sharing in the many complicated problems which today beset the lives of individuals, families and nations . . . helping the Christian people in the constant struggle between good and evil, to ensure that it 'does not fall,' or if it has fallen, that it 'rises again'" (*Redemptoris Mater*, 52).

Today's liturgy helps us to reflect deeply on life and death, on the victory of life over death. On this earth, in the visible world of creation, man exists "for death"; and yet, in Christ, he is called to communion with God, with the living God who "gives life." He is called to this communion precisely through the death of Christ, the death which "gives life."

Today, all over the world, countless people—people of many countries and continents, languages and races—are sharing sacramentally in the death of Christ. We, here in Texas, journey together with them toward the fulfillment of the Paschal Mystery in life. We journey, conscious of being sinners, conscious of being mortal. But we journey on in hope, in union with the sacrifice of Christ, through Eucharistic communion with him and with love for each other. We live for the Lord! We die for the Lord! We belong to the Lord! Come, Lord Jesus! (cf. Rv 22:20). Amen.

Meeting with Catholic Charities and Social Ministry Organizations Municipal Auditorium

Dear Brothers and Sisters,

I am grateful for your presentation of the vast network of Christian love and human solidarity in which you are engaged. May the Lord sustain you in your zeal. "May mercy, peace and love be yours in ever greater measure" (Jude 1).

"Catholic Charities" is a title that speaks wonderfully well of the generous commitment of the Catholic people of the United States to the cause of human solidarity and Christian love. It gives me great joy to be among you, members of Catholic Charities, U.S.A., your associated agencies, and your colleague organizations in social ministry. Through your efforts, you help to make the loving compassion of our Lord and Savior Jesus Christ present to human needs.

Jesus Christ was born poor, lived poor, and died poor. He loved the poor. In his Kingdom the poor have a special place. The Church cannot be any different. She must be ever more fully aware of her fundamental duty to reflect in her life and action the very love with which God loves his creatures. For what is at stake is the mystery of God's love as explained in the First Letter of John: "We, for our part, love because he first loved us" (1 Jn 4:19). All service has its first moment in God.

You carry on a tradition and you live out a teaching grounded in Sacred Scripture, proclaimed by the Church and relevant to every age. Service to the needy not only builds up social harmony, it reveals God, our Father, the rescuer of the oppressed. In the Old Testament, it was God's love for his people that decreed a special concern for the stranger, the widow, and the orphan. As God had treated his people, so were they to treat others. The year of jubilee and the sabbatical year restored economic balance: slaves were set free, land was returned to its original owners, debts were cancelled (cf. Ex 21ff.; Lv 25). Justice and mercy alike were served. The prophets repeatedly drew attention to the inner qualities of heart that must animate the exercise of justice and service: "Not as man sees does God see, because man sees the appearance but the Lord looks into the heart" (1 Sm 16:7).

In the New Testament, the mystery of God's love is further revealed: "God so loved the world that he gave his only Son" (Jn 3:16). Through the heart of Jesus the fullness of God's infinite mercy appeared in the world. Marveling at the incarnation of God's Son, Mary exclaims that through this child the lowly shall be lifted up, their hunger shall be satisfied, and God's mercy shall be extended to all (cf. Lk 1:46-65). Years later, in announcing his own ministry, Jesus sums up his life's program in the words of Isaiah: "to bring glad tidings to the poor, to proclaim liberty to captives, recovery of sight to the blind and release to prisoners, to announce a year of favor from the Lord" (Lk 4:18-19). Jesus identifies himself with the poor and the defenseless: what we do for them is done for him, the service we fail to render them is service denied to him (cf. Mt 26:31-46).

Gross disparities of wealth between nations, classes, and persons reenact the gospel parable of the rich man and the poor man Lazarus. And with the same dire consequences of which the gospel speaks: "My child, replied Abraham, remember that you were well off in your lifetime, while Lazarus was in misery. Now he has found consolation here, but you have found torment" (Lk 16:25). The warning is as valid today as it was two thousand years ago.

From the beginning, the Church has worked to carry out this teaching in her ministry. It is not necessary here to trace the extremely varied history of Christian service. The Church has always sought to respond to the stranger, the widow, and the orphan; she has founded countless schools, hospitals, hospices, child-care facilities, and shelters. In our own times, the Second Vatican Council has forcefully reaffirmed the Church's vocation, in fidelity to her Lord, to love all those who are afflicted in any way: to recognize in the poor and the suffering the likeness of her poor and suffering founder; to do all she can to relieve their needs, striving to serve Christ in them (cf. *Lumen Gentium*, 8). Twenty years after the Council, the Christian community is more than ever aware that the poor, the hungry, the oppressed, the sick, and the handicapped share in a special way in the cross of Christ and therefore need the Church's ministry.

Works of mercy, justice, and compassion are basic to the history of the Church in the United States. The two American women who have been numbered among the saints, Frances Xavier Cabrini and Elizabeth Ann Seton, have been thus honored principally because of their work for their poorer brothers and sisters. The initiatives of Catholic Charities in the United States go back to before the *Declaration of Independence*. Countless institutions and structures have been established to assist the orphan, the immigrant, the ethnic groups, all persons in need of every race and creed. Countless Americans of all extractions have made the compassionate service of their fellow human beings the whole purpose and method of their lives. In particular, generations of religious, women and men, have consumed themselves in selfless service, under the sign of love.

The Church has always proclaimed a love of preference for the poor. Perhaps the language is new, but the reality is not. Nor has the Church taken a narrow view of poverty and the poor. Poverty, certainly, is often a matter of material deprivation. But it is also a matter of spiritual impoverishment, the lack of human liberties, and the result of any violation of human rights and human dignity. There is a very special and pitiable form of poverty: the poverty of selfishness, the poverty of those who have and will not share, of those who could be rich by giving but choose to be poor by keeping everything they have. These people too need help.

The Christian view is that human beings are to be valued for what they are, not for what they have. In loving the poor and serving those in whatever need, the Church seeks above all to respect and heal their human dignity. The aim of Christian solidarity and service is to defend and promote, in the name of Jesus Christ, the dignity and fundamental human rights of every person. The Church "bears witness to the fact that this dignity cannot be destroyed, whatever the situation of poverty, scorn, rejection or powerlessness to which a human being has been reduced. She shows her solidarity with those who do not count in a society by which they are rejected spiritually and sometimes even physically. She is particularly drawn with maternal affection towards those children who, through human wickedness, will never be brought forth from the womb to the light of day, as also for the elderly, alone and abandoned. The special option for the poor, far from being a sign of particularism or sectarianism, manifests the universality of the Church's being and mission" (*Instruction on Christian Freedom and Liberation*, 68).

For "the poor in spirit" the Church has a very special love. She has inherited it from Christ, who called them "blest" (Mt 5:3). On the one hand, the Church knows, from the words of Christ, that despite all human efforts the poor will always be with us (cf. Mt 26:11). On the other hand, in all her efforts to uplift the poor she knows and proclaims the ambivalence of possessions. Indeed, where the pursuit of wealth is treated as the supreme good, human beings become imprisoned in the hardening of their hearts and in the closing of their minds (*Populorum Progressio*, 19). For this reason too, the Church, in the very act of serving the poor and relieving their sufferings, must also continue to proclaim and serve their higher needs, those of the spirit.

Service to those in need must take the form of direct action to relieve their anxieties and to remove their burdens, and at the same time lead them to the dignity of self-reliance. In this respect, I wish to express the Church's immense gratitude to the many Americans who are working to help their fellow human beings, in all the different forms which relief and development take in today's world. And I solemnly thank the American people for the generous way in which they respond to the appeal for financial support for the many splendid programs of assistance carried out in their name. In the case of the many programs run by the Catholic Church, I wish to invite all who have responsibility for them to ensure that they will always be, and be seen to be, in full accord with Catholic principles of truth and justice.

The organizational and institutional response to needs, whether in the Church or in society, is extremely necessary but it is not sufficient in itself. In this regard, I would repeat a concern I mentioned in my apostolic letter on human suffering: "Institutions are very important and indispensable; nevertheless, no institution can by itself replace the human heart, human compassion, human love, or human initiative, when it is a question of dealing with the sufferings of another. This refers to physical sufferings, but it is even more true when it is a question of the many kinds of moral suffering and when it is primarily the soul that is suffering" (*Salvifici Doloris*, 29).

Furthermore, in the necessary organizational and institutional response to needs, it is essential to avoid reducing human beings to mere units or categories of political or social planning and action. Such a process leads to new and other unjust forms of anonymity and alienation.

Service to the poor also involves speaking up for them and trying to reform structures which cause or perpetuate their oppression. As committed Catholics involved in helping to meet people's many concrete needs, you are still called to reflect on another dimension of a worldwide problem: the relationship between rich societies and poor societies, rich nations and poor nations. Your insights must be prayerfully joined to those of many other people to see what can be done as soon as possible to purify the social structures of all society in this regard.

In the final analysis, however, we must realize that social injustice and unjust social structures exist only because individuals and groups of individuals deliberately maintain or tolerate them. It is these personal choices, operating through structures, that breed and propagate situations of poverty, oppression, and misery. For this reason, overcoming "social" sin and reforming the social order itself must begin with the conversion of our hearts. As the American bishops have said: "The Gospel confers on each Christian the vocation to love God and neighbor in ways that bear fruit in the life of society. That vocation consists above all in a change of heart: a conversion expressed in praise of God and in concrete deeds of justice and service" (*Economic Justice for All: Catholic Social Teaching and the U.S. Economy*, 327).

To many people, mercy and conversion may seem like poor tools for solving social problems. Some are tempted to accept ideologies that use force to carry out their programs and impose their vision. Such means sometimes produce what appear to be successes. But these successes are not real. Force and manipulation have nothing to do with true human development and the defense of human dignity. Catholic social teaching is totally different, not only as regards goals, but also as regards the means to be used. For the Christian, putting right human ills must necessarily take into account the reality of creation and redemption. It means treating every human being as a unique child of God, a brother or sister of Jesus Christ. The path of human solidarity is the path of service; and true service means selfless love, open to the needs of all, without distinction of persons, with the explicit purpose of reinforcing each person's sense of God-given dignity.

Solidarity and service are above all a duty of Christian love which must involve the whole community. When we are tempted to congratulate ourselves on what we have done, we must bear soberly in mind the words of Jesus: "When you have done all you have been commanded to do, say, 'We are useless servants. We have done no more than our duty'" (Lk 17:10). When we are faced with the vastness of this duty of love, with the boundless needs of the poor in America and throughout the world, when we are disappointed by slowness and setbacks in the reform of structures and in our own conversion, let us not lose heart, and let us not settle for what has already been accomplished. Love can overcome great obstacles, and God's love can totally transform the world.

As the Church tries to express Christian solidarity in generous service, she also wishes to draw attention to the importance of worship and prayer and their relationship to service. In looking to the example of Christ, the Church can never forget that all Christ's actions were accompanied by prayer. It is in prayer that the Church develops and evaluates her social consciousness and unceasingly discovers anew her vocation to serve the needy of the world, as Jesus did. Addressing a group of American bishops during their last *ad Limina* visit, I spoke of this specifically Christian and ecclesial dimension of all social and charitable action: "Only a worshiping and praying Church can show herself sufficiently sensitive to the needs of the sick, the suffering, the lonely—especially in the great urban centers—and the poor everywhere. The Church as a community of service has first to feel the weight of the burden carried by so many individuals and families, and then strive to help alleviate these burdens. The discipleship that the Church discovers in prayer she expresses in deep interest for Christ's brethren in the modern world and for their many different needs. Her concern, manifested in various ways, embraces—among others—the areas of housing, education, health care, unemployment, the administration of justice, the special needs of the aged and the handicapped. In prayer, the Church is confirmed in her solidarity with the weak who are oppressed, the vulnerable who are manipulated, the children who are exploited, and everyone who is in any way discriminated against" (*Address of December 3, 1983,* 6).

Catholic Charities and related organizations exist essentially to spread Christian love. It is especially through charitable activities at the parish level that the entire Church in the United States joins in the tasks of mercy, justice, and love. We have seen today how Catholic Charities and all its colleague associations have lent God their own flesh—their hands and feet and hearts—so that his work may be done in our world. For your long and persevering service—creative and courageous and blind to distinctions of race or religion—you will certainly hear Jesus' words of gratitude: ". . . you did it for me" (Mt 25:40).

Gather, transform, and serve! When done in the name of Jesus Christ, this is the spirit of Catholic Charities and of all who work in this cause, because it is the faithful following of the One who did "not come to be served but to serve" (Mk 10:45). By working for a society which fosters the dignity of every human person, not only are you serving the poor, but you are renewing the founding vision of this nation under God! And may God reward you abundantly!

Meeting with Seminarians and Men and Women
Preparing for Religious Life
San Fernando Cathedral

Remove the sandals from your feet,
for the place where you stand is holy ground (Ex 3:5).

These words of God marked the beginning of a new way of life for Moses. The place where he was standing was holy ground, for he was standing in the awesome presence of Almighty God. And on that holy ground, he heard a voice calling him to a special mission of service to the People of God. From that moment forward, Moses' life would be radically altered. He would henceforth place his life at the service of the God of Abraham, Isaac, and Jacob. No longer would his life be his own. He would lead the Chosen People out of slavery in Egypt toward freedom in the Promised Land. In meeting God on holy ground, speaking with him there, and hearing his summons to service, Moses came to a new understanding of himself and entered into a deeper commitment to God and his people. The mission of Moses began under the sign of God's holiness.

Dear brothers and sisters in the Lord, it is a deep joy for me to be with you today in this historic cathedral of San Fernando, the oldest cathedral sanctuary in the United States. It is with great gratitude to God that I meet with you who are preparing to serve the Lord as priests and religious, you who in a singular and remarkable way have, like Moses, heard the voice of God calling you to that "holy ground" of a special vocation in the Church. You have stood in the awesome presence of the Lord and heard him call you by name. And listening to his voice with prayerful discernment, you have joyfully begun your formation for the priesthood or the religious life.

A vocation in the Church, from the human point of view, begins with a discovery, with finding the pearl of great price. You discover Jesus, his person, his message, his call. In the gospel which we have heard today, we reflect on the call of Jesus to the first disciples. The first thing that Andrew did after meeting Jesus was to seek out his brother Simon and tell him: "We have found the Messiah!" Then Philip, in a similar way, sought out Nathanael and told him: "We have found the one Moses spoke of in the Law—the prophets too—Jesus, son of Joseph, from Nazareth" (cf. Jn 1:35-51).

After the initial discovery, a dialogue in prayer ensues, a dialogue between Jesus and the one called, a dialogue which goes beyond words and expresses itself in love.

Questions are an important part of this dialogue. For example, in the gospel account of the call of the disciples, we are told that "when Jesus turned around and noticed them following him, he asked them, 'What are you looking for?' They said to him, 'Rabbi' (which means teacher), 'where do you stay?' 'Come and see,' he answered" (Jn 1:38-39).

What begins as a discovery of Jesus moves to a greater understanding and commitment through a prayerful process of questions and discernment. In this process, our motives are purified. We come face to face with pointed questions such as "What are you looking for?" And we even find ourselves asking questions of Jesus, as Nathanael did: "How do you know me?" (Jn 1:48). It is only when we have reflected candidly and honestly in the silence of our hearts that we begin to be convinced that the Lord is truly calling us.

Yet, even then, the process of discernment is not over. Jesus says to us as he said to Nathanael: "You will see much greater things than that" (Jn 1:50). Throughout our lives, after we have made a sacred and permanent commitment and after our active service of the Lord has begun, we still need the dialogue of prayer that will continually deepen our knowledge and love of our Lord Jesus Christ.

Dear students for the priesthood and candidates for the religious life, you stand in a long line of people who have given themselves totally for the sake of the Kingdom of God, and who have shared our Lord's sacrifice and entered into his paschal victory. For generations, many of the generous priests and religious who have served the Church in Texas have come with immigrants from other lands, or as missionaries from other places. I wish to express my gratitude to God for the contribution which they have made to establishing the Church here. At the same time, I praise the Lord of the harvest for all of you and for the growing number of native-born vocations, and I fervently pray that this increase continues.

Like all those who have gone before you, you will have trials. Your fidelity will be ensured only when you invoke the strength of the Lord, only when you rely on Christ's grace. But if Christ is the center of your lives, the one for whom you live and die, then your generous service to your brothers and sisters will know no limits. You will love those who are difficult to love, and you will enrich the world with the gospel of Jesus Christ.

I would now like to speak to the seminarians. Dear brothers in Christ, as men preparing for priestly ordination, it is important for you to have a clear understanding of the vocation to which you feel called so that your promise of lifelong fidelity may be maturely made and faithfully kept. Your life in the priesthood will closely join you with the Eucharist; you will be ministers of the mysteries of God; you will be expected to preach and teach in the name of the Church.

The Eucharist is the principal reason for the ordained priesthood. As I said in my 1950 *Holy Thursday Letter:* "Through our ordination . . . we priests are united in a singular and exceptional way to the Eucharist. In a certain way we derive from it and exist for it" (2). No work we do as priests is so important. The celebration of the Eucharist is the way that we best serve our brothers and sisters in the world because it is the source and center of the dynamism of their Christian lives. How crucial it is then, for our own happiness and for the sake of a fruitful ministry, that we cultivate a deep love for the Eucharist. During your seminary days, a thorough theological study of the nature of the Eucharistic mystery and an accurate knowledge of liturgical norms will prepare you well to foster the full, conscious, and active participation of the community in the liturgy. The future priest is called to reflect and to profess with the Second Vatican Council that "the other sacraments, as well as every ministry of the Church and every work of the apostolate, are linked with the Holy Eucharist and are directed toward it. For the most Blessed Eucharist contains the Church's entire spiritual wealth, that is, Christ himself" (*Presbyterorum Ordinis*, 5).

The task of preaching the gospel is of supreme importance in the priesthood. And since, as Saint Paul says, "Faith comes through hearing, and what is heard is the word of Christ" (Rom 10:17), seminary formation must aim at fostering a deep understanding of the word of God as it is lived and proclaimed by the Church. Always remember the words of the prophet Jeremiah: "When I found your words, I devoured them; they became my joy and the happiness of my heart, because I bore your name, O Lord" (Jer 16:16).

In order for your preaching to bear fruit in the lives of those whom you will serve, you will have to nourish in your own mind and heart a real internal adherence to the Magisterium of the Church. For, as the Council reminded us, "the task of priests is not to teach their own wisdom but God's word, and to summon all people urgently to conversion and to holiness" (*Presbyterorum Ordinis*, 4).

The priest needs to know the real living conditions of the people he serves, and he must live among them as a true brother in Christ. He can never be separated from the community. But there is a real sense in which, like the apostle Paul, he is, in the very words of Scripture, "set apart to proclaim the gospel of God" (Rom 1:1). In his priestly identity he is commissioned for a special service, a unique service, to the Body of Christ. For this reason, the Second Vatican Council spoke in this way: "By their vocation and ordination, priests of the New Testament are indeed set apart in a certain sense within the midst of God's people. But this is so, not that they may be separated from this people or from any man, but that they may be totally dedicated to the work for which the Lord raised them up. They cannot be ministers of Christ unless they are witnesses and dispensers of a life other than this earthly one" (*Presbyterorum Ordinis*, 3).

Each one of you is called to embrace freely a celibate life for the sake of Jesus and his Kingdom, in order to become a "man for others." If modeled on the generous divine and human love of Jesus for his Father and for every man, woman, and child, your celibacy will mean an enhancement of your life, a greater closeness to God's people, an eagerness to give yourself without reserve. By embracing celibacy in the context of the priesthood, you are committing yourself to a deeper and more universal love. Above all, celibacy means the gift of yourself to God. It will be the response, in Christ and the Church, to the gifts of creation and redemption. It will be part of your sharing, at the deepest level of human freedom and generosity, in the death and resurrection of Jesus. Humanly speaking, this sacrifice is difficult because of our human weaknesses; without prayer it is impossible. It will also require discipline and effort and persevering love on your part. But in your gift of celibacy to Christ and his Church, even the world will be able to see the meaning of the Lord's grace and the power of his Paschal Mystery. This victory must always be visible in your joy.

The Council stressed the essential difference between the ordained priesthood and the priesthood of all the baptized and prescribed a priestly formation in seminaries which is distinct from other forms of formation (cf. *Lumen Gentium*, 10; *Optatam Totius*, 4). At the heart of this essential difference is the truth that Jesus entrusted the Twelve with the authority to proclaim the gospel, celebrate the Eucharist, forgive sins, and provide for the pastoral care of the community. This authority is given for a truly specific purpose and through ordination is shared by the successors of the apostles and their collaborators in the ordained priesthood. It is given for a particular ministry of service to be carried out in imitation of the Son of Man who came to serve. The ministry of the ordained priest is essential to the life and development of the Church; it is an essential service to the rest of the Church. It is clear that those who are preparing for this specific ministry will have special needs and requirements that differ from those of the rest of the community.

All the members of the Church are summoned to share in her mission by reason of their baptism and confirmation. Priests can best assist and encourage others in the service of the gospel by being faithful themselves to their priestly ministry in the Church. "Hence, whether engaged in prayer and adoration, preaching the Word, offering the Eucharistic Sacrifice, ministering the other sacraments, or performing any of the works of the ministry for people, priests are contributing to the extension of God's glory as well as to the development of divine life in people" (*Presbyterorum Ordinis*, 2)

And now I turn to you, my brothers and sisters who are preparing for the religious life. Yours too is a great and specific gift of God's love. To each of you, as to the first disciples, Jesus has said: "Come and see" (Jn 1:39). There is no force or coercion on the part of Christ, but rather an invitation, extended simply and personally, to come and stay in his house, to be in his presence, and with him to praise his Father in the unity of the Holy Spirit.

A religious vocation is a gift, freely given and freely received. It is a profound expression of the love of God for you and, on your part, it requires in turn a total love for Christ. Thus, the whole life of a religious is aimed at strengthening the bond of love which was first forged in the Sacrament of Baptism. You are called to do this in religious consecration through the profession of the evangelical counsels of chastity, poverty, and obedience (cf. c. 573 §§1-2).

During your years of preparation, the Church is eager that you receive a formation that will prepare you to live your religious consecration in fidelity and joy, a formation that is both deeply human and Christian, a formation that will help you to accept ever more generously the radical demands of the gospel and bear public witness to them. Your very life is meant to be a confident and convincing affirmation that Jesus is "the Way, and the Truth, and the Life" (Jn 14:6).

What you must develop, first and foremost, is the habit and discipline of prayer. For who you are is more fundamental than any service you perform. In this regard, the Second Vatican Council said that religious should "seek God before all things" and "combine contemplation with apostolic love" (*Perfectae Caritatis*, 5). This is no easy task, for prayer has many dimensions and forms. It is both personal and communal, liturgical and private. It deepens our union with God and fosters our apostolic love. A climate of silence is needed as well as a personal life style that is simple and ready for sacrifice.

The liturgical life of the community greatly influences the personal prayer of all the members. The Eucharist will always be the source and summit of your life in Christ. It is the sacrament through which the worship of your whole existence is presented to God in union with Christ (cf. c. 607 §1). The Eucharist is the point where the offering of your chastity, poverty, and obedience is made one with the sacrifice of Christ.

In your religious consecration, the Sacrament of Penance is a constant reminder to you of the call of Jesus to conversion and newness of life. Precisely because you are called by your religious profession to bear witness to the holiness of God, you must help the People of God never to lose their sense of sin. To be authentic in following Christ in the perfection of charity, you must be the first to recognize sin in your hearts, to repent, and to glorify God's grace and mercy. Conversion is a lifelong process requiring repentant love. The Sacrament of Penance is the sacrament in which our weakness meets God's holiness in the mercy of Christ.

In a thousand ways, the Church will call you into service in her mission for the Kingdom of God. She needs your talents, your availability to come and go according to the needs of the hour, which are often the needs of the poor. She needs your collaboration in the cause of faith and justice. She needs your work and everything that you can do for the gospel. But, above all, the Church needs what you are; she needs you: men and women consecrated to God, living in union with Christ, living in union with his Church, striving after the perfection of love. Why? Because of the holiness of God! Dear brothers and sisters, what you do is important, but what you are is even more important, more important for the world, more important for the Church, more important for Christ.

In Mary, the Mother of Christ and the Church, you will understand the identity of your own life. She showed throughout her life the meaning of the evangelical counsels, to which your religious consecration is directed. Her words to the angel—"I am the servant of the Lord. Let it be done to me as you say." (Lk 1:38)—show the obedient total surrender which our consecration to God requires and which your vows express.

Of course, the call to holiness is a universal call. All members of the Church, without exception, are summoned by God to grow in personal sanctity and to share in the mission of the Church. A heightened awareness of this truth has been one of the fruits of the Second Vatican Council. And it has helped foster a clearer awareness of the role of the laity in building up the Kingdom as well as a closer collaboration of the laity with the clergy and religious. As persons preparing for the priesthood and religious life, it will be your privilege to help explore still more effective forms of collaboration in the future. But even more important, you will be in a position to encourage the lay people to fulfill that mission which is uniquely their own in those situations and places in which the Church can be the salt of the earth only through them.

The Council spoke very clearly about their special mission. Among other things it stated: "The laity, by their very vocation, seek the Kingdom of God by engaging in temporal affairs and by ordering them according to the plan of God. They live in the world, that is, in each and in all of the secular professions and occupations. They live in the ordinary circumstances of family and social life, from which the very web of their existence is woven" (*Lumen Gentium*, 31). This activity of the laity constitutes a specific contribution to the Body of Christ. Yours is another charism, a different gift to be lived differently, so that, in true diversity, there may be real unity in the work of service.

On this occasion, I cannot fail to express my special gratitude and encouragement to those of you who are responsible for the formation of candidates for the priesthood and religious life. Be assured that all your efforts, work, and sacrifice are deeply appreciated by the Church and by me personally. Your task is a vital one for the future of the Church, and your contribution to the life of the People of God is a lasting one. Certainly, it is crucial that you be steeped in sound doctrine, pastoral experience, and holiness of life. Of great importance is your attitude of faith, and particularly your personal example of filial love for the Church, as well as your loyal adherence to her authentic ordinary Magisterium (cf. *Lumen Gentium*, 25). Saint Paul tells us: "Christ loved the Church. He gave himself up for her to make her holy" (Eph 5:25-26). I pray that your own lives will be always animated by this kind of sacrificial love.

I wish to add a word of deep appreciation to all those parents who sustain and encourage their children in the following of Christ. The prayerful support, understanding, and love that you give them is of immense value.

At this time, I wish to appeal to the Church in the United States for vocations to the priesthood and religious life. The duty of fostering such vocations rests on the whole Christian community, and certainly families have traditionally made the greatest contribution. We must always remember too the impact on vocations that can be made by zealous priests and religious, by their example of generous service, by the witness of their charity, their goodness and their joy. Above all, the key to vocations is persevering prayer, as Jesus himself commanded: "The harvest is good but laborers are scarce. Beg the harvest master to send out laborers to gather his harvest" (Mt 9:37-38).

Dear brothers and sisters, you have come to know the Lord Jesus. You have heard his voice, discovered his love, and answered his call. May he, the Lord Jesus, who has begun this good work in you bring it to completion for the glory of his Father and by the power of his Spirit. Remember always: "the place where you stand is holy ground" (Ex 3:5).

And may the Blessed Virgin Mary help you by her prayers and by the example of her love.

Address to Hispanics on Parish Life
Our Lady of Guadalupe Plaza

Dear Brothers and Sisters in Christ,

This is a moment of great joy for me. I have looked forward to this meeting with you, members of the Hispanic community of San Antonio, present here as representatives of all your Hispanic brothers and sisters in the United States. You are here too as a parish community, and through you therefore my words are addressed to every parish community throughout the United States.

I greet each one of you with love in our Lord and Redeemer Jesus Christ. I am particularly happy to speak to you in the beautiful Spanish language, in this square named in honor of Our Lady of Guadalupe. Our gathering here is a vivid reminder, in the current Marian Year, of the special place of the Mother of the Redeemer in the mystery of Christ and of the Church. It speaks to us of how dear our Blessed Mother has always been to you people of Hispanic culture and how important she continues to be today in your lives of faith and devotion. Marian shrines and places of pilgrimage are a kind of "geography" of faith by which we seek to meet the Mother of God in order to find a strengthening of our Christian life (cf. *Redemptoris Mater*, 28). Popular devotion to the Blessed Virgin Mary is rooted in sound doctrine, and authentic religious experience is appropriate and important in the lives of all Christ's followers.

The Hispanic heritage of San Antonio and the Southwest is very important for the Church. Spanish was the language of the first evangelizers of this continent, precisely in this region. The missions here in San Antonio and throughout the Southwest are visible signs of the many years of evangelization and service carried out by the first missionaries. Their preaching of salvation in Jesus Christ was authenticated by their own integrity of life and by the spiritual and corporal works of mercy and love which they performed. Following their example, thousands of dedicated priests, religious, and lay people have labored to build up the Church here. Today it is your turn, in fidelity to the gospel of Jesus Christ, to build your lives on the rock of your Christian faith. It is your turn to be evangelizers of each other and of all those whose faith is weak or who have not yet given themselves to the Lord. May you be no less zealous in evangelization and in Christian service than your forebears!

Today I wish to speak to you about your parish, which is the place and community in which you nourish and express your Christian life. I wish to speak of the parish as the family of families, for parish life is especially related to the strengths and weaknesses and needs of the families that make it up. There are, of course, many things that

94

could be said about parish life; today it is only possible for me to emphasize certain aspects.

It is useful to begin with a well-known passage from the New Testament which helps us to keep in mind just why the members of a Catholic parish come together in the name of Jesus. In the Acts of the Apostles, we read about the early Christians: "They devoted themselves to the apostles' instruction and the communal life, to the breaking of bread and prayers" (Acts 2:42). Instruction in the faith of the apostles, the building up of a living community, the Eucharist and the other sacraments, and the life of prayer—these are essential factors of the life of every parish.

First, instruction or catechesis. Everyone needs to be instructed in the faith. Saint Paul summarizes it this way: "Everyone who calls on the name of the Lord will be saved. But how shall they call on him in whom they have not believed? And how can they believe unless they have heard of him? And how can they hear unless there is someone to preach?" (Rom 10:13-14). In a parish, the faith is proclaimed and transmitted in many ways: through the liturgy, and especially the Eucharist with its appropriate homilies; through religious instruction in schools and catechetical programs; through adult religious education; through prayer-groups and associations for pastoral activity; through the Catholic press.

There are two things that I wish to emphasize about transmitting the faith. Catechesis has an objective content. We cannot invent the faith as we go along. We must receive it in and from the universal community of faith, the Church to whom Christ himself has entrusted a teaching office under the guidance of the Spirit of Truth. Every catechist must sincerely and reverently be able to apply to himself or herself the words of Jesus: "My doctrine is not my own, it comes from him who sent me" (Jn 7:16; cf. *Catechesi Tradendae*, 6). Likewise, every baptized person, precisely by reason of being baptized, has the right to receive the authentic teaching of the Church regarding doctrinal and moral aspects of Christian life (cf. c. 229; *Catechesi Tradendae*, 14).

The other point I wish to make about instruction in the faith is that family catechesis precedes, accompanies, and enriches all other forms of catechesis (cf. *Catechesi Trandendae*, 68). This means that the parish, in considering its catechetical programs, should give particular attention to its families. But above all, it means that the family itself is the first and most appropriate place for teaching the truths of the faith, the practice of Christian virtues, and the essential values of human life.

The second aspect of parish life that is contained in the text from the Acts of the Apostles concerns the parish's task of building up a living community. I have already said that every parish is a family of families. The vitality of a parish greatly depends on the spiritual vigor, commitment, and involvement of its families. The family in fact is the basic unit of society and of the Church. It is "the domestic church." Families are those living cells which come together to form the very substance of parish life. Some are healthy and filled with the love of

God which is poured forth into our hearts through the Holy Spirit who has been given to us (cf. Rom 5:5). In some, there is little energy for the life of the Spirit. Some have broken down altogether. The priests and their collaborators in a parish must try to be very close to all families in their need for pastoral care and provide the support and spiritual nourishment they require.

The pastoral care of families is a vast and complex field of the Church's ministry, but it is a most urgent and pressing service. Each parish must be fully committed to it, especially in the face of so much breakdown and undermining of family life in society. I appeal to all priests—pastors, associates, and all concerned—to the permanent deacons, and to the religious and lay leaders to do everything possible, working together, to serve the family as effectively as possible. This involves proclaiming the whole truth about marriage and family life: the exclusive nature of conjugal love; the indissolubility of marriage; the Church's full teaching on the transmission of life and the respect due to human life from the moment of conception until natural death; the rights and duties of parents with regard to the education of their children, especially their religious and moral education, including proper sex education. Parents and family members must, moreover, be helped, and sustained in their struggle to live by the sacred truths of faith. The Church must furnish families with the spiritual means of persevering in their sublime vocation and of growing in the special holiness to which Christ calls them.

Just as the parish is responsible for the family, so the family must be aware of its obligations to the parish, which is the larger family. Today, Catholic couples and families must think especially of the service which they have a duty to render to other couples and families, especially those who experience problems. This apostolate of couple to couple and family to family can be carried out in many ways: prayer, good example, formal or informal instruction or counseling, and material assistance of many sorts (cf. *Familiaris Consortio*, 71). I appeal to you the Catholic families of the United States: be true families—united, reconciled, and loving; and be true Catholic families—prayerful communities living the Catholic faith, open to the needs of others, taking part fully in the life of the parish and of the Church at large.

Another fundamental aspect of parish life is the worthy celebration of the sacraments, including sacramental marriage. This sacrament forms the stable basis of the whole Christian community. Without it, Christ's design for human love is not fulfilled, his plan for the family is not followed. It is precisely because Christ established marriage as a sacrament and willed it to be a sign of his own permanent and faithful love for the Church that the parish must explain to the faithful why all trial marriages, merely civil marriages, free unions, and divorces do not correspond to Christ's plan.

The sacramental life of the Church is centered above all upon the Eucharist, which celebrates and brings about the unity of the Christian community, unity with God and unity with one another. In the Mass, the sacrifice of the cross is perpetuated throughout the centuries until Christ comes again. The Body and Blood of the Lord are given to us as our spiritual food. The parish community has no greater task or privilege than to gather, like Christ's first disciples, for "the breaking of the bread" (Acts 2:42).

I now repeat especially to all parishes the invitation already addressed to the whole Church: to promote and foster public and private devotion to the Holy Eucharist also outside of Mass (cf. *Inaestimabile Donum*, 20ff.). For, in the words of the Second Vatican Council: "The most blessed Eucharist contains the Church's entire spiritual wealth, that is, Christ himself" (*Presbyterorum Ordinis*, 5).

The sacramental life of a parish extends also to the other sacraments which mark the important moments of the life of individuals and families, and of the entire parochial community. I wish to mention in particular the Sacrament of Penance and the important need for Catholics to confess their sins regularly. In recent years, many have grown neglectful of this wonderful gift by which we obtain Christ's forgiveness of our sins. The state of the Sacrament of Penance in each parish and in each local Church is a good indicator of the authentic maturity of the faith of the priests and people. It is necessary that Catholic families instill in their members a deep love of this beautiful means of reconciliation with our heavenly Father, with the Church, and with our neighbor. Parents, more by example than by words, should encourage their children to go to confession regularly. Parishes need to encourage families to do this; they need to support them through proper catechesis. Needless to say, priests, who are the ministers of God's grace in this sacrament, should make certain that the sacrament is conveniently available in its authorized forms.

Finally, I refer briefly to the life of prayer as it manifests itself within the Christian community. This is an area in which the interaction between the family and the parish is especially clear and profound. Prayer begins in the home. The prayers that serve us well in life are often those learned at home when we were children. But prayer in the home also serves to introduce the children to the liturgical prayer of the whole Church, it helps all to apply the Church's prayer to everyday events and to the special moments of a family's experience (cf. *Familiaris Consortio*, 61).

Everyone involved in parish life should be concerned to encourage and support family prayer by every means available; and families themselves should be making efforts to engage in family prayer and to integrate that prayer into the prayer-life of the wider ecclesial community.

I am happy to know that the number of Hispanic priests and men and women religious is growing. But many more are needed. Young Hispanics: Is Christ calling you? Hispanic families: Are you willing to give your sons and daughters to the Church's service? Do you ask the Lord to send laborers into his harvest? Christ needs Hispanic laborers for the great harvest of the Hispanic community and the whole Church.

And finally, I wish to encourage all families and parishes not to be inward-looking, not to dwell on themselves. Jesus commands to serve our neighbor, to reach out to those in need. And I ask you especially to reach out to those brothers and sisters in the faith who have drifted away because of indifference or who have been hurt in some way. I invite all you who are unsure about the Church or who doubt that you will be welcome to come home to the family of families, to come home to your parish. You belong there! It is our family in the Church, and the Church is the household of God in which there are no strangers or aliens (cf. Eph 2:19).

We are gathered in front of a parish which is dedicated to Our Lady of Guadalupe, Mother of Jesus, Mother of the Church, Mother of the Americas, and in particular of Mexico. When Jesus died on the cross, he entrusted his Mother to his beloved disciple, John. The gospel tells us that from that moment the disciple took her into his home (cf. Jn 19:27). What better way is there for you to celebrate this Marian Year than by taking Mary, the Mother of the Redeemer, into your homes! This means imitating her faith and discipleship; it means keeping her present in your family prayers, especially the family rosary; turning to her, asking her intercession for the grace of conversion and renewal; entrusting yourselves and your families to her maternal care.

> May God bless each and every one of you.
> May he bless every family and parish.
> May the Blessed Virgin of Guadalupe love and protect
>   the Hispanic people of the land.
> *Viva la Virgen de Guadalupe!*

PHOENIX, ARIZONA

Monday, September 14, 1987

Meeting with Catholic Health Care Leaders
Convention Center in Civic Plaza

Dear Brothers and Sisters, Leaders in Catholic Health Care,

In the joy and peace of our Lord Jesus Christ I greet you and thank you for your warm welcome. This meeting gives us the opportunity to honor and give thanks to God for one of the most extensive and fundamental works of the Catholic Church in the United States, all that is embraced in the term "Catholic health care". I am pleased to be able to express to you who represent so many of your country's health care organizations the esteem, support, and solidarity of the whole Church. In you, Jesus Christ continues his healing ministry, "curing the people of every disease and illness" (cf. Mt 4:23).

This is the high dignity to which you and your colleagues are called. This is your vocation, your commitment, and the path of your specific witness to the presence of God's Kingdom in the world. Your health care ministry, pioneered and developed by congregations of women religious and by congregations of brothers, is one of the most vital apostolates of the ecclesial community and one of the most significant services which the Catholic Church offers to society in the name of Jesus Christ. I have been told that membership in the Catholic Health Association extends to 620 hospitals and 300 long-term care facilities; that Catholic hospital beds number 11 percent of the total number in the country; that Catholic institutions administer approximately 17 percent of the health care throughout the nation, and that they cared for nearly 46 million people last year. I am grateful to Sister Mary Eileen Wilhelm and to your president, Mr. Curley for illustrating to us this immense network of Christian service.

Because of your dedication to caring for the sick and the poor, the aged and the dying, you know from your own daily experience how much illness and suffering are basic problems of human existence. When the sick flocked to Jesus during his earthly life, they recognized in him a friend whose deeply compassionate and loving heart responded to their needs. He restored physical and mental health to many. These cures, however, involved more than just healing sickness. They were also prophetic signs of his own identity and of the coming of the Kingdom of God, and they very often caused a new spiritual awakening in the one who had been healed.

The power that went out from Jesus and cured people of his own time (cf. Lk 6:19) has not lost its effect in the two thousand year history of the Church. This power remains, in the life and prayer of the Church, a source of healing and reconciliation. Ever active, this power confirms the identity of the Church today, authenticates her proclamation of the Kingdom of God, and stands as a sign of triumph over evil.

With all Catholic health care the immediate aim is to provide for the well-being of the body and mind of the human person, especially in sickness or old age. By his example, Christ teaches the Christian "to do good by his or her suffering and to do good to those who suffer" (*Salvifici Doloris*, 30). This latter aspect naturally absorbs the greater part of the energy and attention of health care ministry. Today in the United States, Catholic health care extends the mission of the Church in every State of the Union, in major cities, small towns, rural areas, on the campuses of academic institutions, in remote outposts, and in inner-city neighborhoods. By providing health care in all these places, especially to the poor, the neglected, the needy, the newcomer, your apostolate penetrates and transforms the very fabric of American society. And sometimes you yourselves, like those you serve, are called to bow, in humble and loving resignation to the experience of sickness or to other forms of pain and suffering.

All concern for the sick and suffering is part of the Church's life and mission. The Church has always understood herself to be charged by Christ with the care of the poor, the weak, the defenseless, the suffering, and those who mourn. This means that, as you alleviate suffering and seek to heal, you also bear witness to the Christian view of suffering and to the meaning of life and death as taught by your Christian faith.

In the complex world of modern health care in industrialized society, this witness must be given in a variety of ways. First, it requires continual efforts to ensure that everyone has access to health care. I know that you have already examined this question in the report of your task force on health care of the poor. In seeking to treat patients equally, regardless of social and economic status, you proclaim to your fellow citizens and to the world Christ's special love for the neglected and powerless. This particular challenge is a consequence of your Christian dedication and conviction, and it calls for great courage on the part of Catholic bodies and institutions operating in the field of health care. It is a great credit to your zeal and efficiency when, despite formidable costs, you still succeed in preventing the economic factor from being the determinant factor in human and Christian service.

Similarly, the love with which Catholic health care is performed and its professional excellence have the value of a sign testifying to the Christian view of the human person. The inalienable dignity of every human being is, of course, fundamental to all Catholic health care. All who come to you for help are worthy of respect for all have been created in the image and likeness of God. All have been redeemed by Christ and, in their sufferings, bear his cross. It is fitting that our meeting is taking place on the Feast of the Triumph of the Cross. Christ took upon himself the whole of human suffering and radically transformed it through the Paschal Mystery of his passion, death, and resurrection. The triumph of the cross gives human suffering a new dimension, a redemptive value (cf. *Salvifici Doloris*, 24). It is your privilege to bear constant witness to this profound truth in so many ways.

The structural changes which have been taking place within Catholic health care in recent years have increased the challenge of preserving and even strengthening the Catholic identity of the institutions and the spiritual quality of the services given. The presence of dedicated women and men religious in hospitals and nursing homes has ensured in the past, and continues to ensure in the present, that spiritual dimension so characteristic of Catholic health care centers. The reduced number of religious and new forms of ownership and management should not lead to a loss of a spiritual atmosphere or to a loss of a sense of vocation in caring for the sick. This is an area in which the Catholic laity, at all levels of health care, have an opportunity to manifest the depth of their faith and to play their own specific part in the Church's mission of evangelization and service.

As I have said, Catholic health care must always be carried out within the framework of the Church's saving mission. This mission she has received from her divine founder, and she has accomplished it down through the ages with the help of the Holy Spirit who guides her into the fullness of truth (cf. Jn 16:13; *Lumen Gentium*, 4). Your ministry therefore must also reflect the mission of the Church as the teacher of moral truth, especially in regard to the new frontiers of scientific research and technological achievement. Here too you face great challenges and opportunities.

Many times in recent years the Church has addressed issues related to the advances of biomedical technology. She does so not in order to discourage scientific progress or to judge harshly those who seek to extend the frontiers of human knowledge and skill, but in order to affirm the moral truths which must guide the application of this knowledge and skill. Ultimately, the purpose of the Church's teaching in this field is to defend the innate dignity and fundamental rights of the human person. In this regard the Church cannot fail to emphasize the need to safeguard the life and integrity of the human embryo and fetus.

The human person is a unique composite—a unity of spirit and matter, soul and body, fashioned in the image of God and destined to live forever. Every human life is sacred, because every human person is sacred. It is in the light of this fundamental truth that the Church constantly proclaims and defends the dignity of human life

101

from the moment of conception to the moment of natural death. It is also in the light of this fundamental truth that we see the great evil of abortion and euthanasia.

Not long ago, in its *Instruction on Respect for Human Life in Its Origin and on the Dignity of Procreation*, the Congregation for the Doctrine of the Faith once more dealt with certain vital questions concerning the human person. Once more it defended the sanctity of innocent human life from the moment of conception onward. Once again it affirmed the sacred and inviolable character of the transmission of human life by the procreative act within marriage. It explained that new technologies may afford new means of procreation, but "what is technically possible is not for that very reason morally admissible" (Introduction, 4). To place new human knowledge at the service of the integral well-being of human persons does not inhibit true scientific progress but liberates it. The Church encourages genuine advances in knowledge, but she also insists on the sacredness of human life at every stage and in every condition. The cause she serves is the cause of human life and human dignity.

In the exercise of your professional activities you have a magnificent opportunity, by your constant witness to moral truth, to contribute to the formation of society, a moral vision. As you give the best of yourselves in fulfilling your Christian responsibilities, you will also be aware of the important contribution you must make to building a society based on truth and justice. Your service to the sick enables you with great credibility to proclaim to the world the demands and values of the gospel of Jesus Christ, and to foster hope and renewal of heart. In this respect, your concern with the Catholic identity of your work and of your institutions is not only timely and commendable, it is essential for the success of your ecclesial mission.

You must always see yourselves and your work as part of the Church's life and mission. You are indeed a very special part of the People of God. You and your institutions have precise responsibilities toward the ecclesial community, just as that community has responsibilities toward you. It is important at every level—national, state, and local—that there be close and harmonious links between you and the bishops, who "preside in place of God over the flock whose shepherds they are, as teachers of doctrine, priests of sacred worship, and officers of good order" (*Lumen Gentium*, 20). They for their part wish to support you in your witness and service.

I have come here today to encourage you in your splendid work and to confirm you in your vital apostolate. Dear brothers and sisters, for your dedication to meeting the health care needs of all people, especially the poor, I heartily congratulate you. You embody the legacy of those pioneering women and men religious who selflessly responded to the health care needs of a young and rapidly expanding country by developing an extensive network of clinics, hospitals, and nursing homes.

Today you are faced with new challenges, new needs. One of these is the present crisis of immense proportions which is that of AIDS and AIDS-related Complex (ARC). Besides your professional contribution and your human sensitivities toward all affected by this disease, you are called to show the love and compassion of Christ and his Church. As you courageously affirm and implement your moral obligation and social responsibility to help those who suffer, you are, individually and collectively, living out the parable of the Good Samaritan (cf. Lk 10:30-32).

The Good Samaritan of the parable showed compassion to the injured man. By taking him to the inn and giving of his own material means, he truly gave of himself. This action, a universal symbol of human concern, has become one of the essential elements of moral culture and civilization. How beautifully the Lord speaks of the Samaritan! He "was neighbor to the man who fell in with the robbers" (Lk 10:36). To be "neighbor" is to express love, solidarity, and service, and to exclude selfishness, discrimination, and neglect. The message of the parable of the Good Samaritan echoes a reality connected with today's Feast of the Triumph of the Cross: "the kindness and love of God our Savior appeared . . . that we might be justified by his grace and become heirs, in hope, of eternal life" (Ti 3:4-7). In the changing world of health care, it is up to you to ensure that this "kindness and love of God our Savior" remains the heart and soul of Catholic health services.

Through prayer and with God's help, may you persevere in your commitment, providing professional assistance and selfless personal care to those who need your services. I pray that your activities and your whole lives will inspire and help all the people of America, working together, to make this society a place of full and absolute respect for the dignity of every person, from the moment of conception to the moment of natural death. And may God, in whom "we live and move and have our being" (Acts 17:28), sustain you by his grace. God bless you and your families and your contribution to America!

Address at Saints Simon and Jude Cathedral

Dear Bishop O'Brien, Dear Brothers and Sisters in Christ,

It is a joy for me to come to the Cathedral of Saints Simon and Jude, and to be with you who make up this local church in Phoenix. This house of prayer and worship, this mother church of the diocese, is named after two of the twelve apostles, two men of courageous faith who personally received from our Risen Savior the mandate to preach the gospel to the ends of the earth. Jesus said to them and the rest of the Twelve: "Go, therefore, and make disciples of all the nations.

103

Baptize them in the name of the Father, and of the Son, and of the Holy Spirit. Teach them to carry out everything I have commanded you" (Mt 28:19-20).

Simon and Jude responded wholeheartedly to this summons and spent the rest of their lives seeking "to open up for all people a free and sure path to full participation in the mystery of Christ" (*Ad Gentes*, 5).

The Church, built as she is on the foundation of the apostles and prophets (cf. Eph 2:20), has inherited the same mission that Jesus first entrusted to the Twelve. The Church is by her very nature missionary, "for it is from the mission of the Son and the mission of the Holy Spirit that she takes her origin, in accordance with the decree of God the Father" (*Ad Gentes*, 2). She has the honor and privilege, and also the obligation, of bringing the Good News of salvation to all nations, to every person. As the bishops of the United States stated last November in their pastoral statement on world mission: "We are faithful to the nature of the Church to the degree that we love and sincerely promote her missionary activity" (*To the Ends of the Earth*, 2).

The Church in Phoenix, like every other local church in the world, is the fruit of evangelization. The gospel was first brought to Arizona 300 years ago by the renowned Jesuit missionary, Father Eusebio Kino, also known as the "Apostle of Sonora and Arizona." At great personal sacrifice Father Kino worked tirelessly to establish missions throughout this area so that the Good News concerning our Lord Jesus Christ might take root among the people living here.

And the gospel did take root, and numerous other missionaries came after Father Kino to continue the evangelizing effort. Perhaps the most zealous among these was the Franciscan, Francisco Garces. With particular love for the Indian people, he sought to present the gospel to them in a way adapted to their culture; at the same time he also encouraged them to live in harmony and peace among themselves. So completely was his life patterned on that of our Lord, that he ended his labors here by shedding his blood for the gospel.

The missionary efforts continued down through the years, and the Church became firmly established in Arizona. The rich fruit of this evangelization is clearly evident today in this quickly growing Diocese of Phoenix and in the expanding dioceses of the surrounding area. The gospel has truly taken root here and has brought forth fruit in abundance.

And yet, the work of evangelization is not over. On earth it will never be over. Indeed so much remains to be done. Let us not forget the words of the Second Vatican Council which said that missionary activity is "a supremely great and sacred task of the Church" (*Ad Gentes*, 29). The duty of carrying forward this work rests on the whole Church and on every member of the Church.

The Church, at the close of the twentieth century, has need of many more missionaries with the zeal of Father Kino and Father Garces, persons of heroic faith like Saint Isaac Jogues, Saint John Neumann and Saint Frances Cabrini, who are willing to leave their own homeland to bring the message of salvation to people in other lands, especially to those who have never heard the word of God.

Who will meet this need? The gospel message has still not been heard by two-thirds of the world's population. Who will respond to God's missionary call at the end of the twentieth century? Jesus says: "Whoever loves father or mother, son or daughter more than me is not worthy of me" (Mt 10:37). We must be worthy of Christ.

Not everyone is asked to leave home and loved ones for this task, but all are called to bear the burden, to do their part. As the American bishops have said so well: "Jesus' great commission to the first disciples is now addressed to us. . . . This mission to the peoples of all nations must involve all of us personally in our parishes and at the diocesan and universal levels of the Church" (*To the Ends of the Earth*, 3).

Missionaries in foreign countries deserve our prayerful support and material help. American Catholics have been especially generous in the past, a generosity and interest that show your genuine missionary spirit. The practice of "twinning" between American parishes and dioceses and those of Africa and Asia has been of great benefit. With gratitude I commend you, and in the name of the Universal Church I ask your continued help and prayers. Great assistance has been given to the missions by mission aid societies such as the Society for the Propagation of the Faith and the Association of the Holy Childhood. Nor can we ever forget the generous missionary work that has been carried out for decades by religious institutes and missionary societies of the United States, and also by generous *Fidei Donum* priests and by lay missionaries. The reward of those who have sacrificed everything to spread the gospel will be great in heaven.

Dear brothers and sisters, the Letter to the Hebrews tells us that God the Father considered it fitting to make Christ, our leader in the work of salvation, "perfect through suffering" (Heb 2:10). In a similar way, he led the apostles Simon and Jude through the suffering of martyrdom to perfection in eternity. In every age of the Church, God makes his chosen ones "perfect through suffering," bringing them to the fullness of life and happiness by giving them on earth a share in the cross of Christ.

It is easy to understand that God's plan for us passes along the way of the Holy Cross, because it was so for Jesus and his apostles. Brothers and sisters, never be surprised to find yourselves passing under the shadow of the cross. Christian life finds its whole meaning in love, but love does not exist for us without effort, discipline and sacrifice in every aspect of our life. We are willing to give in proportion as we love, and when love is perfect the sacrifice is complete. God so loved the world that he gave his only Son, and the Son so loved us that he gave his life for our salvation.

On this day when Catholics around the world celebrate the triumph of the cross, the Church invites us to look once again at the meaning of our Christian discipleship, to understand the sacrifices it involves, and place all our hope in our Crucified and Risen Savior.

Triumphant Cross of Christ, inspire us to continue the task of evangelization!
Glorious Cross of Christ, strengthen us to proclaim and live the gospel of salvation!
Victorious Cross of Christ, our only hope, lead us to the joy and peace of the Resurrection and eternal life! Amen.

Meeting with Native Americans
Veterans' Memorial Coliseum

Presentation by Mrs. Alfretta M. Antone

Your Holiness, Pope John Paul II,

We welcome you and thank you for this sacred time together. We are affirmed and encouraged by your support of native peoples throughout the world. We respect you as a great spiritual leader and pray that you can help us on our road of life today.

As we approach five hundred years of Catholic Christianity in the Americas, we pray that all who come to this land will respect our grandparents who have lived on this land for over fifty thousand years. Upon initial contact with Europeans, we shared the land given us by our Creator and taught others how to survive here. History, however, stands as a witness to the use and abuse we have experienced in our homelands.

Today, little remains of the gifts and richness which our Creator has shared with us, the original peoples of these lands. We ask you to intervene with all people of good will to preserve our homelands for our families, our children, and the generations to follow us.

We choose not only to survive, but to live fully. We want to live in harmony with all people and all of creation. We choose to keep alive for all generations the ways of living carved in the stones and bones of our ancestors. We are open to share and receive whatever is good for the life of the human family with all people of good will. Our traditions, our languages, our cultures with their rich teachings and values, our songs and dances, our stories and paintings, our art and ways of living, celebrate who we are as people of many tribes.

We pray that our governments and all our rights as distinct peoples be honored and respected. We ask Your Holiness to do all in your prayer, power, and influence to help us secure, for our present and future generations, the following:

First, that our people be recognized, respected, and treated as equals;

Second, that our people determine our own destiny, develop our own lands and resources, plan and make our own decisions in all matters that are properly our own;

Third, that our sacred ways and prayers be respected;

Fourth, that we all learn to live in harmony as brothers and sisters on our Mother Earth;

Fifth, that racism, bigotry, and a sense of superiority be laid to rest in our times;

Sixth, that the United States and other governments honor the solemn agreements and treaties they have made with us which safeguard our lands, waters, and other natural resources;

Seventh, that just compensation be given for our lands which were taken illegally through theft or violation of treaties with our ancestors;

Eighth, that governments, churches, and all people of good will share the goods and resources of Mother Earth so that our people can walk tall, side by side with all people;

Ninth, that the Native American people be given the opportunity for a fair share in the resources of the world to provide the necessary housing, health care, and general well-being;

Tenth, that our people share equally in the educational, health, and social benefits of the Americas;

Eleventh, that our youth be given the necessary support and encouragement to work for a just present and future of our people;

Twelfth, that our people be strengthened in our resolve to overcome the alcohol and drug dependencies which have brought us such great suffering.

We recognize that our Native brothers and sisters come from many distinct tribes. We pray that we can work together in unity and mutual respect for both our individual and common good.

We also recognize that many of our Native brothers and sisters have exercised their freedom of religion by following either their own traditional sacred ways, another world religion, or other Christian traditions. Many of us have chosen the Roman Catholic way of walking with Jesus, speaking his truth and living his life of grace.

As Roman Catholics, we Native Peoples ask Your Holiness to

strengthen and affirm us. Until recent times, many of our people have turned away from the Church. Holy Father, we have always respected the one God, who made all and who is without equal beginning. The Creator has given us a way of life on Mother Earth. As Catholic Natives, we have come to know Jesus as the Son of God, who loves us and lives with us. The Holy Spirit works in many ways through our people. We are encouraged by the support the Roman Catholic Church gives us in affirming the beauty and value of our traditional prayers and ceremonies.

Our people are sharing their own cultural gifts in living and celebrating the mysteries of our Catholic faith. Our languages, which we treasure, are now even spoken by some of the missionaries. Yet, we still need your help and guidance in certain areas:

> *First*, as Native Peoples, we seek to follow Jesus Christ in the languages and cultures which God has given us.

> *Second*, we seek a fuller participation in the life of the Universal Church as bishops, priests, deacons, religious, catechists, and in all lay ministries.

> *Third*, we seek a fuller inclusion of our cultural gifts and languages in the sacramental life of the Church.

> *Fourth*, we seek the canonization of Blessed Kateri Tekakwitha. This young Mohawk woman has given our people a beautiful example of a Native person living out the Christian gospel. Through her help, our people are being gathered to the Church.

Your Holiness, as Native Peoples, we are affirmed in our journey and encouraged in our work through your love and support of us. We pray that God will continue to bless you and your ministry.

In the name of all Native Americans, we ask Your Holiness for your blessing and guidance as we walk together with God, as we live here on Mother Earth and for all time to come.

John Paul II's Response

Dear Brothers and Sisters,

I have greatly looked forward to this visit with you, the original peoples of this vast country. I greet you with love and respect. I thank you for inviting me to be with you and for sharing with me some aspects of your rich and ancient culture.

I have listened to your concerns and hopes. As your representatives spoke, I traced in my heart the history of your tribes and nations. I was able to see you as the noble descendants of countless generations of inhabitants of this land, whose ways were marked by great respect for the natural resources of land and river, of forest and plain and desert. Here your forefathers cherished and sought to pass on to each new generation their customs and traditions, their history, and way of life. Here they worshipped the Creator and thanked him for his gifts. In contact with the forces of nature they learned the value of prayer, of silence and fasting, of patience, and courage in the face of pain and disappointment.

The early encounter between your traditional cultures and the European way of life was an event of such significance and change that it profoundly influences your collective life even today. That encounter was a harsh and painful reality for your peoples. The cultural oppression, the injustices, the disruption of your life, and of your traditional societies must be acknowledged.

At the same time, in order to be objective, history must record the deeply positive aspects of your peoples' encounter with the culture that came from Europe. Among these positive aspects I wish to recall the work of the many missionaries who strenuously defended the rights of the original inhabitants of this land. They established missions throughout this southwestern part of the United States. They worked to improve living conditions and set up educational systems, learning your languages in order to do so. Above all, they proclaimed the Good News of salvation in our Lord Jesus Christ, an essential part of which is that all men and women are equally children of God and must be respected and loved as such. This gospel of Jesus Christ is today, and will remain forever, the greatest pride and possession of your people.

One priest who deserves special mention among the missionaries is the beloved Fray Junipero Serra, who travelled throughout lower and upper California. He had frequent clashes with the civil authorities over the treatment of Indians. In 1773 he presented to the viceroy in Mexico City a representation, which is sometimes termed a "Bill of Rights" for Indians. The Church had long been convinced of the need to protect them from exploitation. Already in 1537, my predecessor Pope Paul III proclaimed the dignity and rights of the native peoples of the Americas by insisting that they not be deprived of their freedom or the possession of their property (*Pastorale Officium*, May 29, 1537: DS 1495). In Spain the Dominican priest, Francisco de Vitoria, became the staunch advocate of the rights of the Indians and formulated the basis for international law regarding the rights of peoples.

Unfortunately not all the members of the Church lived up to their Christian responsibilities. But let us not dwell excessively on mistakes and wrongs, even as we commit ourselves to overcoming their present effects. Let us also be grateful to those who came to this land, faithful to the teachings of Jesus, witnesses of his new commandment of love. These men and women with good hearts and good minds shared knowledge and skills from their own cultures, and shared their most precious heritage, the faith, as well. Now, we are called to learn from the mistakes of the past and we must work together for reconciliation and healing, as brothers and sisters in Christ.

It is time to think of the present and of the future. Today, people are realizing more and more clearly that we all belong to the one human family, and are meant to walk and work together in mutual respect, understanding, trust, and love. Within this family each people preserves and expresses its own identity and enriches others with its gifts of culture, tradition, customs, stories, song, dance, art, and skills.

From the very beginning, the Creator bestowed his gifts on each people. It is clear that stereotyping, prejudice, bigotry, and racism demean the human dignity which comes from the hand of the Creator and which is seen in variety and diversity. I encourage you, as native people belonging to the different tribes and nations in the East, South, West, and North, to preserve and keep alive your cultures, your languages, the values and customs which have served you well in the past and which provide a solid foundation for the future. Your customs that mark the various stages of life, your love for the extended family, your respect for the dignity and worth of every human being, from the unborn to the aged, and your stewardship and care of the earth: these things benefit not only yourselves but the entire human family.

Your gifts can also be expressed even more fully in the Christian way of life. The gospel of Jesus Christ is at home in every people. It enriches, uplifts, and purifies every culture. All of us together make up the People of God, the Body of Christ, the Church. We should all be grateful for the growing unity, presence, voice, and leadership of Catholic Native Americans in the Church today.

Jesus speaks of the word of God as the seed which falls on good ground and produces abundant fruit (cf. Mt 13:4ff.). The seed has long since been planted in the hearts of many of you. And it has already produced the fruits which show its transforming power, the fruits of holiness. The best known witness of Christian holiness among the native peoples of North America is Kateri Tekakwitha, whom I had the privilege, seven years ago, of declaring "Blessed" and of holding up to the whole Church and the world as an outstanding example of Christian life. Even when she dedicated herself fully to Jesus Christ, to the point of taking the prophetic step of making a vow of perpetual virginity, she always remained what she was, a true daughter of her people, following her tribe in the hunting seasons and continuing her devotions in the environment most suited to her way of life, before a rough cross carved by herself in the forest. The gospel of Jesus Christ, which is the great gift of God's love, is never in contrast with what is noble and pure in the life of any tribe or nation, since all good things are his gifts.

I would like to repeat what I said at my meeting with native peoples at the Shrine of Saint Anne de Beaupré during my visit to Canada in

1984: "Your encounter with the gospel has not only enriched you; it has enriched the Church. We are well aware that this has not taken place without its difficulties and, occasionally, its blunders. However, and you are experiencing this today, the gospel does not destroy what is best in you. On the contrary, it enriches as it were from within, the spiritual qualities and gifts that are distinctive of your cultures." The American bishops' statement on Native Americans rightly attests that our Catholic faith is capable of thriving "within each culture, . . . within each nation, . . . within each race, while remaining the prisoner of none" (*Statement of U.S. Catholic Bishops on American Indians*, 8).

Here too I wish to urge the local churches to be truly "catholic" in their outreach to native peoples, and to show respect and honor for their culture and all their worthy traditions. From your ranks have come a bishop, a number of priests, many permanent deacons, men and women religious, and lay leaders. To all of you who have an active part in the Church's ministry I wish to express my gratitude and support. But the Church has some special needs at this time. And for this reason I directly appeal to you, especially to you young Native Americans, to discover if Jesus is calling you to the priesthood or to the religious life. Hear him and follow him! He will never let you down! He will lead you, in the Church, to serve your own peoples and others in the best way possible, in love and apostolic generosity.

At the same time I call upon your native Catholic communities to work together to share their faith and their gifts, to work together on behalf of all your peoples. There is much to be done in solving common problems of unemployment, inadequate health care, alcoholism, and chemical dependency. You have endured much over hundreds of years and your difficulties are not yet at an end. Continue taking steps toward true human progress and toward reconciliation within your families and your communities, and among your tribes and nations.

One day Jesus said: "The thief comes only to steal and slaughter and destroy. I came that they might have life and have it to the full" (Jn 10:10).

Surely the time has come for the native peoples of America to have a new life in Jesus Christ—the new life of adopted children of God, with all its consequences: A life in justice and full human dignity! A life of pride in their own good traditions, and of fraternal solidarity among themselves and with all their brothers and sisters in America! A deeper life in charity and grace, leading to the fullness of eternal life in heaven!

All consciences must be challenged. There are real injustices to be addressed and biased attitudes to be changed. But the greatest challenge is to you yourselves as Native Americans. You must continue to grow in respect for your own inalienable human dignity, for the gifts of creation and redemption as they touch your lives and the lives of your peoples. You must unyieldingly pursue your spiritual and moral goals. You must trust in your own future.

As Catholic Native Americans, you are called to become instruments of the healing power of Christ's love, instruments of his peace. May the Church in your midst—your own community of faith and fellowship—truly bear witness to the new life that comes from the cross and resurrection of our Lord and Savior Jesus Christ!

Homily at Phoenix Eucharist
Sun Devil Stadium, Arizona State University

The Son of Man must be lifted up (Jn 3:14).

Dear Brothers and Sisters,

On this day when I have the joy of celebrating the Eucharist with you here in Phoenix, let our first thoughts be directed to the victorious cross of our Savior, to the Son of Man who is lifted up! Let us adore and praise Christ, our Crucified and Risen Lord. To him, and to the Father and the Holy Spirit, be glory and thanksgiving now and forever!

How good it is to join our voices in praise of God on this Feast of the Triumph of the Cross. And how appropriate to celebrate the feast here in the city of Phoenix, which bears the name of an ancient symbol often depicted in Christian art to represent the meaning of the victorious cross. The phoenix was a legendary bird that, after dying, rose again from its own ashes. Thus, it came to be a symbol of Christ who, after dying on the cross, rose again in triumph over sin and death.

We can rightly say that, by divine providence, the Church in Phoenix has been called in a particular way to live the mystery of the victory of the cross. Certainly, the cross of Christ has marked the progress of evangelization in this area since its beginning: from the day, 300 years ago, when Father Eusebio Kino first brought the gospel to Arizona. The Good News of salvation has brought forth great fruit here in Phoenix, in Tucson, and throughout this whole area. The cross is indeed the Tree of Life.

The Son of Man must be lifted up (Jn 3:14).

Today the Church makes special reference to these words of Christ as she celebrates the Feast of the Triumph of the Cross. Beyond the particular historical circumstances that contributed to the introduction of this feast in the liturgical calendar, there remain these words that Christ spoke to Nicodemus during that conversation which took place at night: "The Son of Man must be lifted up."

112

Nicodemus, as we know, was a man who loved God's word and who studied the word with great attention. Prompted by his hunger for the truth, by his eagerness to understand, Nicodemus came to Jesus at night to find answers to his questions and doubts. It is precisely to him, to Nicodemus, that Jesus speaks these words which still echo in a mysterious way: "The Son of Man must be lifted up, that all who believe may have eternal life in him" (Jn 3:14-15).

Nicodemus could not have known at this point that these words contain, in a certain sense, the summary of the whole Paschal Mystery which would crown the messianic mission of Jesus of Nazareth. When Jesus spoke of being "lifted up" he was thinking of the cross on Calvary: being lifted up on the cross, being lifted up by means of the cross. Nicodemus could not have guessed this at the time. And so Christ referred to an event from the history of the Old Testament which he knew about, namely, Moses lifting up the serpent in the desert.

It was an unusual event that took place during Israel's journey from Egypt to the Promised Land. This journey that lasted 40 years was full of tests: the people "tested" God with their infidelity and lack of trust; in turn this provoked many tests from the Lord in order to purify Israel's faith and deepen it. Near Mount Hor a particular test took place, which was that of the poisonous serpents. These serpents "bit the people" with the result that many of them died (Nm 21:6). Then Moses, ordered by the Lord, "made a bronze serpent and mounted it on a pole, and whenever anyone who had been bitten by a serpent looked at the bronze serpent, he recovered" (Nm 21:9).

We might ask: Why such a test? The Lord had chosen Israel to be his own; he had chosen this people in order to initiate them gradually into his plan of salvation.

Jesus of Nazareth explains the salvific designs of the God of the covenant. The bronze serpent in the desert was the symbolic figure of the Crucified One. If someone who had been bitten looked upon the serpent "lifted up" by Moses on a high pole, that person was saved. He remained alive, not because he had looked upon the serpent, but because he had believed in the power of God and his saving love. Thus when the Son of Man is lifted up on the cross of Calvary, "all who believe will have eternal life in him" (cf. Jn 3:15).

There exists then a profound analogy between that figure and this reality, between that sign of salvation and this reality of salvation contained in the cross of Christ. The analogy becomes even more striking if we keep in mind that the salvation from physical death, caused by the poison of the serpents in the desert, came about through a serpent. Salvation from spiritual death, the death that is sin and that was caused by man, came about through a Man, through the Son of Man "lifted up" on the cross.

In this nighttime conversation, Jesus of Nazareth helps Nicodemus to discover the true sense of God's designs. While Jesus is speaking, the fulfillment of these divine designs belongs to the future, but at this point the future is not far away. Nicodemus himself will be a witness to this fulfillment. He will be a witness to the paschal events in Jerusalem. He will be a witness to the cross, upon which the One who speaks with him this night—the Son of Man—will be lifted up.

Jesus goes on even further. The conversation becomes even deeper: Why the cross? Why must the Son of Man be "lifted up" on the wood of the cross? Because "God so loved the world that he gave his only Son that whoever believes in him may not die but may have eternal life" (Jn 3:16). Yes, eternal life. This is the type of salvation that Jesus is speaking about: eternal life in God.

And then Jesus adds: "God did not send the Son into the world to condemn the world, but that the world might be saved through him" (Jn 3:17). Many thought that the Messiah would be first of all a severe judge who would punish, "separating the wheat from the chaff" (cf. Mt 3:12). If at one moment he will have to come as judge—at the end of the world, now "in the fullness of time" (cf. Gal 4:4) he comes to be judged himself by the sins of the world, and therefore because of the sins of the world. And thus, Christ lifted up on the cross becomes the redeemer of the human race, the redeemer of the world.

Jesus of Nazareth prepares Nicodemus, the eager student of the Scriptures, so that in time he will understand the saving mystery contained in the cross of Christ. And we know that, in time, Nicodemus did understand, but not during that night.

What, then, does this "being lifted up" mean?

In the second reading of today's liturgy, taken from Saint Paul's Letter to the Philippians, "being lifted up" means first of all "being brought low." The apostle writes about Christ, saying: "Though he was in the form of God, he did not deem equality with God something to be grasped at. Rather, he emptied himself and took the form of a slave, being born in the likeness of men" (Phil 2:6-7). The God-man! God becoming man. God taking on our humanity: this is the first dimension of "being brought low," and at the same time it is a "lifting up." God is brought low, so that man may be lifted up. Why? Because "God so loved the world." Because he is love!

Then the apostle writes: "(Christ) was known to be of human estate, and it was thus that he humbled himself, obediently accepting death, death on a cross" (Phil 2:7-8). This is the second and the definitive dimension of being brought low. It is the dimension of being emptied which confirms in the strongest way the truth of those words: "God so loved the world that he gave his only Son." He gave. This emptying is itself the gift. It is the greatest gift of the Father. It surpasses all other gifts. It is the source of every gift. In this absolute lowering, in this emptying, is the beginning and source of every "lifting up," the source of the lifting up of humanity.

The cross was "lifted up" on Golgotha. And Jesus was nailed to the cross, and was therefore lifted up with it. To the human eye, this was the culmination of humiliation and disgrace. But in the eyes of God it was different. It was different in the eternal designs of God.

The apostle continues: "Because of this, God highly exalted him and bestowed on him the name above every other name, so that at

Jesus' name every knee must bend in the heavens, on the earth, and under the earth, and every tongue proclaim to the glory of God the Father: Jesus Christ is Lord" (Phil 2:9-11).

Christ is the Lord! This will be confirmed in the resurrection, but it is already contained in the crucifixion. Precisely in the crucifixion.

To be crucified, humanly speaking, is to be disgraced and humiliated. But from God's point of view it means being lifted up. Indeed, to be lifted up by means of the cross. Christ is the Lord, and he becomes Lord of everything and everyone in this elevation by means of the cross. It is in this way that we look upon the cross, with the eyes of faith, instructed by the word of God, guided by the power of God.

Here then is the mystery of the triumph of the cross.

This mystery reaches us in a particular way and with a special power when the Church celebrates the Sacrament of the Anointing of the Sick, as she does this evening. By means of this sacrament, and through all her pastoral service, the Church continues to care for the sick and dying as Jesus did during his earthly ministry. Through the laying on of hands by the priest, the anointing with oil and the prayers, our brothers and sisters are strengthened with the grace of the Holy Spirit. They are enabled to bear their sufferings with courage and thus to embrace the cross and follow after Christ with stronger faith and hope.

This holy anointing does not prevent physical death nor does it promise a miraculous healing of the human body. But it does bring special grace and consolation to those who are dying, preparing them to meet our loving Savior with lively faith and love, and with firm hope for eternal life. It also brings comfort and strength to those who are not dying but who are suffering from serious illness or advanced age. For these the Church seeks healing of both body and soul, praying that the whole person may be renewed by the power of the Holy Spirit.

Every time that the Church celebrates this sacrament, she is proclaiming her belief in the victory of the cross. It is as if she were repeating the words of Saint Paul: "I am certain that neither death nor life, neither angels nor principalities, neither the present nor the future, nor powers, neither height nor depth nor any other creature will be able to separate us from the love of God that comes to us in Christ Jesus, our Lord" (Rom 8:38-39).

From the very early days until now, Phoenix has been a city to which people have come for health care, for relief of suffering, for new beginnings and fresh starts. Today as in the past, the Church welcomes such people, offering them love and understanding. She is grateful to the sick and elderly for the special mission which they fulfill in the Kingdom of our Savior. Your hospitality, which I myself have also received, reflects the beautiful saying in Spanish: "*mi casa, su casa.*" I pray that you will always remain faithful to this tradition of Christian community and generous service.

By such fidelity to your Christian heritage, through the Sacrament

115

of the Anointing of the Sick, and in the celebration of the Holy Eucharist, you express your deep conviction that suffering and death are not the last words of life. The last word is the Word made flesh, the Crucified and Risen Christ.

The responsorial psalm of today's liturgy exhorts us:

> Hearken, my people, to my teaching;
> Incline your ears to the words of my mouth . . .
> I will utter mysteries from of old (Ps 78:1-2).

It was exactly in this way that Christ revealed the mystery of salvation to Nicodemus, and to us. And to all people. The words which follow, in that same psalm, also refer to us:

> But they flattered him with their mouths
> and lied to him with their tongues,
> Though their hearts were not steadfast toward him,
> nor were they faithful to his covenant (Ps 78:36-37).

And nevertheless:

> While he slew them they sought him
> and inquired after God again;
> Remembering that God was their rock
> and the Most High God, their Redeemer (Ps 78:34-35).

And this is how God continues among us, from one generation to the next, as our rock, our Redeemer. This is the mystery of the triumph of the cross, the rock of our salvation.

> Let us fix our gaze upon the cross!
> Let us be reborn from it!
> Let us return to God!

May the humiliation of Christ—his being brought low by means of the cross—serve once again to lift up humanity toward God. *Sursum corda!* Lift up your hearts! Amen.

LOS ANGELES, CALIFORNIA

Tuesday, September 15, 1987

Address at Saint Vibiana's Cathedral

Dear Archbishop Mahony, Dear Cardinal Manning,
Dear Brothers and Sisters,

I greet you today in the name of our Lord Jesus Christ. Through his love and mercy we are gathered together in the Church to offer praise and thanksgiving to our heavenly Father. Grace and peace be to all of you—the clergy, religious, and laity of this city named in honor of Our Lady of the Angels. May she continue to assist you in praising God both now and forever with the angels, the patroness of this cathedral, Saint Vibiana, and all the saints.

I wish to join my voice to the chorus of praise offered to God in the name of Jesus in so many languages and by people of different races and ethnic origins in this great metropolis. It is his name above all that unites us in one household of faith, hope, and love. It is the name of Jesus that transcends every division and heals every antagonism within the human family.

As the successor of Peter, I come to you today in the name of Jesus. It cannot be otherwise, since every true minister of the gospel preaches not himself or any message of human origin, but he preaches Jesus Christ as Lord (cf. 2 Cor 4:5). To the fears, doubts, and struggles of individuals and nations, the Church seeks to apply the healing power of that name which belongs to him who alone is the Word of God (cf. Rv 19:13).

In a world filled with competing ideologies and so many false and empty promises, the name of Jesus Christ brings salvation and life. The Hebrew word "Jesus" means "Savior," as the angel said to Joseph in his dream: "You are to name him Jesus because he will save his people from their sins" (Mt 1:21). At the very beginning of the Church's mission, Saint Peter proclaims that "there is no salvation in anyone else, for there is no other name in the whole world given to men by which they are to be saved" (Acts 4:12). This name is a source of life for those who believe (cf. Jn 20:31); it delivers us from evil and leads us to the truth that alone can set us free (cf. Jn 8:32).

The name of Jesus is therefore a cry of deliverance for all humanity.

117

It has the power to comfort and heal the sick (cf. Acts 3:6; Jas 5:14-15), to cast out demons (cf. Mk 16:17; Lk 10:17; Acts 16:18), and to work every kind of miracle (cf. Mt 7:22; Acts 4:30). Most importantly, it is in the name of Jesus and through his power that our sins are forgiven (cf. 1 Jn 2:12).

The name of Jesus is at the heart of Christian worship in this cathedral and in every church throughout the world: "Where two or three are gathered in my name, there am I in their midst" (Mt 18:20). The name of Jesus is at the heart of all Christian prayer: "All you ask the Father in my name he will give you" (Jn 15:16). It is a motivation for charity because as Jesus himself explained, "Whoever gives you a cup of water to drink because you bear the name of Christ, will by no means lose his reward" (Mk 9:41). It calls forth the gift of the Holy Spirit, "the Paraclete, whom the Father will send in my name" (Jn 14:26).

My dear brothers and sisters, we are called Christians, and therefore the name of Jesus Christ is also our name. At the baptismal font we received a "Christian name" which symbolizes our communion with Christ and his saints. Our identification with him is reflected in the rule of life which Saint Paul proposes in the Letter to the Colossians: "Whatever you do, whether in speech or in action, do it in the name of the Lord Jesus. Give thanks to God the Father through him" (Col 3:17). We are obliged not only to give thanks, but also to speak and act in the name of Jesus, even at the risk of being ill-treated, persecuted, and hated "for the sake of the name" as Jesus foretold (Acts 5:41; cf. also Mk 13:13; Lk 21:12).

As citizens of the United States, you must give thanks to God for the religious liberty which you enjoy under your Constitution, now in its two hundredth year. However, freedom to follow your Catholic faith does not automatically mean that it will be easy to "speak and act" in the name of the Lord Jesus with a conscience formed by the word of God authentically interpreted by the Church's teaching (cf. *Dei Verbum*, 9f). In a secularized world, to speak and act in the name of Jesus can bring opposition and even ridicule. It often means being out of step with majority opinion. Yet if we look at the New Testament, we find encouragement everywhere for perseverance in this testing of our faith. As the First Letter of Saint Peter tells us: "If anyone suffers for being a Christian . . . he ought not to be ashamed. He should rather glorify God in virtue of that name" (1 Pt 4:6). And Jesus himself says, "In the world you will have trouble, but take courage, I have conquered the world" (Jn 16:33).

Is not this message extremely important for young people who are trying to live a responsible moral life in the face of a tide of popular culture and peer pressure that is indifferent, if not hostile, to Christian morality? And for their parents, who face daily pressures in the conduct of both their private and public life? And for the clergy and religious who may sometimes find it difficult to speak the full truth of the Church's teaching because it is a "hard saying" that many will not readily accept?

Dear brothers and sisters, the name of Jesus, like the Word of God that he is, is a two-edged sword (cf. Heb 4:12). It is a name that means salvation and life; it is a name that means a struggle and a cross, just as it did for him. But it is also the name in which we find strength to proclaim and live the truth of the gospel: not with arrogance, but with confident joy; not with self-righteousness, but with humble repentance before God; never with enmity, and always with charity.

Dear people of this great Archdiocese of Los Angeles, with its many problems, its enormous challenges, and its immense possibilities for good: The name of Jesus is your life and your salvation. It is your pride and joy, and the pride and joy of your families and your parishes. In this name you find strength for your weaknesses and energy for daily Christian living. In your struggle against evil and the Evil One, and in your striving for holiness, the name of Jesus is the source of your hope, because in the name of Jesus you are invincible!

Continue, then, dear Catholic people of Los Angeles to invoke this holy name of Jesus in your joys and your sorrows; continue to teach this name to your children, so that they in turn can teach it to their children, until the Lord Jesus himself comes in glory to judge the living and the dead!

Address at Universal Amphitheatre

Dear Young Friends,

I think that you already know, without my saying it, how happy I am to be with you today. Wherever I travel around the world, I always make it a point to meet with young people. A few days ago I was with them in New Orleans and today I enjoy being with you. From my early days as a young priest, I have spent many hours talking with students on university campuses or while hiking along lakes or in the mountains and hills. I have spent many evenings singing with young men and women like yourselves. Even now as pope, during the summer months, various groups of young people come to Castel Gandolfo for an evening and we sing and talk together.

As you probably know, I often say that you who are young bring hope to the world. The future of the world shines in your eyes. Even now, you are helping to shape the future of society. Since I have always placed high hopes in young people, I would like to speak to you today precisely about hope.

We cannot live without hope. We have to have some purpose in life, some meaning to our existence. We have to aspire to something. Without hope, we begin to die.

Why does it sometimes happen that a seemingly healthy person, successful in the eyes of the world, takes an overdose of sleeping pills and commits suicide? Why, on the other hand, do we see a seriously disabled person filled with great zest for life? Is it not because of hope? The one has lost all hope; in the other, hope is alive and overflowing. Clearly, then, hope does not stem from talents and gifts, or from physical health and success! It comes from something else. To be more precise, hope comes from someone else, someone beyond ourselves.

Hope comes from God, from our belief in God. People of hope are those who believe God created them for a purpose and that he will provide for their needs. They believe that God loves them as a faithful Father. Do you remember the advice that Jesus gave his disciples when they seemed to be fearful of the future? He said: "Do not be concerned for your life, what you are to eat, or for your body, what you are to wear. Life is more important than food and the body more than clothing. Consider the ravens: they do not sow, they do not reap, they have neither cellar nor barn—yet God feeds them. How much more important you are than the birds!" (Lk 12:22-24). Yes, God knows all our needs. He is the foundation for our hope.

But what about people who do not believe in God? This is indeed a serious problem, one of the greatest problems of our time—atheism, the fact that many of our contemporaries have no faith in God. When I visited Australia last year, I told a group of children: "The hardest thing about being pope is to see that many people do not accept the love of Jesus, do not know who he really is and how much he loves them. . . . (Jesus) does not force people to accept his love. He offers it to them and leaves them free to say yes or no. It fills me with joy to see how many people know and love our Lord, how many say yes to him. But it saddens me to see that some people say no" (November 29, 1986). Without faith in God, there can be no hope, no lasting, authentic hope. To stop believing in God is to start down a path that can lead only to emptiness and despair.

But those who have the gift of faith live with confidence about things to come. They look to the future with anticipation and joy, even in the face of suffering and pain; and the future that they are ultimately looking toward is everlasting life with the Lord. This kind of hope was very prominent in the life of Saint Paul who once wrote: "We are afflicted in every way possible, but we are not crushed; full of doubts, we never despair. We are persecuted but never abandoned; we are struck down but never destroyed . . . We do not lose heart, because our inner being is renewed each day" (2 Cor 4:8-9,16). Only God can renew our inner self each day. Only God can give meaning to life, God who has drawn near to each of us in "Christ Jesus our hope" (1 Tm 1:1).

In the New Testament there are two letters ascribed to Saint Peter. In the first of these, he said: "Venerate the Lord, that is, Christ, in your hearts. Should anyone ask you the reason for this hope of yours, be ever ready to reply" (1 Pt 3:15). Dear young friends, I pray that your faith in Christ will always be lively and strong. In this way, you will always be ready to tell others the reason for your hope; you will be messengers of hope for the world.

I am often asked, especially by young people, why I became a priest. Maybe some of you would like to ask the same question. Let me try briefly to reply.

I must begin by saying that it is impossible to explain entirely. For it remains a mystery, even to myself. How does one explain the ways of God? Yet, I know that, at a certain point in my life, I became convinced that Christ was saying to me what he had said to thousands before me: "Come, follow me!" There was a clear sense that what I heard in my heart was no human voice, nor was it just an idea of my own. Christ was calling me to serve him as a priest.

And you can probably tell, I am deeply grateful to God for my vocation to the priesthood. Nothing means more to me or gives me greater joy than to celebrate Mass each day and to serve God's people in the Church. That has been true ever since the day of my ordination as a priest. Nothing has ever changed it, not even becoming pope.

Confiding this to you, I would like to invite each of you to listen carefully to God's voice in your heart. Every human person is called to communion with God. That is why the Lord made us, to know him and love him and serve him and, in doing this, to find the secret to lasting joy.

In the past the Church in the United States has been rich in vocations to the priesthood and religious life. And it could be especially true today. At the same time, the Church needs the gospel witness of holy lay people, in married life and in the single state. Be assured that the Lord knows each of you by name and wishes to speak to your heart in a dialogue of love and salvation. God continues to speak to young people on the banks of the Mississippi River and on the slopes of the Rocky Mountains. God continues to speak in the cities on the West Coast of America and across the rolling hills and plains. God continues to speak to every human person.

Dear young people of America, listen to his voice. Do not be afraid. Open up your hearts to Christ. The deepest joy there is in life is the joy that comes from God and is found in Jesus Christ, the Son of God. He is the hope of the world. Jesus Christ is your hope and mine!

Meeting with Communications Leaders
The Registry Hotel Ballroom

Ladies and Gentlemen of the Communications Industry, Dear Friends,

I am very pleased to be here with you. I would like to be able to greet each one of you personally and to express my regard for you individually. Although this is not possible, I wish to express my sincere respect for all the categories of the media that you represent—the film industry, the music and recording industry, radio, electronic news, television, and all those who inform the world through the written word—and for the diverse functions that you perform as workers, writers, editors, managers, and executives. I greet you in the full range of your activities, from the very visible to the relatively hidden.

My visit to Los Angeles, and indeed to the United States, would seem incomplete without this meeting, since you represent one of the most important American influences on the world today. You do this in every area of social communications and contribute thereby to the development of a mass popular culture. Humanity is profoundly influenced by what you do. Your activities affect communication itself: supplying information, influencing public opinion, offering entertainment. The consequences of these activities are numerous and diverse. You help your fellow citizens to enjoy leisure, to appreciate art and to profit from culture. You often provide the stories they tell and the songs they sing. You give them news of current events, a vision of humanity and motives for hope. Yours is indeed a profound influence on society. Hundreds of millions of people see your films and television programs, listen to your voices, sing your songs, and reflect your opinions. It is a fact that your smallest decisions can have global impact.

Your work can be a force for great good or great evil. You yourselves know the dangers, as well as the splendid opportunities open to you. Communication products can be works of great beauty, revealing what is noble and uplifting in humanity and promoting what is just and fair and true. On the other hand communications can appeal to and promote what is debased in people: dehumanized sex through pornography or through a casual attitude toward sex and human life; greed through materialism and consumerism or irresponsible individualism; anger and vengefulness through violence or self-righteousness. All the media of popular culture which you represent can build or destroy, uplift, or cast down. You have untold possibilities for good, ominous possibilities for destruction. It is the difference between death and life—the death or life of the spirit. And it is a matter of choice. The challenge of Moses to the people of Israel is applicable to all of us today: "I set before you life and death. . . . Choose life" (Dt 30:19).

There is something of great interest for all of us in the Constitution of the United States. The same amendment that guarantees freedom of speech and freedom of the press also guarantees freedom of religious practice. The link between the art of human expression and the exercise of religion is profound. Social communications in fact provide an important first step in uniting human beings in mutual love, and this first step is also a step to God, "for God is love" (1 Jn 4:8). Religious practice for its part fosters communication with God. But it also fosters human communication, since human communication is part of that relationship of love for neighbor that is mandated in both the Old and New Testaments.

It is easy to see why the Church has recognized and taught that people have a right to communicate. Linked to this right is the right to information, about which the Second Vatican Council speaks in these words: "Because of the progress of modern society and the increasing interdependence of its members, it is clear that information has become very useful and generally necessary. . . . There exists therefore in human society a right to information on the subjects that are of concern to people" (Inter Mirifica, 5).

In this way, then, the Church recognizes the need for freedom of speech and freedom of the press, just as does your Constitution. But she goes further. Rights imply corresponding duties. The proper exercise of the right to information demands that the content of what is communicated be true and, within the limits set by justice and charity, complete (cf. ibid.). Your very profession invites you to reflect on this obligation to truth and its completeness. Included here is the obligation to avoid any manipulation of truth for any reason. This manipulation in fact takes place when certain issues are deliberately passed over in silence, in order that others may be unduly emphasized. It also occurs when information is altered or withheld so that society will be less able to resist the imposition of a given ideology.

The obligation to truth and its completeness applies not only to the coverage of news, but to all your work. Truth and completeness should characterize the content of artistic expression and entertainment. You find a real meaning in your work when you exercise your role as collaborators of truth, collaborators of truth in the service of justice, fairness, and love.

Your industry not only speaks to people and for people; it makes communication possible among them. In this we see how your activities transcend the categories of both rights and duties and confer upon you inestimable privileges. Just before joining you this afternoon, I met with young people in several cities by using satellite links. For me this is just one example of how your industry can help foster communication and unite people in fraternal love. It is within your power to use technology to promote what is deeply human and to direct it to the work of peace. You have marvelous tools which others lack. They must be employed in the service of people's right to communicate.

In today's modern world there is always the danger of communication becoming exclusively one-way, depriving audiences of the opportunity to participate in the communication process. Should that happen with you, you would no longer be communicators in the full, human sense. The people themselves, the general public whom you serve, should not be excluded from having the opportunity for public dialogue.

In order to foster such a dialogue, you yourselves, as communicators, must listen as well as speak. You must seek to communicate with people, and not just speak to them. This involves learning about people's needs, being aware of their struggles and presenting all forms of communications with the sensitivity that human dignity requires— your human dignity and theirs. This applies especially to all audio-visual programs.

At the basis of all human rights is the dignity of the human person created in the image and likeness of God (Gn 1:27). A recognition of this human dignity is also a part of your civil tradition in the United States, and is expressed in the declaration of your nation's independence: all people are created equal in their human dignity and are endowed by their Creator with inalienable rights to life, liberty, and the pursuit of happiness. All other rights too are rooted in human dignity, including the right to maintain one's privacy and not to be exploited in the intimacy of one's family.

The fundamental dignity of the human person is still more strongly proclaimed by the Church. She raises her voice on behalf of people everywhere, declaring the dignity of every human being, every man, woman, and child. None is excluded because all bear the image of God. Physical and mental handicaps, spiritual weaknesses, and human aberrations cannot obliterate the dignity of man. You will understand why the Church attaches such importance to this principle found on the first page of the Bible; it will later become the basis of the teaching of Jesus Christ as he says: "Always treat others as you would like them to treat you" (Mt 7:12).

In particular, social communications must support human dignity because the world is constantly tempted to forget it. Whether in news or in drama, whether in song or in story, you are challenged to respect what is human and to recognize what is good. Human beings must never be despised because of limitations, flaws, disorders, or even sins.

Twenty years ago, my predecessor Pope Paul VI, speaking to a gathering much like this one, told that creative community in Rome: "It is a fact that when, as writers and artists, you are able to reveal in the human condition, however lowly or sad it may be, a spark of goodness, at that very instant a glow of beauty pervades your whole work. We are not asking that you should play the part of moralists, but we are expressing confidence in your mysterious power of opening up the glorious regions of light that lie behind the mystery of human life" (*Allocution of May 6, 1967*).

As you do precisely this: open up the glorious regions of light that lie behind the mystery of human life, you must ask yourselves if what you communicate is consistent with the full measure of human dignity. How do the weakest and the most defenseless in society appear in your words and images: the most severely handicapped, the very old, foreigners and the undocumented, the unattractive and the lonely, the sick and the infirm? Whom do you depict as having, or not having human worth?

Certainly your profession subjects you to a great measure of accountability—accountability to God, to the community, and before

124

the witness of history. And yet at times it seems that everything is left in your hands. Precisely because your responsibility is so great and your accountability to the community is not easily rendered juridically, society relies so much on your good will. In a sense the world is at your mercy. Errors in judgment, mistakes in evaluating the propriety and justice of what is transmitted, and wrong criteria in art can offend and wound consciences and human dignity. They can encroach on sacred fundamental rights. The confidence that the community has in you honors you deeply and challenges you mightily.

I would encourage you in yet another way: to respect also your own dignity. All that I have said about the dignity of human beings applies to you.

Daily cares oppress you in ways different from those arising in other kinds of work. Your industry reflects the fast pace of the news and changing tastes. It deals with vast amounts of money that bring with them their own problems. It places you under extreme pressure to be successful, without telling you what "success" really is. Working constantly with images, you face the temptation of seeing them as reality. Seeking to satisfy the dreams of millions, you can become lost in a world of fantasy.

At this point, you must cultivate the integrity consonant with your own human dignity. You are more important than success, more valuable than any budget. Do not let your work drive you blindly; for if work enslaves you, you will soon enslave your art. Who you are and what you do are too important for that to happen. Do not let money be your sole concern, for it too is capable of enslaving art as well as souls. In your life there must also be room for your families and for leisure. You need time to rest and be re-created, for only in quiet can you absorb the peace of God.

You yourselves are called to what is noble and lofty in human living, and you must study the highest expressions of the human spirit. You have a great part in shaping the culture of this nation and other nations. To you is entrusted an important portion of the vast heritage of the human race. In fulfilling your mission you must always be aware of how your activities affect the world community, how they serve the cause of universal solidarity.

The Church wishes you to know that she is on your side. For a long time she has been a patron and defender of the arts; she has promoted the media and been in the forefront of the use of new technology. The first book for the printing press of Johannes Gutenberg, the inventor of movable type, was the inspired word of God, the Bible. Vatican Radio was established under the direction of the inventor of radio, Guglielmo Marconi.

Today, too, the Church stands ready to help you by her encouragement and to support you in all your worthy aims. She offers you her challenge and her praise. I pray that you will welcome that help and never be afraid to accept it.

Ladies and gentlemen of the communications industry, I have set before you the broad outlines of a choice for good within the framework of your profession. I ask you to choose the common good. It means honoring the dignity of every human being.

I am convinced that to a great extent we can share a common hope, rooted in a vision of the human race harmoniously united through communication. I am sure too that all of you, whether Christian or not, will permit me to allude to the great fascination that surrounds the mystery of the communicating word. For Christians, the communicating word is the explanation of all reality as expressed by Saint John: "In the beginning was the Word; the Word was in God's presence, and the Word was God" (Jn 1:1). And for all those who hold the Judeo-Christian tradition, the nobility of communication is linked to the wisdom of God and expressed in his loving revelation. Thus the Book of Deuteronomy records God's communication to Israel: "You shall love the Lord your God with all your heart, and with all your soul, and with all your strength. Take to heart these words which I enjoin on you today" (Dt 6:6).

Ladies and gentlemen, as communicators of the human word, you are the stewards and administrators of an immense spiritual power that belongs to the patrimony of mankind and is meant to enrich the whole of the human community. The challenge that opens up before you truly requires generosity, service, and love. I am sure that you will strive to meet it. And, as you do, I pray that you will experience in your own lives a deep satisfaction and joy. And may the peace of God dwell in your hearts.

Homily at Los Angeles Eucharist
Los Angeles Coliseum

And you yourself shall be pierced with a sword (Lk 2:35).

Dear Brothers and Sisters of the Archdiocese of Los Angeles and of the Dioceses of Orange, San Diego, San Bernardino, and Fresno,

The Church's meditation today focuses on the sufferings of Mary, the Mother standing at the foot of her Son's Cross. This brings to completion yesterday's Feast of the Triumph of the Cross. Jesus had said, "Once I am lifted up, I will draw all men to myself" (Jn 12:32). These words were fulfilled when he was "lifted up" on the cross.

The Church, which constantly lives this mystery, feels very deeply the suffering of the Mother on Golgotha. The agony of the Son who in his terrible pain entrusts the whole world to his Father, that agony is united with the agony in the heart of the Mother there on Calvary.

Today's gospel reminds us that, when Jesus was only 40 days old, Simeon had foretold this agony in the heart of the Mother when he said: "And you yourself shall be pierced with a sword" (Lk 2:35).

The entire mystery of obedience to the Father is encompassed by the Son's agony: "he humbled himself, obediently accepting even death, death on a cross" (Phil 2:8), as yesterday's liturgy proclaimed. And today we read in the Letter to the Hebrews: "In the days when he was in the flesh, (Christ) offered prayers and supplications with loud cries and tears to God, who was able to save him from death" (Heb 5:7). These words have special application to the agony in the Garden of Gethsemane when he prayed: "My Father, if it is possible, let this cup pass me by" (Mt 26:39-42). The author of the Letter to the Hebrews immediately adds that Christ "was heard because of his reverence" (Heb 5:7). Yes, he was heard. He had said, "not as I will but as you will" (Mt 26:39). And so it came to pass.

The agony of Christ was, and still is, the mystery of his obedience to the Father. At Gethsemane. On Calvary. "Son though he was," the text continues, "he learned obedience from what he suffered" (Heb 5:9). This includes Christ's obedience even unto death, the perfect sacrifice of redemption. "And when perfected, he became the source of eternal salvation for all who obey him" (Heb 5:9).

As we celebrate Our Lady of Sorrows during this Marian Year, let us call to mind the teaching of the Second Vatican Council concerning the presence of Mary, the Mother of God, in the mystery of Christ and of the Church. Let us recall in particular the following words: "The Blessed Virgin advanced in her pilgrimage of faith and loyally persevered in her union with her Son unto the cross, where she stood, in keeping with the divine plan" (*Lumen Gentium*, 58).

Mary's pilgrimage of faith! It is precisely at the foot of the cross that this pilgrimage of faith, which began at the Annunciation, reaches its high point, its culmination. There it is united with the agony of Mary's maternal heart. "Suffering grievously with her only-begotten Son . . . she lovingly consented to the immolation of this victim which she herself had brought forth" (*Lumen Gentium*, 58). At the same time, the agony of her maternal heart also represents a fulfillment of the words of Simeon: "And you yourself shall be pierced with a sword" (Lk 2:35). Surely these prophetic words express the "divine plan" by which Mary is destined to stand at the foot of the cross.

Today's liturgy makes use of the ancient poetic text of the sequence which begins with the Latin words *Stabat Mater*:

By the Cross of our salvation
Mary stood in desolation
While the Savior hung above.
All her human powers failing,
Sorrow's sword, at last prevailing,
Stabs and breaks her heart of love. . . .

Virgin Mary, full of sorrow,
From your love I ask to borrow

Love enough to share your pain.
Make my heart to burn with fire,
Make Christ's love my one desire,
Who for love of me was slain.

The author of this sequence sought, in the most eloquent way
humanly possible, to present the "compassion" of the Mother at the
foot of the cross. He was inspired by those words of Sacred Scripture
about the sufferings of Mary which, though few and concise, are
deeply moving.

It is appropriate that Mary's song of praise, the *Magnificat*, should
also find a place in our celebration: "My being proclaims the greatness
of the Lord . . . For he has looked upon his servant in her lowliness
. . . God who is mighty has done great things for me . . . His mercy
is from age to age . . . Even as he promised our fathers, Abraham
and his descendants forever" (Lk 1:46-55).

Can we not suppose that these words, which reflect the fervor and
exultation of the young mother's heart, still ring true at the foot of
the cross? That they still reveal her heart now that she finds herself
in agony with her Son? Humanly speaking, it does not seem possible
to us. However, within the fullness of divine truth, the words of the
Magnificat actually find their ultimate meaning in the light of Christ's
Paschal Mystery, from the cross through the resurrection.

It is precisely in this Paschal Mystery that the "great things" which
God who is mighty has done for Mary find their perfect fulfillment,
not only for her, but for all of us and for all of humanity. It is precisely
at the foot of the cross that the promise is fulfilled which God once
made to Abraham and to his descendants, the people of the Old
Covenant. It is also at the foot of the cross that there is an overflow
of the mercy shown to humanity from generation to generation by
him whose name is holy.

Yes, at the foot of the cross, the "humility of the Lord's servant"—
the one upon whom "God has looked" (cf. Lk 1:48)—reaches its full
measure together with the absolute humiliation of the Son of God.
But from that same spot the "blessing" of Mary by "all ages to come"
also begins. There, at the foot of the Cross, to use the description of
the prophet Isaiah in the first reading, the Virgin of Nazareth is fully
"clothed with a robe of salvation" (cf. Is 61:10): she whom already at
the Annunciation the archangel hailed as "full of grace" (Lk 1:28); she
who was redeemed in the most perfect manner; she who was conceived without stain in view of the merits of her Son. At the price of
the cross. In virtue of Christ's Paschal Mystery.

Dear brothers and sisters of Los Angeles and Southern California,
it is a joy for me to celebrate this liturgy today with you. California
has been a symbol of hope and promise for millions of people who
continue to come here to make a home for themselves and their
families. Today the people of California play a major role in shaping
the culture of the United States, which has such a profound influence
on the rest of the world. Your state also leads in research and tech-

nology designed to improve the quality of human life and to transcend the limitations which impede human freedom and progress.

Yet amid the many blessings that you enjoy within this beautiful and prosperous state, I know that the mention of Mary as a Mother of sorrows and suffering still strikes a responsive chord in your hearts. This is because all of us, in some way, experience sorrow and suffering in our lives. No amount of economic, scientific, or social progress can eradicate our vulnerability to sin and to death. On the contrary, progress creates new possibilities for evil as well as for good. Technology, for example, increases what we can do, but it cannot teach us the right thing to do. It increases our choices, but it is we who must choose between evil and good. Besides moral suffering, physical, and emotional sufferings are part of every human life. The gospel message is certainly no enemy of human progress or of the promotion of our temporal welfare, but neither does the Paschal Mystery allow us to run away from human sorrow and suffering.

The message of the crucified Son and of his Mother at the foot of the cross is that the mysteries of suffering, love, and redemption are inseparably joined together. In bitterness and alienation from God and our fellow human beings we will never find the answer to the question, the "why?" of suffering. Calvary teaches us that we will find an answer only through the "obedience" mentioned in the Letter to the Hebrews. It is not obedience to a cruel or unjust god of our own making, but obedience to the God who "so loved the world that he gave his only Son" (Jn 3:16). Jesus prayed: "not as I will, but as you will . . . your will be done" (Mt 26:39,42). And Mary began her pilgrimage of faith with the words, "I am the servant of the Lord. Let it be done to me as you say" (Lk 1:38).

Looking upon the suffering Son and Mother in the light of Scripture, we cannot equate their obedience with fatalism or passivity. Indeed, the gospel is the negation of passivity in the face of suffering (*Salvifici Doloris*, 30). What we find is a loving act of self-giving on the part of Christ for the salvation of the world, and on the part of Mary as an active participant from the beginning in the saving mission of her Son. When we have striven to alleviate or overcome suffering, when like Christ we have prayed that "the cup pass us by" (cf. Mt 26:39), and yet suffering remains, then we must walk "the royal road" of the cross. As I mentioned before, Christ's answer to our question "why" is above all a call, a vocation. Christ does not give us an abstract answer, but rather he says, "Follow me!" He offers us the opportunity through suffering to take part in his own work of saving the world. And when we do take up our cross, then gradually the salvific meaning of suffering is revealed to us. It is then that in our sufferings we find inner peace and even spiritual joy (cf. *Salvifici Doloris*, 26).

The Letter to the Hebrews also speaks of being made perfect through suffering (cf. Heb 5:8-10). This is because the purifying flames of trial and sorrow have the power to transform us from within by unleashing our love, teaching us compassion for others, and thus drawing us closer to Christ. Next to her Son, Mary is the most perfect example of this. It is precisely in being the Mother of Sorrows that she is a mother to each one of us and to all of us. The spiritual sword that pierces her heart opens up a river of compassion for all who suffer.

My dear brothers and sisters, as we celebrate this Marian Year in preparation for the Third Millennium of Christianity, let us join the Mother of God in her pilgrimage of faith. Let us learn the virtue of compassion from her whose heart was pierced with a sword at the foot of the cross. It is the virtue that prompted the Good Samaritan to stop beside the victim on the road, rather than to continue on or to cross over to the other side. Whether it be the case of the person next to us or of distant peoples and nations, we must be Good Samaritans to all those who suffer. We must be the compassionate "neighbor" of those in need, not only when it is emotionally rewarding or convenient, but also when it is demanding and inconvenient (cf. *Salvifici Doloris*, 28-30). Compassion is a virtue we cannot neglect in a world in which the human suffering of so many of our brothers and sisters is needlessly increased by oppression, deprivation, and underdevelopment—by poverty, hunger, and disease. Compassion is also called for in the face of the spiritual emptiness and aimlessness that people can often experience amid material prosperity and comfort in developed countries such as your own. Compassion is a virtue that brings healing to those who bestow it, not only in this present life but in eternity: "Blessed are they who show mercy, mercy shall be theirs" (Mt 5:7).

Through the faith of Mary, then, let us fix our gaze on the mystery of Christ. The mystery of the Son of Man, written in the earthly history of humanity, is at the same time the definitive manifestation of God in that history.

Simeon says: "This child is destined to be the downfall and the rise of many in Israel, a sign that will be opposed" (Lk 2:34). How profound these words are! How far down these words reach into the history of man! Into the history of us all: Christ is destined for the ruin and the resurrection of many! Christ is a sign of contradiction! Is this not also true in our time? In our age? In our generation?

And standing next to Christ is Mary. To her Simeon says: " . . . so that the thoughts of many hearts may be laid bare. And you yourself shall be pierced with a sword" (Lk 2:35).

> Today we ask for humility of heart and for a clear conscience:
> before God
> through Christ.
>
> Yes, we ask that the thoughts of our hearts may be laid bare.
> We ask that our consciences may be pure:
> before God
> through the Cross of Christ
> in the heart of Mary. Amen.

Meeting with the Bishops of the United States
Our Lady Queen of the Angels Minor Seminary

Welcome by Archbishop John L. May

Most Holy Father, we your brother bishops of the United States welcome you today with all our hearts. With the psalmist we sing in our hearts, "O how good and how pleasant it is for brothers to be together as one."

We are grateful for your coming this second time to our land and to our people. We are amazed and edified by your ongoing care for all the churches in these worldwide pastoral visits of yours. It is difficult enough, we know, to make faithful pastoral visits to the parishes of one diocese. Your pastoral zeal is a beautiful encouragement to us and we are grateful.

Especially today we thank you, Holy Father, for the generous period of time you are giving to this visit with us bishops. Your hospitality during our *Ad Limina* visits has been beautiful and we want to reciprocate.

Very graciously you have acceded to our request for a discussion with us. It is my privilege and joy to present our spokesmen to you: His Eminence, Joseph Cardinal Bernardin of Chicago, Archbishop Daniel Pilarczyk of Cincinnati, Archbishop John Quinn of San Francisco, and Archbishop Rembert Weakland of Milwaukee. We look forward to their presentations and the response of Your Holiness and our fraternal discussion together. With Peter, your predecessor and patron, we can truly say, "Lord, it is good for us to be here!"

The Relationship of the Universal Church and the Particular Churches
Presented by Joseph Cardinal Bernardin

Your presence among us today, Holy Father, brings into clear focus the nature of the Church as a *communio*: a communion of particular churches in which and from which exists the one and unique Catholic Church; a communion which is not fully the Church unless united

131

with the Bishop of Rome. This communion over which you preside as Peter's successor brings together the strength of our unity in faith and the richness of our diversity as a world church rooted in every region and culture of the earth.

Just as there is but one faith, one Lord, one baptism, so there can be but one loyalty—to the Word of God perennially proclaimed in the Church entrusted to the episcopal college with you, our Holy Father, as its visible head and perpetual source of unity. Today, in your presence we celebrate our unity, and we reaffirm our fidelity to the affection for you. Each day, when we pray at Mass with our priests and people for John Paul, our pope, and for ourselves as shepherds of our particular churches, we acknowledge this wonderful mystery, the Church, which is always one in its diverse manifestations.

In the name of my brother bishops, I assure you that the Church in the United States has always been and will always be one, holy, Catholic, and apostolic. Our realization of the mystery of the Church, of course, is situated in the context of our American culture. We live in an open society where everyone prizes the freedom to speak his or her mind. Many tend to question things, especially those matters which are important to them, as religion is. They want to know the reasons why certain decisions are made, and they feel free to criticize if they do not agree or are not satisfied with the explanations. They see this as an integral part of the call to live their lives as responsible, educated adults. It is also important to know that many Americans, given the freedom they have enjoyed for more than two centuries, almost instinctively react negatively when they are told that they must do something, even though in their hearts they may know they should do it. As a result, the impression is sometimes given that there is a certain rebelliousness in many American Catholics, that they want to "go it alone."

I will readily admit that these cultural phenomena, which are not unique to our country, can have problematic ecclesial implications. We must address this reality. However, the majority of the Catholics in the United States have a deep faith and accept the Church as described in the conciliar documents. They contribute to the life of their parish and diocese, as well as the broader Church. In a special way, they support you and want to be united with you as pastor of the universal Church.

As with any living organism which values both its unity and diversity, there are bound to be misunderstandings and tensions at times. Tension in itself need not be debilitating or destructive. Often it is a sign of growth. We know that in the Apostolic Church reflected in the New Testament and in the young Church described by the Fathers, there were disagreements and conflicting points of view.

It was largely for this reason that the Lord gave the Church the ministry of the *episkopoi* or overseers to provide for the unity of the particular churches, and the Petrine ministry to promote and protect the unity of the Universal Church. Thus, the Church was provided with those who would have authority to make the decisions necessary

132

for the Church to remain one. The Holy Spirit, present in the Church and working in a particular way through the college of bishops in union with Peter and his successors, has successfully guided the Church through 20 centuries marked by both harmony and strife.

The practical question that must be addressed today, as before, (and it was openly discussed at the 1985 Extraordinary Synod) is how to maintain our unity while affirming the diversity in the local realizations of the Church; how to discern a proper balance between freedom and order. The Second Vatican Council invited us to engage in a discernment which identifies and confirms the elements of truth and grace found in our respective cultures, purifying them of what is evil and elevating them by restoring them to Christ. Faithful to this invitation, we have confronted the realities of our modern age: instant worldwide communication, the desire of people to exercise more control over their lives and destiny, the rising expectations of both men and women and the insistence that their rights be respected, a heightened national consciousness among peoples even as the world becomes more of a global village. Here in the United States, particularly, we tend at times to overemphasize our own experience, not always giving adequate recognition to the insights and experiences of others.

In this context we can appreciate two unfortunate tendencies which affect the relationship between the Universal Church and the particular churches of our country. When the Holy See reaffirms a teaching which has been part of our heritage for centuries, or applies it to today's new realities, it is sometimes accused of retrogression, or making new and unreasonable impositions on people. In like manner, when someone questions how a truth might be better articulated or lived today, he or she is sometimes accused of rejecting the truth itself or portrayed as being in conflict with the Church's teaching authority. As a result, both sides are sometimes locked into what seem to be adversarial positions. Genuine dialogue becomes almost impossible.

I know that this is a great concern of yours. You have been given the grace of the Petrine Office, and we know that it is your duty to confirm and support the brethren in their understanding and acceptance of the legacy given to us by the Lord himself. And this you do in an extraordinarily generous and effective way. But at times you are misunderstood; some allege that you do not understand the actual situation in which the Church finds herself in the different parts of the world today.

It is also painful for us, as the shepherds of our particular churches, when we are cast in an adversarial position with the Holy See, or with certain groups within our own dioceses. Sometimes this is done by persons who do not understand us; sometimes, however, by people at either extreme who simply oppose some of the teachings of the Second Vatican Council.

Thus far, Holy Father, I have spoken of our *communio*, of the distinct but complementary responsibilities of the pope and the bishops in a Church that is one but diverse, of some unique aspects of our experience in the United States, and of some of the tensions we face.

But how will we resolve some of the problems I have noted so that the Universal Church and the particular churches can share the full benefit of their *communio* which acknowledges the hierarchical structures and responsibilities of the Church but is also enriched by a fruitful exchange between the two? The Church in the United States has much to contribute to the Universal Church. I am thinking, for example, of our role in the development of the documents on religious freedom and ecumenism of the Second Vatican Council. But how much we have to learn from the Universal Church whose experience touches every corner of the world and reaches back for 20 centuries!

I do not presume to have a complete answer to this question. But perhaps some brief reflections might help us.

First, there has to be in the whole body of the Church a much greater trust in the promise of the risen Christ to be present with his Church and in the living action of the Holy Spirit. We are part of a mystery, a unique convergence of the divine and human. For this reason, we cannot rely only on secular models—although we can surely learn from them.

Second, we must be able to speak with one another in complete candor, without fear. This applies to our exchanges with the Holy See as well as among ourselves as bishops. Even if our exchange is characterized by some as confrontational, we must remain calm and not become the captives of those who would use us to accomplish their own ends.

Third, in such a mutual exchange—conducted with objectivity, honesty, and openness—we can discern what will truly enhance the Church's unity and what will weaken or destroy it. Sometimes, the outcome of our endeavors will not be immediately evident, but this in itself should not deter us, because we must allow for growth and development in certain areas of the Church's life and ministry.

Fourth, we must affirm and continue to grow in our appreciation of the conciliar vision of collegiality as both a principle and a style of leadership in the Church. Here in the United States our national conference has been a visible expression of that collegiality. It has served to enhance the pastoral role of each bishop precisely because it provides a framework and a forum for us to share ideas, to teach and elucidate sound Catholic doctrine, set pastoral directions, and develop policy positions on contemporary social issues. I believe that we are learning how to balance this dimension of collegiality with the collegiality of the bishops of the Universal Church in union with you as head of the episcopal college.

Finally, we must constantly reaffirm, as we do today, that we are "the Roman Catholic Church. The papacy belongs to the binding content of our faith itself, in its proper place within the hierarchy of truths and in our own Christian life . . . " (Karl Rahner, SJ, *The Shape of the Church to Come*, Part 2, c.2).

Holy Father, on behalf of my brother bishops, I wish to express gratitude for the opportunity to share with you some thoughts which are so central to our ministry as pastors of the Church. In my name and theirs, I reaffirm our affection and fidelity. May the grace of the Lord Jesus Christ, and the love of God, and the fellowship of the Holy Spirit be with us all!

John Paul II's Response

Dear Brothers in Our Lord Jesus Christ,

Before beginning to respond in the context of our fraternal exchanges, I wish to express to you my deep gratitude: gratitude for your many invitations to make this pastoral visit, gratitude for your presence here today, and gratitude for the immense amount of preparation which this visit required. Over and above all this, I thank you for your daily toil, and your partnership with me in the gospel. In a word, I thank you for "your work of faith and labor of love and steadfastness of hope in our Lord Jesus Christ" (1 Thes 1:3).

Cardinal Bernardin has given us an introduction to the extremely important reality of *communio*, which is the best framework for our conversation. As bishops, we can never tire of prayerfully reflecting on this subject. Since, as the Extraordinary Session of the Synod of Bishops in 1985 indicated, "the ecclesiology of communion is the central and fundamental idea of the Council's documents" (*Relatio Finalis*, C, 1), it follows that we must return time and again to those same documents in order to be imbued with the profound theological vision of the Church which the Holy Spirit has placed before us, and which constitutes the basis of all pastoral ministry in the Church's pilgrimage through human history.

The program of our collegial ministry cannot be other than to release into the lifestream of ecclesial life all the richness of the Church's self-understanding, which was given by the Holy Spirit to the community of faith in the celebration of the Second Vatican Council. The renewal of Catholic life which the Council called for is to be measured not primarily in terms of external structures, but in deeper understanding and more effective implementation of the core vision of her true nature and mission which the Council offered to the Church at the close of the Second Millennium of the Christian era. That renewal depends on the way the Council's fundamental insights are authentically received in each particular church and in the Universal Church.

At the heart of the Church's self-understanding is the notion of *communio*: primarily, a sharing through grace in the life of the Father given us through Christ and in the Holy Spirit. "God chose us in him"—in Christ—"before the world began, to be holy and blameless in his sight, to be full of love" (Eph 1:4). This communion has its origin in a divine call, the eternal decree which predestined us to share the image of the Son (cf. Rom 8:28-30). It is realized through sacramental union with Christ and through organic participation in all that constitutes the divine and human reality of the Church, the Body of Christ, which spans the centuries and is sent into the world to embrace all people without distinction.

It is clear that in the decades since the Council this "vertical dimension" of ecclesial communion has been less deeply experienced by many who, on the other hand, have a vivid sense of dimension." Unless, however, the entire Christian community has a keen awareness of the marvelous and utterly gratuitous outpouring of "the kindness and love of God our savior" which saved us "not because of any righteous deeds we had done, but because of his mercy" (Ti 3:4-5), the whole ordering of the Church's life and the exercise of her mission of service to the human family will be radically weakened and never reach the level intended by the Council.

The ecclesial body is healthy in the measure in which Christ's grace, poured out through the Holy Spirit, is accepted by the members. Our pastoral efforts are fruitful, in the last analysis, when the People of God—we bishops with the clergy, religious and laity—are led to Christ, grow in faith, hope, and charity, and become authentic witnesses of God's love in a world in need of transfiguration.

Cardinal Bernardin has stated very well that just as there is but one faith, one Lord, one baptism, so there can be but one loyalty to the word of God perennially proclaimed in the Church, entrusted to the Episcopal College with the Roman Pontiff as its visible head and perpetual source of unity. The word of God, which is the power of God leading all who believe to salvation (cf. Rom 1:16; *Dei Verbum*, 17), is fully revealed in the Paschal Mystery of the death and resurrection of Jesus Christ. This Paschal Mystery brings about a salvation that is transcendent and eternal: "He died for us, that all of us . . . together might live with him" (1 Thes 5:10). It is the Church's task therefore, while she seeks in every way possible to increase her service to the human family in all its needs, to preach Christ's call to conversion and to proclaim redemption in his blood.

The "vertical dimension" of ecclesial communion is of profound significance in understanding the relationship of the particular churches to the Universal Church. It is important to avoid a merely sociological view of this relationship. "In and from such individual churches there comes into being the one and only Catholic Church" (*Lumen Gentium*, 23), but this Universal Church cannot be conceived as the sum of the particular churches, or as a federation of particular churches.

In the celebration of the Eucharist these principles come fully to the fore. For, as the Council document on the liturgy specifies: "the principal manifestation of the Church consists in the full, active participation of all God's holy people in the same liturgical celebrations, especially in the same Eucharist, in one prayer, at one altar, at which the bishop presides, surrounded by his presbyterate and by his ministers" (*Sacrosanctum Concilium*, 41). Wherever a community gathers around the altar under the ministry of a bishop, there Christ is present and there, because of Christ, the one, holy, Catholic, and apostolic Church gathers together (cf. *Lumen Gentium*, 26).

The Catholic Church herself subsists in each particular church, which can be truly complete only through effective communion in faith, sacraments, and unity with the whole Body of Christ. Last November, in my letter to you during your meeting in Washington, I dealt at some length with this aspect of communion. At that time I wrote: "The very mystery of the Church impels us to recognize that the one, holy, Catholic, and apostolic Church is present in each particular church throughout the world. And since the successor of Peter has been constituted for the whole Church as pastor and as Vicar of Christ (cf. *Lumen Gentium*, 22), all the particular churches—precisely because they are Catholic, precisely because they embody in themselves the mystery of the Universal Chruch—are called to live in communion with him.

"Our own relationship of ecclesial communion—*collegialitas effectiva et affectiva*—is discovered in the same mystery of the Church. It is precisely because you are pastors of particular churches in which there subsists the fullness of the Universal Church that you are, and must always be, in full communion with the successor of Peter. To recognize your ministry as 'vicars and delegates of Christ' for your particular churches (cf. *Lumen Gentium*, 27) is to understand all the more clearly the ministry of the Chair of Peter, which 'presides over the whole assembly of charity, protects legitimate variety, and at the same time sees to it that differences do not hinder unity but rather contribute to it' " (*Lumen Gentium*, 13; *Letter of November 4, 1986*).

In this perspective too, we must see the ministry of the successor of Peter, not only as a "global" service, reaching each particular church from "outside" as it were, but as belonging already to the essence of each particular church from "within." Precisely because this relationship of ecclesial communion—our *collegialitas effectiva et affectiva*—is such an intimate part of the structure of the Church's life, its exercise calls for each and every one of us to be completely one in mind and heart with the will of Christ regarding our different roles in the College of Bishops. The Council took pains not only to formulate these roles but also to place the exercise of authority in the Church in its proper perspective, which is precisely the perspective of *communio*. In this respect also the Council was, in the words of the Extraordinary Synod, "a legitimate and valid expression and interpretation of the deposit of faith as it is found in Sacred Scripture and in the living tradition of the Church" (*Relatio Finalis*, I, 2).

As I also wrote to you last year, I have endeavored to fulfill my role as successor of Peter in a spirit of fraternal solidarity with you. I wish only to be of service to all the bishops of the world and, in obedience to my specific responsibility at the service of the Church's unity and universality, to confirm them in their own collegial ministry. I have always been greatly encouraged in this task by your fraternal support and your partnership in the gospel, for which I express to you again my profound gratitude. It is of great importance to the Church that in the full power of the Church's communion we continue to proclaim together Jesus Christ and his gospel. In this way we ourselves live fully, as successors of the apostles, the mystery of ecclesial communion. At the same time through our ministry we enable the faithful to enter ever more deeply into the Church's life of communion with the Most Holy Trinity.

Moral Teaching and the New Realities
Presented by Archbishop John R. Quinn

Most Holy Father,

Recognizing the privilege which has been given to me in addressing Your Holiness on the moral teaching of the Church, I would begin by stating my belief that moral theology is an example of human wisdom struggling to understand God's revelation about how we live. Notwithstanding the promised presence and guidance of the Holy Spirit in the Church, this struggle, so dramatically portrayed in the opening sections of *Gaudium et Spes* (cf. 4—10), is unavoidable for several reasons:

1. We are limited human creatures wrestling with a word the infinite God has spoken.

2. We are affected by the reality of sin.

3. We are profoundly affected by rapid and pervasive change.

The distinguished American theologian, Father John Courtney Murray, SJ, who made such a signal contribution to the council, captures this struggle between human wisdom and God's revelation in the following words:

> . . . (H)istory . . . does change . . . the human reality. It evokes situations that never happened before. It calls into being relationships that had not existed. It involves human life in an increasing multitude of institutions of all kinds, which proliferate in response to new human needs and desires, as well as in consequence of the creative possibilities that are inexhaustibly resident in human freedom . . . "The nature of man is susceptible of change," St. Thomas repeatedly states. History continually changes the community of mankind and alters the modes of communication between man and man, as these take form "through external acts." In this sense,

138

the nature of man changes in history, for better or for worse, at the same time that the fundamental structure and human nature, and the essential destinies of the human person, remain untouched and intact.[1]

As all this happens, continually new problems are being put to the wisdom of the wise, at the same times that the same old problems are being put to every man, wise or not. The issue is always the same: What is man or society to do, here and now, in order that personal or social action may fulfill the human inclination to act according to reason?

Father Murray, then, anticipating the thought of *Gaudium et Spes* (4-10), here describes one of the fundamental challenges for moral theology: there are "new human needs and desires," new realities, which confront both believers and the Church as a community of moral discourse.

The Church, of course, meets these new human realities with a critical posture. *Gaudium et Spes* itself teaches:

Faith throws new light on everything, manifests God's design for man's total vocation, and thus directs the mind to solutions which are fully human (11).

This perspective of faith in the midst of earthly contingencies continually affirms the supernatural dignity of the human person. The Church is called to be the sign and safeguard of the transcendence of the human person (*Gaudium et Spes*, 46) and must therefore scrutinize the signs of the times and interpret them in the light of the gospel. "Thus, in language intelligible to each generation, she can respond to the perennial questions which men ask about this present life and the life to come, and about the relationship of one to the other. We must, therefore, recognize and understand the world in which we live, its expectations, its longings and its often dramatic characteristics" (ibid., 4).

This need to scrutinize the signs of the times and to struggle, in light of the Word of God, with the great human questions led the Council to call for moral theology to "be renewed by livelier contact with the Mystery of Christ and the history of salvation . . . . It should show the nobility of the Christian vocation of the faithful" (*Optatam Totius*, 16).

The Council thus calls moral theology to a more evident grounding in the Mystery of Christ and a more effective relationship to authentic Christian discipleship. As the Church encounters new and changing realities, moral theology confronts the dual task of the conversion of the mind and the conversion of the heart. In the United States, the first challenge, the conversion of the mind, is to convey to American

---

1. John Courtney Murray, SJ. "Natural Law and the Public Consensus." *Natural Law and Modern Society.* John Cogley, ed. (Cleveland: World Publishing Company, 1962) pp. 66-67.

Catholics that the revolutionary changes which have occurred in personal and societal life in the twentieth century are not grounds for dismissing Church teaching as outmoded, but rather that these changes point all the more strongly to the value of the Church's tradition in interpreting new human realities. The second challenge of moral theology, the conversion of the heart, is to convey to American Catholics the reality that the Christian moral life is challenging, but not onerous; that it is a call to holiness by a God who understands our weaknesses and walks with us in our struggle to live out the values of the gospel; that it is not a set of abstract rules designed to constrict our lives, but a call to pilgrimage and conversion that can enrich our lives. The Christian moral life thus conceived, can be summed up in the beautiful words of St. Thomas' hymn: *"Per tuas semitas, duc nos quo tendimus ad lucem quam inhabitas"* (*Office of Corpus Christi*, "Sacris Solemniis").

The New Realities Facing the Church in the United States

Most Holy Father,

Turning now to more practical aspects of the matter, I would like, in a brief and summary fashion, to touch on some of these critical new realities as the Church faces them in the United States:

1. The fact that the United States is a major military power in the world.

2. Pervasive divorce and family instability which so greatly harm the ability of the family to be the basic transmission belt of civilization and religion.

3. The immensely high standard of living enjoyed by a great part of American society and the responsibilities as well as the human problems this standard of living creates.

4. The development of new medical technologies which aid both in the generation and prolongation of life, and the shocking paradox that the noble profession of medicine, the servant of human life and well-being, has also become a destroyer of human life through widespread abortion.

5. The constantly developing insights of the psychological and sociological sciences into the nature of human sexuality and of the human emotional life.

6. The sexual revolution which has created a permissive climate in which sexual activity is declared to have a value independent of other human responsibilities and moral exigencies.

7. The dramatically altered and changing social status of women

with its concomitant impact on personal meaning and social identity.

8. The increased, widespread high level of education among American Catholics and its impact on their understanding of and expectations about their role in the Church.

Our constant effort as pastors to focus the moral tradition of the Church faithfully on these complex and rapidly changing issues is a source of tremendous difficulties. We accept the great transcendent moral imperatives of the gospel and the Church's perennial teaching. We recognize our grave obligation to teach courageously and bear witness to the whole, and not just part, of the gospel, even in the face of ridicule and opposition. At the same time, we also recognize that we cannot fulfill our task simply by an uncritical application of solutions designed in past ages for problems which have qualitatively changed or which did not exist in the past.

Rooted in the Mystery of Christ, guided by the teaching of the Church, and calling to a life of authentic discipleship, moral theology must respond to these new human realities in a manner which at once reflects what newness there is in these issues, the legitimate development of the human sciences, the enduring nature of the human person, the tradition of moral wisdom in the Church, and the absolute claims of the gospel.

The Church has indeed met this challenge in some remarkable ways. For instance, the 1987 *Instruction on Respect for Human Life in Its Origin and on the Dignity of Procreation* of the Congregation for the Doctrine of the Faith speaks to the moral seriousness of certain technological aspects of modern reproductive medicine stating forthrightly:

> The human being is to be respected and treated as a human person from the moment of conception; and therefore from that same moment his rights as a person must be recognized, among which in the first place is the inviolable right of every innocent human being of life (I:1).

In the area of sexual morality, both *Gaudium et Spes* and *Humanae Vitae* underlined the meaning of the "special sacrament" that is marriage witnessing to the intrinsic relationship between the procreative and unitive meanings of the marital union.

The Congregation for the Doctrine of the Faith's 1986 *Letter to Bishops of the Catholic Church on the Pastoral Care of Homosexual Persons*, while affirming the consistent moral teaching of the Church against homosexual acts, at the same time affirmed the fundamental dignity and freedom of homosexual persons by making clear their "transcendent nature" and "supernatural vocation" which invests homosexual persons with an "intrinsic dignity . . . (which) must always be respected in word, in action, and in law" (7, 10).

The 1983 pastoral letter of the American bishops, *The Challenge of*

Peace: God's Promise and Our Response confronts the moral dimensions of the nuclear arms race as a "new urgency" underlining the uniquely "destructive nature of the modern war" (231).

The 1986 document of the American bishops, *Economic Justice for All: Catholic Social Teaching and the U.S. Economy,* faces the moral implications of what it means to be "among the most economically powerful nations on earth" (6).

These examples from the social, medical, and sexual moral teaching of the Holy See and of the American bishops indicate the Church's dialogue with the new human realities and the Church's careful effort to lay new foundations for a critical mediation of the moral tradition in a transformed cultural and social context.

Moral and Pastoral Reflections

Most Holy Father,

These examples of the Church's wisdom struggling with God's revelation suggest some important moral and pastoral reflections.

First. The recent pastoral letters of the American bishops just referred to employ a moral pedagogy which distinguishes "universally binding moral principles found in the teaching of the Church" from "specific applications, observations and recommendations which allow for diversity of opinion on the part of those who assess the factual data of situations differently" ("Summary," 9). It is a pedagogy which distinguishes between principles and prescriptions in moral teaching, but does not thereby deny the value of prescriptions. Nor does it mean to imply that there are not or cannot be binding prescriptions in the Church. As Karl Rahner has noted, "The only defense of the inheritance of the past is the conquest of the future. But, for that we need . . . practical prescriptions, not only abstract principles."[2]

Second. We as pastors are greatly concerned that some particular areas of the Church's teaching in both sexual and social morality are at times subjected to negative criticism in our country and sometimes even by Catholics of good will. This can, in some instances, be ascribed to the permissive, narcissistic, and consumer qualities of our society. Indeed, in such a setting, people's sensitivity to these kinds of difficult and challenging moral teachings can be dulled, their ability to hear and willingness to listen, reduced. Nevertheless, we bishops feel that this problem must be mentioned in any presentation of the current situation of the moral teaching of the Church, and we regard it as a continuing incentive to search more carefully for more effective ways of translating the Church's teaching into more attractive language— even when presenting the difficult or corrective teachings of the gospel—so that " . . . in language intelligible to each generation, (the

---

2. Karl Rahner, SJ. *The Practice of Faith.* (Crossroad, 1984) n. 48. "Principles and Prescriptions." pp. 225-228.

Church) can respond to the perennial questions which men ask . . . " (*Gaudium et Spes*, 4).

Third. We firmly believe that an authoritative teaching office has been entrusted to us in our communion with you as Bishop of Rome and successor of Peter. In fulfillment of this sacred responsibility, we have experienced the value of dialogue, as elaborated by Paul VI in *Ecclesiam Suam*. We have found it an effective mode of coming to understand more fully the nature of the moral questions posed by our times, to formulate various responses, to deepen insight into the *sensus fidelium* and to fulfill in an efficacious manner our teaching office. Dialogue and discussion, of course, are never a substitute for the decisions of the Magisterium. But they are, and have been, as Cardinal Newman has so effectively shown, its indispensable prolegomenon.

Fourth. The Church's Magisterium needs to encourage moral theologians in their difficult task as Your Holiness has done, for example, in speaking to scholars at The Catholic University of America in 1979, in *Laborem Exercens* and in your commentaries of Genesis. We are grateful for the unselfish assistance we bishops continually receive from them in carrying out the public and pastoral work of the Church.

Conclusion

Most Holy Father,

As moral theology continues its struggle to understand God's revelation, new human problems and realities are constantly developing. But we do not forget that the revelation of God par excellence is found in the cross of Christ which makes God's folly wiser than human wisdom. Often human wisdom in a given age appears to have the last word. But the cross brings a perspective that changes judgments radically. And the Church's moral teaching is there to see to it that the cross is allowed to be the hermeneutic it is intended to be in moral theology which, otherwise, is in danger of becoming a discipline "which tells me what God has no right to expect of me." The gospel, we can never forget, is always a call to "more." "I tell you, unless your holiness surpasses that of the scribes and the pharisees, you shall not enter the kingdom of God," Jesus said. (Mt. 5:20)

Moral theology, then, like the Church itself, should bring "to mankind light kindled from the gospel, and put at its disposal those saving resources which the Church, herself, under the guidance of the Holy Spirit, receives from her Founder . . . (It should) offer to mankind the honest assistance of the Church to foster that brotherhood of all men which corresponds to their destiny . . . (and) seek but a solitary goal: to carry forward the work of Christ Himself under the lead of the befriending Spirit. And Christ entered this world to give witness to the truth, to rescue and not to sit in judgment, to serve and not to be served" (*Gaudium et Spes*, 3).

143

John Paul II's Response

Archbishop Quinn has spoken of the Church as a community that wishes to remain faithful to the moral teaching of our Lord Jesus Christ. To proclaim a body of moral teaching is in fact an inseparable part of the Church's mission in the world. From the beginning, the Church under the guidance of the Holy Spirit has striven to apply God's revelation in Christ to all the many aspects of our living in this world, knowing that we are called to "lead a life worthy of the Lord and pleasing to him in every way" (Col 1:10).

It is sometimes reported that a large number of Catholics today do not adhere to the teaching of the Church on a number of questions, notably sexual and conjugal morality, divorce and remarriage. Some are reported as not accepting the Church's clear position on abortion. It has also been noted that there is a tendency on the part of some Catholics to be selective in their adherence to the Church's moral teachings. It is sometimes claimed that dissent from the Magisterium is totally compatible with being a "good Catholic" and poses no obstacle to the reception of the sacraments. This is a grave error that challenges the teaching office of the bishops of the United States and elsewhere. I wish to encourage you in the love of Christ to address this situation courageously in your pastoral ministry, relying on the power of God's truth to attract assent and on the grace of the Holy Spirit which is given both to those who proclaim the message and to those to whom it is addressed.

We must also constantly recall that the teaching of Christ's Church, like Christ himself, is a "sign of contradiction." It has never been easy to accept the gospel teaching in its entirety, and it never will be. The Church is committed, both in faith and morals, to make her teaching as clear and understandable as possible, presenting it in all the attractiveness of divine truth. And yet the challenge of the gospel remains inherent in the Christian message transmitted to each generation. Archbishop Quinn has made reference to a principle with extremely important consequences for every area of the Church's life: " . . . the revelation of God par excellence is found in the cross of Christ which makes God's folly wiser than human wisdom. Often human wisdom in a given age appears to have the last word. But the cross brings a perspective that changes judgments radically." Yes, dear brothers, the cross, in the very act of revealing mercy, compassion, and love, changes judgments radically.

A number of other general points may be made. First, the Church is a community of faith. To accept faith is to give assent to the word of God as transmitted by the Church's authentic Magisterium. Such assent constitutes the basic attitude of the believer, and is an act of the will as well as of the mind. It would be altogether out of place to try to model this act of religion on attitudes drawn from secular culture.

144

Within the ecclesial community, theological discussion takes place within the framework of faith. Dissent from Church doctrine remains what it is, dissent; as such it may not be proposed or received on an equal footing with the Church's authentic teaching.

Moreover, as bishops we must be especially responsive to our role as authentic teachers of the faith when opinions at variance with the Church's teaching are proposed as a basis for pastoral practice. I wish to support you as you continue to engage in fruitful dialogue with theologians regarding the legitimate freedom of inquiry which is their right. You rightly give them sincere encouragement in their difficult task and assure them how much the Church needs and deeply appreciates their dedicated and constructive work. They, on their part, will recognize that the title Catholic theologian expresses a vocation and a responsibility at the service of the community of faith, and subject to the authority of the pastors of the Church. In particular your dialogue will seek to show the inacceptability of dissent and confrontation as a policy and method in the area of Church teaching.

Speaking on your behalf, Archbishop Quinn has shown full awareness of the seriousness of the challenge facing your teaching ministry. He has spoken of the dual task of the conversion of the mind and the conversion of the heart. The way to the heart very often passes through the mind, and throughout the length and breadth of the Church there is need today for a new effort of evangelization and catechesis directed to the mind. Elsewhere I have mentioned the relationship between the gospel and culture. Here I wish to underline the importance of the formation of the mind at every level of Catholic life.

Catholic children and young people need to be given an effective opportunity to learn the truths of the faith, in such a way that they become capable of formulating their Catholic identity in terms of doctrine and thought. Here the Catholic press can make a magnificent contribution to raising the general level of Catholic thought and culture. Seminaries, especially, have the responsibility of ensuring that future priests should acquire a high level of intellectual preparation and competence. Continuing education programs for priests, religious, and laity play an important part in stimulating a necessary and serious intellectual approach to the multitude of questions confronting faith in our contemporary world.

A crucial aspect of this "apostolate of the mind" concerns the duty and right of bishops to be present in an effective way in Catholic colleges and universities and institutes of higher studies in order to safeguard and promote their Catholic character, especially in what affects the transmission of Catholic doctrine. It is a task which requires personal attention on the part of bishops, since it is a specific responsibility stemming from their teaching office. It implies frequent contacts with teaching and administrative personnel, and calls for providing serious programs of pastoral care for students and others within the academic community. Much is already being done, and I take the opportunity to encourage you to seek ways of intensifying these apostolates.

One of the greatest services we bishops can render to the Church is to consolidate present and future generations of Catholics in a sound and complete understanding of their faith. The ecclesial community will thus be wonderfully strengthened for all aspects of Christian moral living and for generous service. The intellectual approach that is needed, however, is one intimately linked to faith and prayer. Our people must be aware of their dependence on Christ's grace and on the great need to open themselves ever more to its action. Jesus himself wants us all to be convinced of his words: "Apart from me you can do nothing" (Jn 15:5).

The Role of the Laity in Society and the Church in the U.S.A.
Presented by Archbishop Rembert G. Weakland, OSB

Perhaps the first question that should be asked is: Who are the Catholic laity in the U.S.A. today? They form 28 percent of the total population of the nation (up eight percent from 1947) and are moving rapidly into the upper echelons of society, business, and politics. Products of the fine Catholic educational tradition of the Church in the U.S.A., they continue to place weight on further education; Catholics represent a higher percentage of students in the nation's colleges than their percentage in the general population. Thus, it can be assumed they will continue to take a prominent role in U.S. society and culture in the future. This picture stands in striking contrast to their position before the Second World War when they were mostly working-class immigrants, considering themselves second-class citizens at best. Now the Church in the U.S.A. can boast of having the largest number of educated faithful in the world.

Most sociologists analyzing the rise of Catholics in U.S. society note that they remain very much attached to their Church. It is true that since the Second World War Mass attendance on a weekly basis declined perceptibly. In 1958, 74 percent said they had attended Mass in the past seven days; while in 1985, 53 percent answered the question positively, 71 percent saying they went to Mass at least once a month. This figure has been stable for the last ten years. The defection rate today is not much different than in the 1950s. More admit to increased reading of the Bible, more attendance at other church functions, and surveys show a remarkable increase in confession in the last ten years (up from 18 percent in 1977 who said they had been to confession in

146

the past eight weeks to 23 percent in 1986 who said they had gone to confession in the last 30 days). There exists a high rate of contentment with the changes of Vatican Council II, especially among the intellectuals. It should also be noted that the rise in social status among Catholics did not alter perceptibly their concern for social problems and their more open stance in that regard.

"Today American Catholics no longer worry about being accepted— they worry about how to lead."[1]

Yet, these trends pose new challenges to episcopal leadership. Five areas will be mentioned.

One. The faithful are more inclined to look at the intrinsic worth of an argument proposed by the teachers in the Church than to accept it on the basis of the authority itself. Since so often that teaching touches areas where many of the faithful have professional competency (from medical-moral issues to complex economic ones, for example), they wish to be able to contribute through their own professional skills to solving the issues. This demands a new kind of collaboration and a wider range of consultation on the part of the teaching office of the Church. Before their peers, Catholic intellectuals are also more sensitive to the credibility of the Church if such competency is not maintained.

Two. Moreover, in the area of political issues Catholics in the U.S.A. are jealous of their tradition of freedom and deeply resent being told how to vote on a issue or for which candidate to vote. In fact, any interference might have just an opposite effect on them. This poses the delicate balance to the bishops of teaching correct doctrine but of avoiding what could look like taking sides in partisan disputes or using their religious authority in a way that might seem to interfere in the political process.

In all of these cases an authoritarian style is counterproductive, and such authority for the most part then becomes ignored.

Three. The faithful are demanding more help from the teaching authority of the Church on how to bring the gospel to their professional or work world, their societal and political involvement. They sense the dualism between their private life and morality and their other commitments. They realize the complexity of these issues, are not looking for facile solutions but only to be prodded, encouraged, and sustained in their search. More than anything, they are looking for a spirituality that integrates their life, that does not condemn the technological world in which they live and work, that helps them sift the good from the bad, that permits them to reinforce the good. They sense the tensions between their work concerns and their family responsibilities and seek help from their faith to unify all these demands with the gospel imperatives.

Four. The faithful want to contribute their skills and knowledge to the life and growth of the Church. They often feel there are not

---

1. George Gallup, Jr. and Jim Castelli, *The American Catholic People: Their Beliefs, Practices, and Values.* (New York, 1987) p. 2.

sufficient opportunities for them to use their professional skills within the Church, that they are held back by a fear that can look like clericalism or clerical control on the part of Church leadership.

Five. Women, in particular, seek to be equal partners in sharing the mission of the Church. The Church in the U.S.A. owes a tremendous debt to the religious women who built the educational and health systems that have been among the strengths of our Church. There are no words to explain so much pain on the part of so many competent women today who feel they are second-class citizens in a Church they love. That pain turns easily to anger and is often shared and transmitted to the younger generation of men and women. Women do not want to be treated as stereotypes of sexual inferiority, but want to be seen as necessary to the full life of a Church that teaches and shows by example the co-discipleship of the sexes as instruments of God's Kingdom. They seek a Church where the gifts of women are equally accepted and appreciated. Many of them do not yet see the Church imaging such a co-discipleship but fear that it is still one of male superiority and dominance.

Catholic women repudiate those forms of feminism that undermine the importance of family or that go contrary to their nature; but many do not see the Church as yet striving for a structure where women are considered as equal partners, where the feminine is no longer subordinate but seen in a holistic mutuality with the masculine as forming the full image of the Divine.

In your *Angelus* talk at Castel Gandolfo on August 16th, you rightly pointed out, Holy Father, that the gospel is "rich in the presence of women," and that, "even if women are not called to the typical mission which the Lord entrusted to the apostles as their own (namely, as you have clearly stated often, that involving ordination to the priesthood), nevertheless women are given roles of great importance in relationship to the spreading of the Good News of the Kingdom." You rightly point out the role of Mary herself as exemplar. Women today want to reclaim that scriptural sense of co-discipleship.

For a complete picture of the pastoral tasks facing the bishops of the U.S.A., one would have to say something of the charismatic renewal and its impact; on the discovery of the Bible in the personal life of the faithful; on the fundamentalist trends in the U.S.A.; on the many social concerns movements (e.g., The Catholic Worker) and spiritual renewal movements in general (e.g., RENEW). Negatively, one would also have to say something of the large number of divorces and the breakup of so many families. The influence of affluence on societal values and the possible evils of consumerism and waste would also have to be mentioned as pastoral concerns.

But no picture would be complete without speaking of other groups which add so much to the vitality and spiritual richness of the Church in the U.S.A.: the Hispanic, Black, and Asian communities. All of these in recent decades have provided a new dimension to Church life. For example, the Hispanic and Black Catholics have evolved a pastoral plan that meets their special needs as they take their place in American society and contribute to the life of the whole Church. All of these groups can be special targets of fundamentalist sects that seek to offer them a sense of community, material help, and uncomplicated assurance of salvation. (It should be noted in honesty that such fundamentalist temptations are also found at all levels of U.S. Catholic society.) These groups, however, are facing the challenges of U.S. culture realistically under good leadership and are a young and rejuvenating element in the Church in the U.S.A.

The Catholic Church has a clear duty to fight racism as it opens its doors to these newer cultural expressions of the faith; it is evident that goodwill does not seem to be enough here. The Church must also fight for the rights of so many of these populations who live in poverty and are without work; the Church must also continue its educational thrust among them.

One of the pastoral problems the Catholic Church faces in the U.S.A. is to remain very conscious of the needs of the less fortunate. As the majority of Catholics rise to positions of power and prestige, they must be challenged to use their influence to create a more equal society and to assume a larger international leadership role as well. We bishops have attempted to do this with our recent pastoral letters. They reflect this new situation of our faithful and challenge them to bring the gospel, not just into consonance with their personal lives, but also to the world situation in which we all live and where lay Catholics in the U.S.A. can and should assume a more positive role of moral leadership.

John Paul II's Response

The Synod to be held this coming month in Rome will undoubtedly deal in further detail with the many important points raised by Archbishop Weakland in his presentation on the role of the laity. These remarks, like my own, particularly concern the Catholic laity in the United States. It has been stated that "the Church in the United States of America can boast of having the largest number of educated faithful in the world." This statement has many implications. The situation which it describes is cause for humble rejoicing and gratitude because it represents a major achievement: the sustained educational effort by the Church in this country for many, many decades. At the same time the education of the faithful offers great promise and potential in the years ahead. For "it can be assumed they will continue to take a prominent role in U.S. society and culture in the future."

Primarily through her laity, the Church is in a position to exercise great influence upon American culture. This culture is a human creation. It is created through shared insight and communication. It is built by an exchange among the people of a particular society. And culture, while having a certain dynamic endurance, is always changing and developing as a way of life. Thus the American culture of today stands in continuity with your culture of 50 years ago. Yet it has changed; it has been greatly influenced by attitudes and currents of thought.

But how is the American culture evolving today? Is this evolution being influenced by the gospel? Does it clearly reflect Christian inspiration? Your music, your poetry and art, your drama, your painting and sculpture, the literature that you are producing are all those things which reflect the soul of a nation being influenced by the spirit of Christ for the perfection of humanity?

I realize these are difficult questions to answer, given the complexity and diversity of your culture. But they are relevant to any consideration of the role of the Catholic laity, "the largest number of educated faithful in the world." And it is above all the laity, once they have themselves been inspired by the gospel, who bring the gospel's uplifting and purifying influence to the world of culture, to the whole realm of thought, and artistic creativity, to the various professions and places of work, to family life, and to society in general. As bishops, with the task of leading the laity and of encouraging them to fulfill their ecclesial mission in the world, we must continue to support them as they endeavor to make their specific contribution to the evolution and development of culture and to its impact on society.

With reference to this question, and in such areas as politics, economics, mass media, and international life, the service we bring is primarily a priestly service: the service of preaching and teaching the word of God with fidelity to the truth, and of drawing the laity ever more into the dialogue of salvation. We are charged to lead our people to holiness, especially through the grace of the Eucharist and the whole sacramental life. The service of our pastoral leadership, purified in personal prayer and penance, far from bearing an authoritarian style in any way, must listen and encourage, challenge and at times correct. Certainly, there is no question of condemning the technological world but rather of urging the laity to transform it from within so that it may receive the imprint of the gospel.

We serve our laity best when we make every effort to provide for them, and in collaboration with them, a comprehensive and solid program of catechesis with the aim of "maturing the initial faith and of educating the true disciple of Christ by means of a deeper and more systematic knowledge of the person and the message of our Lord Jesus Christ" (*Catechesi Tradendae*, 19). Such a program will also assist them in developing that habit of discernment which can distinguish the spirit of the world from the Spirit of God, and which can distinguish authentic culture from elements that degrade human dignity. It can provide them a solid basis for growing in their knowledge and love of Jesus Christ through continual conversión and personal commitment to the demands of the gospel.

In speaking of the laity, I feel a particular desire to support you in all you are doing on behalf of family life. Archbishop Weakland has mentioned "the large number of divorces and the breakup of so many families" as a special pastoral problem. I know that all of us feel great sadness and deep pastoral concern for all those whose lives are affected in this way.

As you will recall, on the occasion of your *Ad Limina* visits, four years ago, I spoke at some length on the topic of marriage. Without repeating all that I said on that occasion, I wish to encourage you to continue in your many zealous and generous efforts to provide pastoral care to families. I also urge you in the face of all the trends which threaten the stability of marriage, the dignity of human love, and the dignity of human life, as well as its transmission, never to lose confidence and courage. Through the grace given us as pastors we must endeavor to present as effectively as possible the whole teaching of the Church, including the prophetic message contained in *Humanae Vitae* and in *Familiaris Consortio*.

The faithful teaching of the intrinsic relationship between the unitive and procreative dimensions of the marriage act is of course only a part of our pastoral responsibility. With pastoral solicitude for couples *Familiaris Consortio* pointed out that "the ecclesial community at the present time must take on the task of instilling conviction and offering practical help to those who wish to live out their parenthood in a truly responsible way. . . . This implies a broader, more decisive and more systematic effort to make the natural methods of regulating fertility known, respected, and applied" (No. 35).

On the occasion of the last *Ad Limina* visits I stated: "Those couples who choose the natural methods perceive the profound difference, both anthropological and moral, between contraception and natural family planning. Yet they may experience difficulties; indeed they often go through a certain conversion in becoming committed to the use of the natural methods, and they stand in need of competent instruction, encouragement, and pastoral counseling and support. We must be sensitive to their struggles and have a feeling for the needs that they experience. We must encourage them to continue their efforts with generosity, confidence, and hope. As bishops we have the charism and the pastoral responsibility to make our people aware of the unique influence that the grace of the sacrament of marriage has on every aspect of married life, including sexuality" (cf. *Familiaris Consortio*, 33). The teaching of Christ's Church is not only light and strength for God's People, but it uplifts their hearts in gladness and hope.

"Your episcopal conference has established a special program to expand and coordinate efforts in the various dioceses. But the success of such an effort requires the abiding pastoral interest and support of each bishop in his own diocese, and I am deeply grateful to you for what you do in this most important apostolate" (*Address of September 24, 1983*).

My profound gratitude to you extends to the many other areas in which, with generous dedication, you have worked for and with the laity. These include your persevering efforts at promoting peace, fostering justice, and supporting the missions. In the area of the defense of human life, you have worked with exceptional commitment and constancy. Already during the *Ad Limina* visits of 1978, Paul VI drew attention to this activity of yours, assuring you of the appreciation of the Holy See. Because of their exceptional importance, I wish to quote at some length his words of strong support for you and make them my own:

> In the name of Jesus Christ, we thank you for your ministry at the service of life. We know that you have labored precisely in order that the words of the Good Shepherd would be fulfilled:"that they may have life and have it to the full." Under your leadership, so many of the Catholic people —priests, deacons, religious and laity— have joined in numerous initiatives aimed at defending, healing, and promoting human life.

> With the enlightenment of faith, the incentive of love, and an awareness of your pastoral accountability, you have worked to oppose whatever wounds, weakens, or dishonors human life. Your pastoral charity has found a consistent expression in so many ways—all related to the question of life, all aimed at protecting life in its multiple facets. You have endeavored to proclaim in practice that all aspects of human life are sacred.

> In this regard, your efforts have been directed to the eradication of hunger, the elimination of subhuman living conditions, and the promotion of programs on behalf of the poor, the elderly, and minorities. You have worked for the improvement of the social order itself. At the same time, we know that you have held up to your people the goal to which God calls them: the life above, in Christ Jesus (cf. Phil 3:14).

> Among your many activities at the service of life there is one which, especially at this juncture of history, deserves our strongest commendation and our firmest support: it is the continuing struggle against what the Second Vatican Council calls the 'abominable crime' of abortion (*Gaudium et Spes*, 51). Disregard for the sacred character of life in the womb weakens the very fabric of civilization; it prepares a mentality, and even a public attitude, that can lead to the acceptance of other practices that are against the fundamental rights of the individual. This mentality can, for example, completely undermine concern for those in want, manifesting itself in insensitivity to social needs; it can produce contempt for the elderly, to the point of advocating euthanasia; it can prepare the way for those forms of genetic engineering that go against life, the dangers of which are not yet fully known to the general public.

> It is therefore very encouraging to see the great service you render to humanity by constantly holding up to your people the value of human life. We are confident that, relying on the words of the

Good Shepherd, who inspires your activity, you will continue to exercise leadership in this regard, sustaining the entire ecclesial community in their own vocation at the service of life.

It is also a source of worldwide honor that, in your country, so many upright men and women of differing religious convictions are united in a profound respect for the laws of the Creator and Lord of life, and that, by every just means at their disposal, they are endeavoring, before the witness of history, to take a definitive stand for human life" (*Address of May 26, 1978*).

Nine years have passed since these words were spoken and yet they are still relevant today—relevant in their prophetic vision, relevant in the needs they express, relevant in the defense of life.

In his encyclical *Pacem in Terris*, Pope John XXIII placed the question of the advancement of women in the context of the characteristics of the present day, "the signs of the times." He made it clear that the cause in question was one of human dignity. This is indeed the aim of all the Church's efforts on behalf of women: to promote their human dignity. The Church proclaims the personal dignity of women as women—a dignity equal to that of men's dignity. This dignity must be affirmed in its ontological character, even before consideration is given to any of the special and exalted roles fulfilled by women as wives, mothers, or consecrated women.

There are many other aspects involved in the question of women's equal dignity and responsibility, which will undoubtedly be properly dealt with in the forthcoming Synod of Bishops. At the basis of all considerations are two firm principles: the equal human dignity of women and their true feminine humanity. On the basis of these two principles *Familiaris Consortio* has already enunciated much of the Church's attitude toward women, which reflects the "sensitive respect of Jesus toward the women that he called to his following and his friendship" (22). As I have stated and as Archbishop Weakland has pointed out, women are not called to the priesthood. Although the teaching of the Church on this point is quite clear, it in no way alters the fact that women are indeed an essential part of the gospel plan to spread the Good News of the Kingdom. And the Church is irrevocably committed to this truth.

Lay, Religious, and Clerical Vocations in the United States
Presented by Archbishop Daniel E. Pilarczyk

Most Holy Father, I have been asked to speak about certain implications of lay, religious, and clerical vocations in the United States. With your permission, I would like to address these issues by positing a single question and treating it in a format that is familiar to us all.

Quaeritur. Whether the ministry of the Church in the United States is in a state of turmoil and crisis.

Et videtur quod sit.

Primo. The number of vocations to religious life has declined considerably. In 1962, there were 173 thousand women religious in the United States and 12 thousand religious brothers. In 1986, there were 114 thousand sisters and seven thousand brothers.

Secundo. The number of diocesan and religious priests has increased since 1962 from 56 thousand to 57 thousand but this latter number also includes many thousand priests who are retired because of infirmity and age. Moreover, during this same period, the number of Catholics in our country has increased by nearly 10 million, changing the ratio of priest to Catholics from 771 to 920.

Tertio. The number of seminarians and candidates for religious life has declined to the point where it seems clear that there will be far fewer priests and religious to minister to the faithful of our country in the years ahead.

Quarto. The rise of lay ministry within the Church has led some to voice serious concern about the clericalization of the laity and the laicizing of the clergy.

Quinto. Questions continue to be voiced about the wisdom of the Church's discipline of priestly celibacy and about the Church's teaching on the ordination of women, as well as about certain other Church teachings.

Sexto. Our society is becoming increasingly secular and therefore increasingly inhospitable to Christian belief, with the result that ministry to believers and unbelievers alike is more demanding than it was in the past.

Sed contra.

Primo. We have witnessed the development of an intense and lively participation of lay persons and non-clerical religious in the ministry of the Church, a participation which includes lay teachers in our Catholic schools, and, in our parishes, full-time catechetical directors (directors of religious education), youth ministers, home visitors, business managers, and general pastoral ministers.

Secundo. We have been blessed with some eight thousand permanent deacons in our country since the Second Vatican Council.

Tertio. There is an increased understanding of and appreciation for religious life on the part of bishops and priests, thanks, in large part, to the pontifical commission which you yourself established, Holy Father.

Quarto. Various kinds of spiritual renewal programs have grown up within the Church over the past two decades which have led hundreds of thousands of our people to a deeper knowledge and a greater assimilation of their Catholic faith.

Quinto. There is an increasingly urgent awareness on the part of almost every segment of the Church in our country of the need to undertake greater efforts of evangelization.

Sexto. Thanks to the collaboration of other persons in the Church's ministry, priests no longer have to attend personally to every single task in their parishes and are freer to focus their energies on specifically priestly activities such as preaching, liturgical celebration, and leadership of the Christian community.

Respondeo dicendum, first of all, Holy Father, that no brief overview of the ministerial realities of the Church in our country can do justice to the breadth and variety of the Church's life here. I suspect that every bishop in this room could and would add several other items of concern and of encouragement to the list which I have presented.

Next, I would be untrue to my mandate if I did not observe that certain aspects of our present situation are a source of great anxiety for us bishops. Will there be enough priests in the future to do the specifically priestly work that will need doing? How can we better identify and address the real questions of church order and doctrine which face us? Will there be enough material resources (i.e. money) to offer appropriate wages and suitable health and retirement benefits to the increasing number of lay persons who work in and for the Church? Sometimes we are afraid as we look toward the future which seems to hold so many unknowns.

At the same time, I am convinced, and I believe my brother bishops are also convinced, that what we are experiencing here in our country bears the marks of the work of the Holy Spirit.

What we are experiencing is a broadening of the concept of church vocation and church ministry, a concept which formerly included only priests and religious, but which now includes lay persons in an ever increasing number of capacities and religious in capacities different from those in which they served previously. Most emphatically, the specific roles and implications of ordained ministry and of vowed religious life have to be carefully maintained, as does the urgency of the need for Christian witness by lay persons in the world. But at the same time, we welcome the developments which are making the Church in our country a church of ever deepening participation and collaboration instead of a gathering of the active few and the passive many.

Concomitant with this development is an increasing appreciation for spirituality: for prayer, for Sacred Scripture, for preaching, for the liturgy, for spiritual direction. We are by no means a nation of mystics, but we are increasingly a Catholic community which realizes that external conformity to rites and rules, important as that is, is not enough.

Overall, Holy Father, I believe that the Holy Spirit is hard at work among the dioceses and parishes of our country. One of the implications of the theme that I was asked to develop (lay, religious, and clerical vocations in the United States) is, I believe, that Catholic people in our country have available to them a depth and variety of ministry in the Church far greater than ever before. And for that, we bishops are profoundly grateful to all our collaborators in the Church's ministry and grateful for the opportunity to express our thanks to them in the presence of the Church's universal pastor.

I hope that my presentation does not sound like the prayer of the Pharisee in the temple, grateful that he is not like the rest of sinful humankind (cf. Lk 18:9ff.). God knows that it is not our intent here today to hold up for universal imitation an "American way" of being church. We don't want a merely "American" church. We want a Catholic Church to flourish in our country. God also knows that we have plenty of problems and plenty of loose ends to deal with. At the same time, though, we felt that it was important for us bishops to take the opportunity of being with Your Holiness to speak of some of the very positive implications of lay, religious, and clerical vocations in our country.

And now I am in a position to respond to the original *quaestio* around which I have constructed these remarks. *Quaerebatur* whether the ministry of the Church in the United States is in a state of turmoil and crisis. *Et respondeo* affirmative, but it is not the turmoil and crisis of death and decay, but of development and of life.

Dixi, Beatissime Pater.

John Paul II's Response

My interest in the question of vocations is well known to all of you. It is a recurring theme in my conversations with bishops around the world. It is one of the subjects I frequently speak about in my meetings with young people. It is a crucial factor for the future of the Church as we draw near to the beginning of the third millennium. Therefore, I am very pleased that you have chosen this topic as one of those to be emphasized today.

Archbishop Pilarczyk has presented an "overview of the ministerial realities of the Church in this country," mentioning aspects that offer much consolation to you as bishops and aspects which are cause for pastoral concern. He mentioned that it was important "to speak of some of the very positive implications of lay, religious, and clerical vocations in America." In doing this, he rightly drew attention to the way that the Holy Spirit is at work in your midst, something that we must indeed be ever attentive to and grateful for. As *Lumen Gentium* reminds us, "The Spirit guides the Church into the fullness of truth (cf. Jn 16:13) and gives her unity of fellowship and service. . . . By the power of the gospel the Spirit makes the Church grow, perpetually renews her, and leads her to perfect union with her Spouse" (4).

It is indeed encouraging to note how lay people, in ever-increasing numbers, have become involved in the life of the Church, and how this has led to "a depth and variety of ministry far greater than ever before." Certainly, the more active participation of the laity in the mission of the Church is an eloquent sign of the fruitfulness of the Second Vatican Council, one for which we all give thanks. And I am confident that the forthcoming Synod of Bishops will give fresh impetus to this participation and solid direction for its continued growth and consolidation.

It is important for our people to see clearly that the ministry of the ordained priest and the involvement of the laity in the Church's mission are not at all opposed to one another. On the contrary, the one complements the other. Just as the priestly ministry is not an end in and of itself, but serves to awaken and unify the various charisms within the Church, so too the involvement of the laity does not replace the priesthood, but supports it, promotes it, and offers it space for its own specific service.

At this time, I would like to make a few remarks about vocations to the priesthood and to the religious life.

The insufficient number of seminarians and candidates for religious life is indeed a cause of pastoral concern for all of us, for we know that their public witness to the gospel and their specific roles in the Church are irreplaceable. In many parts of the world the Church is experiencing, as Archbishop Pilarczyk observed, that "society is becoming increasingly secular and therefore increasingly inhospitable to Christian belief." It is especially difficult today for young people to make the generous sacrifices entailed in accepting God's call. Yet it is possible for them to do so through grace and with the support of the community. And it is precisely in this situation that we are called to bear witness to the hope of the Church.

In our pastoral mission we must often evaluate a situation and decide on a course of action. We must do this with prudence and pastoral realism. At the same time we know that today, as always, there are "prophets of doom." We must resist them in their pessimism, and continue in our efforts to promote vocations to the priesthood and the religious life.

Prayer for vocations remains the primary way to success, since Jesus himself left us the commandment: "Beg the harvest master to send out laborers to gather his harvest" (Mt 9:38). I ask you therefore to encourage prayer for vocations among all the people, particularly among priests and religious themselves, but also in families, where the first seeds of vocations are usually planted, and in schools and religious education programs. The prayers of the elderly and the sick have an efficacy that must not be forgotten.

In addition to prayer, young people must be invited. It was Andrew who brought his brother Peter to the Lord. It was Philip who brought Nathanael. And how many of us and of our priests and religious came to hear the Lord's call through the invitation of someone else? Your own presence among the youth is a blessing and an opportune time to extend this invitation to them and to ask young people themselves to pray for vocations.

Just last Thursday, speaking in Miami about vocations to the priesthood, I emphasized the basis of our hope: "There is still one more factor to be considered in evaluating the future of vocations, and it is the power of Christ's Paschal Mystery. As the Church of Christ, we are all called to profess his power before the world; to proclaim that he is able, in virtue of his death and resurrection, to draw young people to himself, in this generation as in the past; to declare that he is strong enough to attract young men even today to a life of self-sacrifice, pure love, and total dedication to the priesthood. As we profess this truth, as we proclaim with faith the power of the Lord of the harvest, we have a right to expect that he will grant the prayers that he himself has commanded to be offered. The present hour calls for great trust in Him who has overcome the world."

I would like to thank you for all you are doing to ensure a solid formation for the priesthood in the United States. The apostolic visitation to the seminaries has been carried out with generous collaboration. And I am grateful for the letters many of you have sent me expressing your appreciation for this initiative and telling me of the many positive effects which have resulted from it.

At the same time, your pastoral interest and personal involvement in seminary training is something that can never end. It is too central a task and too important a priority in the life of the Church. The Church of tomorrow passes through the seminaries of today. With the passing of time, the pastoral responsibility will no longer be ours. But at present the responsibility is ours and it is heavy. Its zealous fulfillment is a great act of love for the flock. In particular, I ask you to be vigilant that the dogmatic and moral teaching of the Church is faithfully and clearly presented to the seminarians and fully accepted and understood by them. On the opening day of the Second Vatican Council, October 11, 1962, John XXIII told his brother bishops: "The greatest concern of the Ecumenical Council is this: that the sacred deposit of Christian doctrine should be more effectively guarded and taught." What Pope John expected of the Council is also a primary concern for priestly formation. We must ensure that our future priests have a solid grasp of the entirety of the Catholic faith; and then we must prepare them to present it in turn to others in ways that are intelligible and pastorally sound.

I cannot let this opportunity pass without expressing once again my gratitude for the great interest you have taken in the religious life. I am pleased to note, as Archbishop Pilarczyk has said, that there is "an increased understanding of and appreciation for religious life on the part of bishops and priests, thanks, in large part, to the pontifical commission" established in 1983.

In asking the commission to study the problem of vocations, I did so "with a view to encouraging a new growth and fresh move forward in this most important sector of the Church's life." The response which you have all made to this request has been most gratifying. And I know you will continue with this important effort. The religious life is a precious gift from the Lord, and we must continue to assure religious of the love and esteem of the Church.

There are many other issues, dear brother bishops, which come to mind as we reflect together in this extraordinary hour of ecclesial communion. All of them touch us in our role as pastors and challenge our apostolic love and zeal.

Because of its importance in the life of the Church, I spoke to the priests in Miami about confession and our own need to receive the sacrament regularly. I also expressed my gratitude for their generous ministry in making confession available to the faithful. In this regard I would ask you as bishops to make every effort to ensure that the important norms of the Universal Church with regard to the use of general absolution are understood and observed in a spirit of faith. In this regard I would ask that the postsynodal apostolic exhortation *Reconciliatio et Paenitentia* continue to be the object of prayerful reflection.

I wish to encourage you also in the pastoral care that you give to homosexual persons. This includes a clear explanation of the Church's teaching, which by its nature is unpopular. Nevertheless your own pastoral experience confirms the fact that the truth, howsoever difficult to accept, brings grace and often leads to a deep inner conversion. No matter what problem individual Christians have, and no matter what degree of response to grace they make, they are always worthy of the Church's love and Christ's truth. All homosexual and other persons striving to fulfill the gospel precept of chastity are worthy of special encouragement and esteem.

From time to time the question of sex education, especially as regards programs being used in schools, becomes a matter of concern to Catholic parents. The principles governing this area have been succinctly but clearly enunciated in *Familiaris Consortio*. First among these principles is the need to recognize that sex education is a basic right and duty of parents themselves. They have to be helped to become increasingly more effective in fulfilling this task. Other educational agencies have an important role, but always in a subsidiary manner, with due subordination to the rights of parents.

Many parents will undoubtedly be heartened by the reference in the pastoral letter of the bishops of California, *A Call to Compassion*, to an absolutely essential aspect of this whole question: "The recovery of the virtue of chastity," they wrote, "may be one of the most urgent needs of contemporary society." We cannot doubt that the Catholic Church in the United States, as elsewhere, is called to make great efforts to assist parents in teaching their children the sublime value of self-giving love; young people need great support in living this fundamental aspect of their human and Christian vocation.

Among your many pastoral obligations is the need to provide for the spiritual care of the military and their dependents. This you do through the Military Ordinariate. The functioning of this extended archdiocese requires the fraternal and sensitive collaboration of all the bishops in permitting and encouraging priests to commit themselves to this worthy ministry. The Church is grateful to all the chaplains who generously serve God's people in this particular situation, with its special needs.

I wish at this time to offer you my encouragement as you seek to guide the Church of God in so many areas, as you seek to lead your people in fulfilling their mission within the United States and well beyond her boundaries. Everything you do to help your people to look outside themselves to Christ in need is a great ecclesial and apostolic service.

My final word is about our pastoral identity as bishops of Jesus Christ and his Church. Because of this identity we are called to holiness and to daily conversion. In speaking to you eight years ago in Chicago I stated: "The holiness of personal conversion is indeed the condition for our fruitful ministry as bishops of the Church. It is our union with Jesus Christ that determines the credibility of our witness to the gospel and the supernatural effectiveness of our activity" (*Discourse of October 5, 1979*). May God give us all this great gift of union with Jesus and allow us to live it together in strength and joy, in the communion of the Church of God.

Meeting with Non-Christian Religious Leaders Japanese Cultural Center

Presentation by Dr. Havanpola Ratanasara Buddhist Representative

His Holiness Pope John Paul II, Archbishop Roger Mahony, Dignitaries of the Multi-Religious Assembly, Ladies and Gentlemen,

I consider it to be a great privilege to receive and greet His Holiness, Pope John Paul II to this great city of Los Angeles, on behalf of all the Buddhist community.

The Buddhist community in Los Angeles consists of nine Asian Buddhist traditions, along with the American community of Buddhists. These peace-loving people of the ancient Buddhist tradition heartily welcome Your Holiness to this city, whose very nature is multiethnic and multireligious.

The religious community in this city is unique in that greater understanding, cooperation, and friendship prevail here than is found in most communities. Los Angeles is truly the city which leads the world in daily interreligious cooperation. Here we do not speak of cooperation; here we enact it every day. The cordial relationship within the multireligious community has been greatly strengthened, largely due to the Second Vatican Council and its passage of *Nostra Aetate*, and to the Vatican's concern for communication and cooperation with the major non-Christian religious traditions. The ecumenical principles enunciated by the Vatican have influenced the attitude of the various religious communities. In the implementation of this principle of interfaith cooperation, His Eminence Cardinal Timothy Manning and Archbishop Roger Mahony should be especially mentioned.

We Buddhists were very pleased to take part in the Peace Day in October 1986, when the religious leaders of the interfaith community of Los Angeles joined together, upon your urging, to take a stand for peace and sanity. We have been especially encouraged by our frequent chance to discuss and debate with leaders of the Catholic community, in events such as the commemorating the 20th anniversary of *Nostra Aetate*. We have found a new spirit of friendship and respect coming from the Catholic community, for which we are most grateful.

We Buddhists the world over have for the past 25 centuries been advocating the great message of the Buddha, i.e. compassion, *Karuna*, and loving kindness, *Metta*, to all beings. Sectarianism, fanaticism, and labialism are actively discouraged in Buddhism. We are always yearning for peace, prosperity, and harmony for all beings, and our goal in life is the improvement of life for all beings, rather than their religious conversion. We live by the principle laid down by our Lord to live purely and to not cause others unhappiness by improper behavior or proselytization. Therefore, we are so very happy when we view the short history of the Vatican under your leadership, Your Holiness. You have shown a tremendous vision, courage, and exemplary leadership worthy of your eminent position. Your Holiness has visited a number of trouble spots at the risk of your own life, with the hope of bringing back sanity among the warring parties. This gesture of Your Holiness is appreciated by the Buddhist community.

Let us urge for peace with a more vigorous voice, with more vigorous actions, and with more vigorous speed. Let us together, as caring, spiritual people who are concerned with all life, be the active, unresting conscience of the world, especially those in power. When the rulers support or initiate cruelty and inhumanity, let us speak up loudly. When they support arms at the expense of human welfare, let us speak up loudly. Let us not remain silent, no matter what people's opinion may be. Let us always speak and act for the improvement of humankind and the environment earth in which we live. Let us speak out against war and the preparation of nations for war, against poverty, against the destruction of planet earth and its life. Let us instead urge peace, security, a pristine and clean earth and space, and a dignity for all humans and for all life forms with whom we share our life. We Buddhists urge Your Holiness to continue your work and fearlessly take the lead whenever it is needed. The

Buddhist community shall always render all assistance, cooperation, and courage in any noble effort which Your Holiness makes.

> May the suffering ones be suffering free,
> May the fear-struck fearless be,
> May the grieving shed all grief,
>   and the sick find health relief.
> May all beings be happy, prosperous and peaceful.

And may Your Holiness always have good health, great courage and determination, and a long life. To you we give our deepest respect and blessing.

Presentation by Dr. Maher Hathout
Islamic Representative

Your Holiness,

Since the time God created the earth and man, through the prehistoric and historic eras, never has the world been on the brink of such dangers, nor its children in the midst of such suffering as we are today.

At a time when half of the world denies God, and most of the other half disobeys him; when the future of our race and our environment are hostage to decisions of fallible men and the touch of a button; when people are dying from over-eating while their brethren starve; when we cannot count the victims of war, and are not allowed to count the prisoners of conscience—those who are jailed because they dare to speak out against tyranny, oppression, racism, and military occupation—when the brokers of death simultaneously sell arms to both sides of a war; when mass propaganda will defame people and religion to stimulate them and set them as targets of prejudice and hate; when people are bombed daily in their homes while the world looks to the other side; when the people of the homeland of Jesus Christ are denied the God-given right of self-determination—it is in these stormy times when the candle flickers, that glimpses of hope become extremely valuable.

We, together, are those glimpses of hope, for these times are the trial of those who believe in God and human decency to come together—to cherish their common ground while realizing and respecting their differences, to have the *Nostra Aetate* not as a mere document but as a personal reality, for God has called upon us.

Ye mankind, I have created thee from a single male and female, and made you into nations and tribes, that ye may befriend (know) each other, not that ye may despise each other.

God save the truth and may God bless you all.

Presentation by Swami Swahananda
Hindu Representative

As a monk of the Ramakrishna Order belonging to Vedanta which is the philosophy of Hinduism, I am very happy to be invited to participate in the welcome of His Holiness the Pope, who is the highly respected leader of the Christian monastic orders and also of the Catholic Church. This meeting shows catholicity, a spirit of harmony, and concern for the whole humanity. His recent efforts to involve the leaders of other religions in promoting peace have endeared him to all. Peace is not merely an urgent necessity for the external world, but also peace within oneself is the persistent need of the soul. Hinduism, along with other religions, gives primacy to this need. The invocations and hymns in the Vedas, the source books of Hinduism, begin and end with the word peace, *Shanti.*

The philosophy of Vedanta long ago harmonized the various religious groups in India and made them into sects of Hinduism. The special message of Vedanta is the harmony of religions, unity of Godhead, divinity of the soul, and unity of existence. Though many Gods are worshipped, they are aspects of the same God. Though man is mortal, he has a spiritual core in him which is indestructible. Though the universe is variegated, there is unity in diversity, one Reality permeating them. All creation is striving to realize the truth of God and regain its harmony. Everyone has a spiritual future. This philosophy gave Hinduism a tremendously liberal and tolerant attitude. Sri Ramakrishna, the prophet of New India, in the recent past, supported this acceptance and harmony by his realization. Naturally, I am very happy that the archdiocese has convened this meeting with leaders of different religions, manifesting the catholic spirit and tolerance which Hinduism prizes so much.

Politics is based on a struggle for power and, therefore, is often unable to bring peace. The root cause of the unrest in the world is man's selfishness and feeling of competition and hatred, which are fed by prevalent mechanistic and materialistic theories and nationalistic ideas. There are hundreds of groups and organizations all over the world working for peace. Often they base their appeal on expediency, self-interest, and survival of man. Though religion takes into consideration all these points, it has a more basic appeal, for it stands

163

for the best in man and speaks of voluntary sacrifice and love. It is religion that imbues the minds of people with love and understanding. Bringing together the leaders of different religions is itself the product of that love and the liberal spirit. This is also manifest in the inter-religious councils. If religions can work together for peace and fight against irreligion, it will be a demonstration of love, free from dis-sension for which religions are ill-reputed. This will be a model for other organizations, social and political. The efforts of the pope and the leaders of religions of the world have a special significance, for they will involve people themselves practicing religious values and will help create a proper climate for peace. May all the political leaders of society, with whom lies the immediate power, heed the message of peace based upon love, unselfishness, and fellow feeling. *Om Shanti, Shanti, Shanti.*

Presentation by Rabbi Alfred Wolf
Jewish Representative

Your Holiness,

It is my privilege to welcome you to Los Angeles on behalf of my coreligionists. While not all of us, in this "City of the Angels" act like angels all of the time, a spirit of harmony and mutual trust binds our Jewish community—the second largest in the United States—to the largest Roman Catholic archdiocese in our nation. Rooted in the past of our multireligious city, this friendship grew under the impact of the Vatican II Council. It spread to include other branches of Chris-tianity, the religions mentioned in *Nostra Aetate* and represented on this dais, as well as Bahais and Sikhs.

Together we, in Los Angeles, have learned some of the lessons which you have taught the world; for you have given mobility to the throne of St. Peter and your travels dwarf the journeys of the apostle Paul. By your world-spanning flights you have conquered the miles separating continents, and by a few steps into a synagogue you have cut through a millennial curtain of contempt. By your personal pres-ence in some of the hidden places of the earth you have linked the concerns of the few and the weak and the distant to the worldwide mission of your Church. You have built a visible bridge between the particular and the universal.

Similarly, we have learned in our local dialogue that the particular fears and hopes of each segment of contemporary humanity are linked to the universal fears and hopes of all times and all places. This may be especially true of Jewish cares and Jewish dreams; for we have been a conspicuous minority in every place and every time ever since the days of our Father Abraham.

We plead with you, as we plead with all our friends, to assist us in the continuing struggle against anti-Semitism wherever and under whatever name it may arise. This is our particular agenda; but it is also our reaffirmation of the universal principle, as stated by our teacher Moses: "The stranger who dwells among you shall be as one born among you and you shall love him as yourself" (Lv 19:34).

We plead with you, as we plead with all people of good will, to fight with us for our people in the Soviet Union and in other lands of oppression to be free to worship in their tradition and free to leave. This is our particular agenda; but it is also our commitment to the universal vision of the Prophet Micah: "They shall sit, every one, under their own vine and fig tree, and none shall make them afraid" (Mi 4:4).

We plead with you, as we plead with the entire civilized world, to aid us in securing for our people in the State of Israel peace within secure borders and full recognition in the family of nations. This is our particular agenda; but it is also our yearning for the fulfillment of Isaiah's universal goal: "They shall beat their swords into plough-shares and their spears into pruning hooks. Nation shall not lift up sword against nation nor learn war any more" (Is 2:4).

When you gathered religious leaders in Assisi to pray for peace, you taught the world that we need not set aside our particular beliefs and traditions to unite for a universal task. You also made us realize that, as representatives of religion, we will have little credibility as peacemakers while religion is still abused as a reason or a pretext for war. May we hope, therefore, that the gathering in Assisi was but a beginning and that you will continue to lead us toward the time when the world's religions will not only pray for peace between the nations but will live in peace with each other, a "United Religions," a guide and model for a real and effective United Nations.

May the Good Lord grant you health, strength, and long life to bring the world closer to harmony and peace.

John Paul II's Response

Dear Brothers and Sisters, Representatives of World Religions and Religious Leaders, Dear Friends,

It is a great joy for me to meet with you, the local representatives of great religions of the world, during the course of my pastoral visit. I wish to thank in particular the Japanese community of Los Angeles for their kind hospitality at this center, which is a symbol of cultural diversity within the United States as well as a symbol of dialogue and interaction at the service of the common good. I understand that the Japanese community has been present in this area of Los Angeles for a century. May God continue to bless you with every good gift now and in the future. I also wish to extend cordial greetings to all religious leaders and to all people of good will who honor us with their presence today.

It is my conviction that we must make use of every opportunity to show love and respect for one another in the spirit of *Nostra Aetate* which, as the theme of our meeting affirms, is indeed alive 22 years after its promulgation among the documents of the Second Vatican Council. This declaration, on the relation of the Catholic Church to Non-Christian religions, speaks of "that which people have in common and of those things which tend to promote fellowship among them" (*Nostra Aetate*, 1). This continues to be the basis of our efforts to develop a fruitful relationship among all the great religions of the world.

As I stated earlier this year, the Catholic Church remains firmly committed to the proclamation of the gospel and to dialogue with people of other religions: proclamation of the gospel, because as *Nostra Aetate* points out, the Church "must ever proclaim Christ, 'the way, the truth, and the life' (Jn 14:6) in whom people find the fullness of religious life, and in whom God has reconciled all things to himself (cf. 2 Cor 5:18-19)" (*Nostra Aetate*, 2); dialogue and collaboration with the followers of other religions, because of the spiritual and moral goods that we share (cf. ibid.). That dialogue "is a complex of human activities, all founded upon respect and esteem for people of different religions. It includes the daily living together in peace and mutual help, with each bearing witness to the values learned through the experience of faith. It means a readiness to cooperate with others for the betterment of humanity, and a commitment to search together for true peace. It means the encounter of theologians and other religious specialists to explore, with their counterparts from other religions, areas of convergence and divergence. Where circumstances permit, it means a sharing of spiritual experiences and insights. This sharing can take the form of coming together as brothers and sisters to pray to God in ways which safeguard the uniqueness of each religious tradition" (*Address to the Members and Staff of the Secretariat for Non-Christians*, April 28, 1987).

Throughout my pontificate it has been my constant concern to fulfill this twofold task of proclamation and dialogue. On my pastoral visits around the world I have sought to encourage and strengthen the faith of the Catholic people and other Christians as well. At the same time I have been pleased to meet with leaders of all religions in the hope of promoting greater interreligious understanding and cooperation for the good of the human family. I was very gratified at the openness and good will with which the World Day of Prayer for Peace in Assisi last October was received, not only by the various Christian churches and ecclesial communities, but by the other religions of the world as well. I was also pleased that another World Day of Prayer subsequently took place in Japan at Mount Hiei.

What I said in Assisi also applies to our meeting today: "The fact that we have come here does not imply any intention of seeking a religious consensus among ourselves or of negotiating our faith convictions. Neither does it mean that religions can be reconciled at the level of a common commitment in an earthly project which would surpass them all. Nor is it a concession to relativism in religious beliefs, because every human being must sincerely follow his or her upright conscience with the intention of seeking and obeying the truth. Our meeting attests only, and this is its real significance for the people of our time, that in the great battle for peace, humanity in its very diversity must draw from its deepest and most vivifying sources where its conscience is formed and upon which is founded the moral action of all people" (*Message to the Participants at the World Day of Prayer for Peace*, Assisi, October 27, 1986).

It is in that spirit that I wish, through you, to greet each of your communities before saying something further about the concern for peace that we all share.

To the Buddhist community, which reflects numerous Asian traditions as well as American, I wish respectfully to acknowledge your way of life, based upon compassion and loving kindness and upon a yearning for peace, prosperity, and harmony for all beings. May all of us give witness to compassion and loving kindness in promoting the true good of humanity.

To the Islamic community, I share your belief that mankind owes its existence to the one, compassionate God who created heaven and earth. In a world in which God is denied or disobeyed, in a world that experiences so much suffering and is so much in need of God's mercy, let us then strive together to be courageous bearers of hope.

To the Hindu community, I hold in esteem your concern for inner peace and for the peace of the world, based not on purely mechanistic or materialistic political considerations, but on self-purification, unselfishness, love, and sympathy for all. May the minds of all people be imbued with such love and understanding.

To the Jewish community, I repeat the Second Vatican Council's conviction that the Church "cannot forget that she received the revelation of the Old Testament through the people with whom God in his mercy established the ancient covenant. Nor can she forget that she draws sustenance from the root of that good olive tree onto which has been grafted the wild olive branches of the Gentiles (cf. Rom 11:17-24; *Nostra Aetate*, 4). With you, I oppose every form of anti-Semitism. May we work for the day when all peoples and nations may enjoy security, harmony, and peace.

Dear brothers and sisters of these religions and of every religion, so many people today experience inner emptiness even amid material prosperity because they overlook the great questions of life: "What is man? What is the meaning and purpose of life? What is goodness and what is sin? What gives rise to suffering and what purpose does it serve? What is the path to true happiness? What is death, judgment, and retribution after death? What, finally, is that ultimate, ineffable mystery which embraces our existence, from which we take our origin and toward which we move?" (*Nostra Aetate*, 1).

These profoundly spiritual questions, which are shared to some degree by all religions, also draw us together in a common concern for man's earthly welfare, especially world peace. As I said at Assisi: "(World Religions) share a common respect of and obedience to conscience, which teaches all of us to seek the truth, to love and serve all individuals and peoples, and therefore to make peace among individuals and among nations" (*Message at the Conclusion of the World Day of Prayer for Peace*, Assisi, October 27, 1986).

In the spirit of the kind words with which you addressed me earlier as an advocate of peace, let us continue to seek peace for the human family through prayer, since peace transcends our human efforts; through penance, since we have not always been "peacemakers"; through prophetic witness, since old divisions and social evils need to be challenged; and through constant initiatives on behalf of the rights of individuals and nations, and on behalf of justice everywhere. The fragile gift of peace will survive only if there is a concerted effort on the part of all, to be concerned with the "glaring inequalities not merely in the enjoyment of possessions but even more in the exercise of power" (*Populorum Progressio*, 9). In this regard world leaders and international bodies have their special role to play. But universal sensitivity is also called for, particularly among the young.

I believe that the *Prayer of Saint Francis of Assisi*, universally recognized as a man of peace, touches the conscience of us all. It is that prayer that best expresses my sentiments in meeting with all of you today:

> Lord, make me an instrument of your peace;
> where there is hatred, let me sow love;
> where there is injury, pardon;
> where there is doubt, faith;
> where there is despair, hope;
> where there is darkness, light;
> and where there is sadness, joy.
>
> O Divine Master,
> grant that I may not so much seek to be consoled as to console;
> to be understood as to understand;
> to be loved as to love;
> for it is in giving that we receive,
> it is in pardoning that we are pardoned,
> and it is in dying that we are born to eternal life.

Homily at Los Angeles Eucharist
Dodger Stadium

*The Lord has made his salvation known in the sight
of the nations* (Ps 98:2).

Dear Brother Bishops, Dear Brothers and Sisters in Christ, People of
this City of Our Lady of the Angels, Once Known as *El Pueblo de
Nuestra Senora de los Angeles,* Citizens of This State of California,

Today, from this City of Los Angeles on the Pacific Coast, in which
are gathered all the bishops of the United States, we return together
to the upper room in Jerusalem. We hear words from the prayer which
Christ pronounced there. Surrounded by his apostles, Jesus prays for
the Church of every time and place. He says to the Father: "I do not
pray for them alone. I pray also for those who will believe in me
through their word" (Jn 17:20). Christ, the one Eternal Priest of the
new and everlasting covenant, prays for us, for all of us gathered
here, for everyone who lives here in Los Angeles on the West Coast
of the United States of America, for everyone in the world. Yes, every
one of us is included in this priestly prayer of the redeemer.
    Jesus says to the Father: "I pray also for those who will believe in
me through their word" (Jn 17:20). This is the Church of all ages that
he is praying for. How many generations of disciples have already
heard these words of Christ! How many bishops, priests, men and
women religious, and how many parents and teachers in the course
of the centuries have passed on this word of salvation! In how many
places of the world, among how many peoples and nations, has this
mystery of the redemption continued to unfold and bear fruit! It is
the word of salvation from which the Church has grown and continues
to grow. This is true for the Universal Church and for each local
church. It is true for the Church in Los Angeles which is visited today
by the Bishop of Rome, the successor of Peter.
    In 1769 Father Junipero Serra and his Franciscan companions brought
the word of God to California. Leaving behind all that was familiar
and dear to them, they freely chose to come to this area to preach
the Good News of our Lord Jesus Christ. This initial effort of evangelization very quickly showed impressive results as thousands of
Native Americans accepted the gospel and were baptized. Soon, a
whole series of missions was established all along El Camino Real,
each of them bearing the name of a saint or a mystery of the Christian
faith: San Diego, San Bernardino, San Gabriel, San Buenaventura,
Santa Barbara, San Fernando, and all the rest.
    Within years of this first missionary effort, immigrants began to
settle in California. Coming mostly from Mexico and Spain, these
early settlers had already been evangelized and thus they brought as

part of their heritage the Catholic and apostolic faith. Little did they know at the time that, in God's providence, they were initiating a pattern which would characterize California for years to come.

Subsequently California has become a haven for immigrants, a new home for refugees and migrants, a place where people from every continent have come together to fashion a society of the most varied ethnic diversity. Many of these, like their earliest predecessors, have brought not only their specific cultural traditions but also the Christian faith. As a result, the Church in California, and particularly the Church in Los Angeles, is truly catholic in the fullest sense, embracing peoples, and cultures of the widest and richest variety.

Today, in the Church in Los Angeles, Christ is Anglo and Hispanic, Christ is Chinese and Black, Christ is Vietnamese and Irish, Christ is Korean and Italian, Christ is Japanese and Filipino, Christ is Native American, Croatian, Samoan, and many other ethnic groups. In this local church, the one Risen Christ, the one Lord and Savior, is living in each person who has accepted the word of God and been washed clean in the saving waters of baptism. And the Church, with all her different members, remains the one Body of Christ, professing the same faith, united in hope and in love.

What does Jesus pray for in the upper room the night before his passion and death? "That all may be one as you, Father, are in me, and I in you; I pray that they may be one in us, that the world may believe that you sent me" (Jn 17:21). "One in us"—the mystery of the inscrutable Divine Being, the mystery of the intimate life of God: the Divine Unity and at the same time the Trinity. It is the divine "We" of the Father, and the Son, and the Holy Spirit. And even though it is not attainable in its absolute fullness, this most perfect Unity is the real model for the Church. According to the teaching of the Second Vatican Council, "the Church shines forth as a people made one by the unity of the Father, the Son, and the Holy Spirit" (*Lumen Gentium*, 4).

It is for this type of unity for the Church of all times that Christ prays in the upper room: "that they may be one, as we are one—I living in them, you living in me—that their unity may be complete. So shall the world know that you sent me, and that you loved them as you loved me" (Jn 17:22-23). This is the unity of the Church's communion which is born from the communion of Three Persons in the Most Holy Trinity.

People of all times and places are called to this communion. This truth of revelation is first presented to us in today's liturgy, through the image of the holy city of Jerusalem found in the reading from the prophet Isaiah, who writes: "Nations shall walk by your light, and kings by your shining radiance. Raise your eyes and look about; they all gather and come to you: your sons come from afar, and your daughters in the arms of their nurses" (Is 60:3-4). Isaiah spoke these words in Jerusalem as he foresaw a great light which would descend upon the city: This light is Christ. The awesome movement toward

Christ of people from all over the world begins as a result of the gospel. Animated by the Holy Spirit, in the power of the cross and resurrection of Christ, this movement of people culminates in a new unity of humanity. Thus, the words of Jesus come to pass: "and I— once I am lifted up from the earth—will draw all men to myself" (Jn 12:32).

The Second Vatican Council gave prominence to this dimension of the unity of the Church, above all in the teaching on the People of God. "This people, while remaining one and unique, is to be spread throughout the whole world and must exist in all ages, so that the purpose of God's will may be fulfilled" (*Lumen Gentium,* 13).

However, that people is at the same time the Body of Christ. The body is yet another image, and in a certain sense another dimension, of the same truth of the unity that we all constitute in Christ under the action of the Holy Spirit. Accordingly, Saint Paul exhorts us: "Make every effort to preserve the unity which has the Spirit as its origin and peace as its binding force. There is but one body and one Spirit, just as there is but one hope given all of you by your call. There is one Lord, one faith, one baptism; one God and Father of all, who is over all, and works through all, and is in all" (Eph 4:3-6). The unity for which Christ prayed in the upper room is realized in this way. It does not come from us, but from God: from the Father, through the Son, in the Holy Spirit.

This unity does not at all erase diversity. On the contrary, it develops it. There is constantly "unity in diversity." Through the work of the one Lord, by means of the one faith and the one baptism, this diversity—a diversity of human persons, of individuals—tends toward unity, a unity which is communion in the likeness of God the Trinity.

The unity of the Body of Christ gives life; at the same time, it serves diversity and develops it. This is the diversity of "everyone" and at the same time of "each one." It is the truth that we find in the letter to the Ephesians where Paul writes: "Each of us has received God's favor in the measure in which Christ bestows it. . . . It is he who gave apostles, prophets, evangelists, pastors, and teachers in roles of service for the faithful to build up the body of Christ" (Eph 4:7,11-12). As such then it is the Holy Spirit who is the source of both the unity and the diversity in the Church: the unity because it finds its origin solely in the Spirit; the diversity since the Spirit bestows the variety of gifts, the variety of vocations and ministries found in the Church, which is the Body of Christ and at the same time the People of God.

The saints whom we honor in today's liturgy, Cornelius and Cyprian, remind us of one concrete example of unity in diversity: the unity of the Universal Church which is served by the successor of Saint Peter, and the diversity of the particular Churches which help to build up the whole Body through the leadership of the local bishops.

Pope Saint Cornelius was called to shepherd the Universal Church in the middle of the third century, a time of religious persecution from without and a time of painful dissension within. His efforts to strengthen the Church's communion were greatly aided by the persuasive talents of the bishop of Carthage, Saint Cyprian, who while caring for his own flock also promoted unity throughout North Africa. These two men of different backgrounds and temperaments were united by a mutual love for the Church and by their zeal for the unity of the faith. How appropriate that we should observe their feast on the day when the present successor of Peter is meeting with the bishops of the United States.

The feast focuses our attention on a basic truth, namely that the unity of the members of the Church is deeply affected by the unity of the bishops among themselves and by their communion with the successor of Peter. The Second Vatican Council put it this way: "The Roman Pontiff, as the successor of Peter, is the perpetual and visible source and foundation of the unity of the bishops and of the multitude of the faithful. The individual bishop, however, is the visible principle and foundation of unity in his particular church, fashioned after the model of the Universal Church. In and from such individual churches there comes into being the one and only Catholic Church" (*Lumen Gentium*, 23).

The Church's concrete methods of evangelization and her efforts to promote peace and justice are shaped to a large extent by the fact that the Church is one and yet diverse. The Good News of Jesus must be proclaimed in the language that particular people understand, in artistic symbols that give meaning to their experience, in ways that correspond as far as possible to their own aspirations and needs, their manner of looking at life, and the way in which they speak to God. At the same time, there must be no betrayal of the essential truth while the gospel is being translated and the Church's teaching is being passed down.

The ethnic universality of the Church demands a keen sensitivity to authentic cultures and a real sense of what is required by the process of inculturation. In this regard, Pope Paul VI stated very accurately the task to be done: "The question is undoubtedly a delicate one. Evangelization loses much of its force and effectiveness if it does not take into consideration the actual people to whom it is addressed, if it does not use their language, their signs and symbols, if it does not answer the questions they ask, and if it does not have an impact on their concrete life. But on the other hand evangelization risks losing if one empties or adulterates its content under the pretext of translating it; if, in other words, one sacrifices this reality and destroys the unity without which there is no universality" (*Evangelii Nuntiandi*, 63).

Closely aligned with the Church's evangelization is her action on behalf of peace and justice, and this too is deeply influenced by her pastoral concern for particular peoples, especially for refugees, immigrants, and the poor. For over two hundred years, the Church has welcomed the waves of new immigrants to the shores of your country. It was the love and compassion of the Church that so many new arrivals first felt when they stepped onto the soil of this young nation.

172

While that continuous pastoral care of the immigrant was focused primarily on the East Coast in the early decades, that pastoral outreach now extends to virtually every major city in the country. Los Angeles, where this evening we celebrate the diversity of peoples who make up your country, has now become the new major point of entry for the latest waves of immigrants.

I commend you, my brother bishops, and all of those working closely with you, for your active collaboration in helping several million undocumented immigrants to become legal residents. This pastoral care of the immigrant in our own day reflects the love of Christ in the gospels and the legitimate work of the Church in carrying on the challenge of the Lord, "I was a stranger and you welcomed me" (Mt 25:35).

The Church faces a particularly difficult task in her efforts to preach the word of God in all cultures in which the faithful are constantly challenged by consumerism and a pleasure-seeking mentality, where utility, productivity, and hedonism are exalted while God and his law are forgotten. In these situations, where directly contradict the truth about God and about humanity itself, the Church's witness must be unpopular. She must take a clear stand on the word of God and proclaim the whole gospel message with great confidence in the Holy Spirit. In this effort, just as in all others, the Church shows herself to be the sacrament of salvation for the whole human race, the people God has chosen to be his channel of peace and reconciliation in a world torn by division and sin.

While the Church's unity is not her own achievement but a precious gift from the Lord, it is nonetheless her serious responsibility to be an instrument for guarding and restoring unity in the human family. She does this by being faithful to the truth and by directly opposing the devil, who is "the Father of lies." She does this by efforts to break down prejudice and ignorance as she fosters new understanding and trust. She also promotes unity by being a faithful channel of Christ's mercy and love.

Today, with the very prayer for unity said by Christ in the upper room, we celebrate the liturgy of the Eucharist here, on the rim of the Pacific, in the city that takes its name from the angels. And with the psalmist, we say: "Sing to the Lord a new song, for he has done wondrous deeds" (Ps 98:1).

Yes, God has done so many wondrous deeds that confirm his salvific action in our world—the "God and Father of all, who is over all, and works through all, and is in all" (Eph 4:6). "The Lord has made his salvation known: . . . he has revealed his justice." He constantly remembers "his kindness and his faithfulness" (Ps 98:2-3). This is the way God is, the God of our faith, the Father of our Lord Jesus Christ.

The angels in heaven see "the face of God" in the beatific vision of glory. All of us, people of this planet, walk in faith toward that same vision. And we walk in hope. We draw the strength of this hope from the same prayer of Christ in the upper room. Did not Christ say in

173

the words addressed to the Father: "I have given them the glory you gave me that they may be one, as we are one—I living in them, you living in me" (Jn 17:22-23)?

"The glory . . . I gave to them." We are called in Christ to share in the glory that is part of the beatific vision of God.

Truly, "all the ends of the earth have seen the salvation by our God." For this reason: "Sing to the Lord a new song!" (Ps 98:3,1). Amen.

MONTEREY, CALIFORNIA

Thursday, September 17, 1987

Homily at Monterey Eucharist
Laguna Seca

Be careful not to forget the Lord, your God (Dt 8:11).

Dear Brothers and Sisters of the Monterey Peninsula, Brothers and Sisters of California and Other Areas of the United States,

Originally these words were addressed by Moses to the Israelite people as they were on the point of entering the promised land—a land with streams of water, with springs and fountains welling up in the hills and valleys, a land producing an abundance of every fruit and food, a land where the people would lack nothing (cf. Dt 8:7-9). Today, these words are addressed to the People of God here in Monterey, in the State of California, against the background of an extraordinary beauty of land and sea, of snowcapped mountains and deep lakes, oak groves and forests of fir and pine and mighty redwoods, a land among the richest and most fruitful of the earth. Yes, today, these words are addressed to all of us gathered here: "Be careful not to forget the Lord, Your God."

These words, pronounced thousands of years ago, have still today a special meaning and relevance. Moses, the great teacher of his people, was concerned that in their future prosperity they might abandon God—the God who brought them out of the land of slavery and guided them through the desert with its parched ground, feeding them with manna along the way (cf. Dt 8:15-16). Moses knew the tendency of the human heart to cry out to the Lord in time of need, but easily "to neglect his commandments and decrees and statutes" (cf. Dt 8:11) in the time of well-being and prosperity. He knew that God is easily forgotten.

In our own day are we not perhaps witnesses of the fact that often in rich societies, where there is an abundance of material well-being, permissiveness and moral relativism find easy acceptance? And where the moral order is undermined, God is forgotten and questions of ultimate responsibility are set aside. In such situations a practical atheism pervades private and public living.

From the moment of original sin, man has been inclined to see himself in the place of God. He often thinks, just as Moses warned he might: "It is my own power and the strength of my own hand that has obtained for me this wealth" (Dt 8:17). He acts as if the One who is the source of all life and goodness were just not there. He ignores a fundamental truth about himself: the fact that he is a creature; that he has been created and owes everything to his Creator, who is also his Redeemer.

In these closing years of the twentieth century, on the eve of the Third Millennium of the Christian era, a part of the human family, the most economically and technically developed part, is being specially tempted, perhaps as never before, to imitate the ancient model of all sin—the original rebellion that expressed itself saying: "I will not serve." The temptation today is to try to build a world for oneself, forgetting the Creator and his design and loving providence. But sooner or later we must come to grips with this: that to forget God, to feign the death of God, is to promote the death of man and of all civilization. It is to threaten the existence of individuals, communities, and all society.

Today's readings from the New Testament are in contrast to such a position. They speak of God's presence which permeates the human heart and the whole of created reality. Jesus teaches that the Reign of God is like the growth of the seed that a man scatters on the ground (cf. Mk 4:26-29). Certainly, human activity is essential. Man "goes to bed and gets up every day. . . . " He plants. And "when the crop is ready he wields the sickle." Even the rich valleys of California would produce nothing without human ingenuity and toil. But the word of God says that "the soil produces of itself first the blade, then the ear, finally the ripe wheat in the ear" (Mk 4:28). As if to say: the growth of the wheat and its maturing, which greatly depends on the fertility of the soil, comes from the nature and vitality of creation itself. Consequently there is another source of growth: the One who is above nature and above the man who cultivates the earth.

In a sense, the Creator "hides himself" in this life-giving process of nature. It is the human person, with the help of intellect and faith, who is called to "discover" and "unveil" the presence of God and his action in all of creation: "So may your way be known upon earth; among all nations, your salvation" (Ps 67:3).

If the parable of the seed indicates the growth of the Kingdom of God in the world, the words of Saint Paul in the second reading speak of how God's generous giving aims at drawing "good works" from the human heart: "God can multiply his favors among you . . . for good works." The whole of human activity must be finalized in works of justice, peace, and love. All human work—including, in a very direct way, the noble work of agriculture in which many of you are engaged—is to be carried out at the service of man and for the glory of God.

The land is God's gift. From the beginning, God has entrusted it to the whole human race as a means of sustaining the life of all those whom he creates in his own image and likeness. We must use the land to sustain every human being in life and dignity. Against the background of the immense beauty of this region and the fertility of its soil, let us proclaim together our gratitude for this gift, with the words of the responsorial psalm: "The earth has yielded its fruit, the Lord our God has blessed us" (Ps 67:7).

As we read in Genesis, human beings earn their bread by the sweat of their brows (Gn 3:17). We toil long hours and grow weary at our tasks. Yet work is good for us. "Through work man not only transforms nature, adapting it to his own needs, but he also achieves fulfillment as a human being and indeed in a sense becomes 'more a human being' " (*Laborem Exercens*, 9).

The value of work does not end with the individual. The full meaning of work can only be understood in relation to the family and society as well. Work supports and gives stability to the family. Within the family, moreover, children first learn the human and positive meaning of work and responsibility. In each community and in the nation as a whole, work has a fundamental social meaning. It can, moreover, either join people in the solidarity of a shared commitment, or set them at odds through exaggerated competition, exploitation, and social conflict. Work is a key to the whole social question, when that "question" is understood to be concerned with making life more human (cf. *Laborem Exercens*, 3).

Agricultural work exemplifies all these principles—the potential of work for the fulfillment of the human person, the 'family' dimension of work, and social solidarity. Agricultural work is—as Pope John XXIII described it—a vocation, a God-given mission, a noble task, and a contribution to civilization (cf. *Mater et Magistra*, 149). God has blessed the United States with some of the richest farm land in the world. The productivity of American agriculture is a major success story. Clearly, it is a history of hard and wearying work, of courage and enterprise, and it involves the interaction of many people: growers, workers, processors, distributors, and finally consumers.

I know too that recently thousands of American farmers have been introduced to poverty and indebtedness. Many have lost their homes and their way of life. Your bishops and the whole Church in your country are deeply concerned; and they are listening to the voices of so many farmers and farmworkers as they express their anxieties over the costs and the risks of farming, the difficult working conditions, the need for a just wage and decent housing, and the question of a fair price for products. On an even wider scale is heard the voice of the poor, who are bewildered in a land of plenty and still experience the pangs of hunger.

All agree that the situation of the farming community in the United States and in other parts of the world is highly complex, and that simple remedies are not at hand. The Church, on her part, while she can offer no specific technical solutions, does present a social teaching

177

based on the primacy of the human person in every economic and social activity. At every level of the agricultural process, the dignity, rights, and well-being of people must be the central issue. No one person in this process—grower, worker, packer, shipper, retailer, or consumer—is greater than the other in the eyes of God.

Giving voice therefore to the sufferings of many, I appeal to all involved to work together to find appropriate solutions to all farm questions. This can only be done in a community marked by a sincere and effective solidarity,—and, where still necessary, reconciliation—among all parties to the agricultural productive process.

And what of our responsibility to future generations? The earth will not continue to offer its harvest, except with faithful stewardship. We cannot say we love the land and then take steps to destroy it for use by future generations. I urge you to be sensitive to the many issues affecting the land and the whole environment, and to unite with each other to seek the best solutions to these pressing problems.

Each one of us is called to fulfill his or her respective duties before God and before society. Since the Church is constrained by her very nature to focus her attention most strongly on those least able to defend their own legitimate interests, I appeal to landowners, growers, and others in positions of power to respect the just claims of their brothers and sisters who work the land. These claims include the right to share in decisions concerning their services and the right to free association with a view to social, cultural, and economic advancement (cf. *Laborem Exercens*, 21). I also appeal to all workers to be mindful of their own obligations of justice and to make every effort to fulfill a worthy service to mankind.

New legislation in your country has made it possible for many people, especially migrant farmworkers, to become citizens rather than remain strangers among you. Many of these people have worked here with the same dream that your ancestors had when they first came. I ask you to welcome these new citizens into your society and to respect the human dignity of every man, woman, and child.

Two hundred years after the Constitution confirmed the United States as a land of opportunity and freedom, it is right to hope that there may be a general and renewed commitment to those policies needed to ensure that within these borders equity and justice will be preserved and fostered. This is an ever present requirement of America's historical destiny.

It is also important for America at this time to look beyond herself and all her own needs to see the even greater needs of the poorer nations of the world. Even as local communities mobilize to work ever more effectively for the integral human advancement of their own members, they must not forget their brothers and sisters elsewhere. We must be careful not to forget the Lord, but we must be careful also not to forget those whom he loves.

The hidden attributes of the Creator are reflected in the beauty of his creation. The beauty of the Monterey Peninsula attracts a great number of visitors; as a result so many of you are involved in the

178

tourist industry. I greet you and encourage you to see your specific work as a form of service and of solidarity with your fellow human beings.

Work, as we have seen, is an essential aspect of our human existence, but so also is the necessary rest and recreation which permits us to recover our energies and strengthen our spirit for the tasks of life. Many worthwhile values are involved in tourism: relaxation, the widening of one's culture and the possibility of using leisure time for spiritual pursuits. These include prayer and contemplation, and pilgrimages, which have always been a part of our Catholic heritage; they also include fostering human relationships within the family and among friends. Like other human activities, tourism can be a source of good or evil, a place of grace or sin. I invite all of you who are involved in tourism to uphold the dignity of your work and to be always willing to bear joyful witness to your Christian faith.

Dear brothers and sisters, it is in the Eucharist that the fruits of our work—and all that is noble in human affairs—become an offering of the greatest value in union with the sacrifice of Jesus Christ, our Lord and Savior. In fostering what is authentically human through our work and through deeds of justice and love, we set upon the altar of the Lord those elements which will be transformed into Christ: "Blessed are you Lord, God, of all creation. Through your goodness we have this bread to offer, which earth has given and human hands have made. It will become for us the bread of life."

I ask you to join with me in praising the Most Holy Trinity for the abundance of life and goodness with which you have been gifted: "The earth has yielded its fruit. God, our God, has blessed us" (Ps 67:7). But may your abundance never lead you to forget the Lord or cease to acknowledge him as the source of your peace and well-being. Your prayer for yourselves and for all your brothers and sisters must always be an echo of the psalm:

> May God have pity on us and bless us;
> may he let his face shine on us (Ps 67:2).

For years to come may the Lord's face shine on this land, on the Church in Monterey, and on all America: "From sea to shining sea." Amen.

Address at Carmel Mission Basilica

Dear Bishop Shubsda, Dear Brothers and Sisters,

I come today as a pilgrim to this Mission of San Carlos, which so powerfully evokes the heroic spirit and heroic deeds of Fray Junipero Serra and which enshrines his mortal remains. This serene and beautiful place is truly the historical and spiritual heart of California. All the missions of El Camino Real bear witness to the challenges and heroism of an earlier time, but not a time forgotten or without significance for the California of today and the Church of today.

These buildings and the men who gave them life, especially their spiritual father, Junipero Serra, are reminders of an age of discovery and exploration. The missions are the result of a conscious moral decision made by people of faith in a situation that presented many human possibilities, both good and bad, with respect to the future of this land and its Native Peoples. It was a decision rooted in a love of God and neighbor. It was a decision to proclaim the gospel of Jesus Christ at the dawn of a new age, which was extremely important for both the European settlers and the Native Americans.

Very often, at crucial moments in human affairs, God raises up men and women whom he thrusts into roles of decisive importance for the future development of both society and the Church. Although their story unfolds within the ordinary circumstances of daily life, they become larger than life within the perspective of history. We rejoice all the more when their achievement is coupled with a holiness of life that can truly be called heroic. So it is with Junipero Serra, who in the providence of God was destined to be the Apostle of California, and to have a permanent influence over the spiritual patrimony of this land and its people, whatever their religion might be. This apostolic awareness is captured in the words ascribed to him: "In California is my life and there, God willing, I hope to die." Through Christ's Paschal Mystery, that death has become a seed in the soil of this state that continues to bear fruit "thirty-or sixty-or a hundred-fold" (Mt 13:9).

Father Serra was a man convinced of the Church's mission, conferred upon her by Christ himself, to evangelize the world, to "make disciples of all the nations, baptizing them in the name of the Father and of the Son and of the Holy Spirit" (Mt 28:19). The way in which he fulfilled that mission corresponds faithfully to the Church's vision today of what evangelization means: " . . . the Church evangelizes when she seeks to convert, solely through the divine power of the message she proclaims, both the personal and collective consciences of people, the activities in which they engage, and the lives and concrete milieux which are theirs" (*Evangelii Nuntiandi*, 18).

He not only brought the gospel to the Native Americans, but as one who lived the gospel he also became their defender and champion. At the age of 60 he journeyed from Carmel to Mexico City to intervene with the viceroy on their behalf—a journey which twice brought him close to death—and presented his now famous *Representacion* with its "bill of rights," which had as their aim the betterment of every phase of missionary activity in California, particularly the spiritual and physical well-being of its Native Americans.

Father Serra and his fellow missionaries shared the conviction found everywhere in the New Testament that the gospel is a matter of life and salvation. They believed that in offering to people Jesus Christ, they were doing something of immense value, importance and dignity. What other explanation can there be for the hardships that they freely and gladly endured, like Saint Paul and all the other great missionaries before them: difficult and dangerous travel, illness and isolation, an ascetical life-style, arduous labor, and also, like Saint Paul, that "concern for all the churches" (2 Cor 11:28) which Junipero Serra, in particular, experienced as "Presidente" of the California missions in the face of every vicissitude, disappointment, and opposition.

Dear brothers and sisters, like Father Serra and his Franciscan brethren, we too are called to be evangelizers, to share actively in the Church's mission of making disciples of all people. The way in which we fulfill that mission will be different from theirs. But their lives speak to us still because of their sure faith that the gospel is true, and because of their passionate belief in the value of bringing that saving truth to others at great personal cost. Much to be envied are those who can give their lives for something greater than themselves in loving service to others. This, more than words or deeds alone, is what draws people to Christ.

This single-mindedness is not reserved for great missionaries in exotic places. It must be at the heart of each priest's ministry and the evangelical witness of every religious. It is the key to their personal sense of well-being, happiness, and fulfillment in what they are and what they do. This single-mindedness is also essential to the Christian witness of the Catholic laity. The covenant of love between two people in marriage and the successful sharing of faith with children require the effort of a lifetime. If couples cease believing in their marriage as a sacrament before God, or treat religion as anything less than a matter of salvation, then the Christian witness they might have given to the world is lost. Those who are unmarried must also be steadfast in fulfilling their duties in life if they are to bring Christ to the world in which they live.

"In him who is the source of my strength I have strength for everything" (Phil 4:13). These words of the great missionary, Saint Paul, remind us that our strength is not our own. Even in the martyrs and saints, as the liturgy reminds us, it is "(God's) power shining through our human weakness" (*Preface of Martyrs*). It is the strength that inspired Father Serra's motto: "always forward, never back." It is the strength that one senses in this place of prayer so filled with his presence. It is the strength that can make each one of us, dear brothers and sisters, missionaries of Jesus Christ, witnesses of his message, doers of his word.

SAN FRANCISCO, CALIFORNIA

Thursday, September 17, 1987

Address at Mission Dolores Basilica

Dear Archbishop Quinn, Dear Brothers and Sisters in Christ,

Thank you for your very kind welcome to San Francisco. It is a joy to be here with all of you. As I begin my pastoral visit to your historic city, I extend fraternal greetings to all the citizens of this metropolitan area. In the love of Christ I greet my brothers and sisters of the Catholic community. And in a special way I welcome this opportunity to be with you who are present in this basilica dedicated to Our Lady of Sorrows. May the grace and peace of God our Father and our Lord Jesus Christ be with you all.

San Francisco! Both in name and by history you are linked to the spirit of Saint Francis of Assisi. And thus, as I come to your city on this pastoral visit, I think of all that Saint Francis means, not only to yourselves but to people all around the world. There is something about this man, who was born over 800 years ago in a little Italian town, that continues in our day to inspire people of vastly different cultures and religions.

Saint Francis was a man of peace and gentleness, a poet and lover of beauty. He was a man of poverty and simplicity, a man in tune with the birds and animals, enchanted by all of God's creation. Above all, Francis was a man of prayer whose whole life was shaped by the love of Jesus Christ. And he wished to live in a way that spoke in the clearest terms of the everlasting love of God.

As I come today then to the city of San Francisco, I come in the spirit of this saint whose whole life proclaims the goodness and mercy of God.

Accordingly, I wish to speak to you about the all-embracing love of God. Saint John says: "Love, then, consists in this: not that we have loved God but that he has loved us and has sent his Son as an offering for our sins" (1 Jn 4:10). God's love for us is freely given and unearned, surpassing all we could ever hope for or imagine. He does not love us because we have merited it or are worthy of it. God loves us, rather, because he is true to his own nature. As Saint John puts

183

it, "God is love, and he who abides in love abides in God, and God in him" (1 Jn 4:15).

The greatest proof of God's love is shown in the fact that he loves us in our human condition, with our weaknesses and our needs. Nothing else can explain the mystery of the cross. The apostle Paul once wrote: "You can depend on this as worthy of full acceptance: that Christ Jesus came into the world to save sinners. Of these, I myself am the worst. But on that very account I was dealt with mercifully, so that in me, as an extreme case, Jesus Christ might display all his patience, and that I might become an example to those who would later have faith in him and gain everlasting life" (1 Tm 1:15-16).

The love of Christ is more powerful than sin and death. Saint Paul explains that Christ came to forgive sin and that his love is greater than any sin, stronger than all my personal sins or those of anyone else. This is the faith of the Church. This is the Good News of God's love that the Church proclaims throughout history, and that I proclaim to you today: God loves you with an everlasting love. He loves you in Christ Jesus, his Son.

God's love has many aspects. In particular, God loves us as our Father. The parable of the prodigal son expresses this truth most vividly. You recall that moment, in the parable, when the son came to his senses, decided to return home and set off for his father's house. "While he was still a long way off, his father caught sight of him and was deeply moved. He ran out to meet him, threw his arms around his neck, and kissed him" (Lk 15:20). This is the fatherly love of God, a love always ready to forgive, eager to welcome us back.

God's love for us as our Father is a strong and faithful love, a love which is full of mercy, a love which enables us to hope for the grace of conversion when we have sinned. As I said in my encyclical on the mercy of God: "The parable of the prodigal son expresses in a simple but profound way the reality of conversion. Conversion is the most concrete expression of the working of love and of the presence of mercy in the human world . . . Mercy is manifested in its true and proper aspect when it restores to value, promotes and draws good from all the forms of evil existing in the world" (*Dives in Misericordia,* 6).

It is the reality of God's love for us as our father that explains why Jesus told us when we pray to address God as "Abba, Father" (cf. Lk 11:2; Mt 6:9).

It is also true to say that God loves us as a mother. In this regard, God asks us, through the prophet Isaiah: "Can a mother forget her infant, be without tenderness for the child of her womb? Even should she forget, I will never forget you" (Is 49:15). God's love is tender and merciful, patient and full of understanding. In the Scriptures, and also in the living memory of the Church, the love of God is indeed depicted and has been experienced as the compassionate love of a mother.

Jesus himself expressed a compassionate love when he wept over Jerusalem, and when he said: "O Jerusalem, Jerusalem. . . . How often would I have gathered your children together as a hen gathers her brood under her wings" (Lk 13:34).

Dear friends in Christ, the love of God is so great that it goes beyond the limits of human language, beyond the grasp of artistic expression, beyond human understanding. And yet, it is concretely embodied in God's Son, Jesus Christ, and in his Body, the Church. Once again this evening, here in Mission Dolores Basilica, I repeat to all of you the ageless proclamation of the gospel: God loves you!

God loves you all, without distinction, without limit. He loves those of you who are elderly, who feel the burden of the years. He loves those of you who are sick, those who are suffering from AIDS and from AIDS-Related Complex. He loves the relatives and friends of the sick and those who care for them. He loves us all with an unconditional and everlasting love.

In the spirit of Saint Francis, then, I urge you all to open your hearts to God's love, to respond by your prayers and by the deeds of your lives. Let go of your doubts and fears, and let the mercy of God draw you to his heart. Open the doors of your hearts to our God who is rich in mercy.

> See what love the Father has bestowed on us
> in letting us be called children of God!
> Yet that is what we are (1 Jn 3:1).

Yes, that is what we are today and forever: children of a loving God!

Meeting with Men and Women Religious
Saint Mary's Cathedral

Presentation by Sister Helen Garvey

It is a privilege, Pope John Paul II, to address you on behalf of the 130 thousand women religious of the United States of America. May the spirit of God be in my heart and on my lips at this special moment in the history of the Church and in the history of women religious.

The life of women religious in this country is a life rich in ministerial service to God's people. It is a life whose very meaning is rooted in spirituality, in an attentive, active response to God's loving presence within us and among us. It is a life grounded in the life and mission

185

of Jesus Christ. The story of the mission of Jesus takes us back almost two thousand years to a synagogue in Nazareth.

Jesus came to Nazareth where he had been reared, and entering the synagogue on the Sabbath as he was in the habit of doing, He stood up to do the reading and found the passage where it was written: "The Spirit of the Lord is upon me; Therefore God has anointed me, sending me to bring glad tidings to the poor, to proclaim liberty to captives, recovery of sight to the blind and release to prisoners, to announce a year of favor from our God." Rolling up the scroll he gave it back to the assistant and sat down. All in the synagogue had their eyes fixed on Him. Then He began by saying to them, "Today this scripture passage is fulfilled in your hearing" (Lk 4: 16-21).

In imitation of Jesus, women religious seek to fulfill this passage to the extent that our very real limitations allow. In a world of expanding technology, in a world of unequal distribution of resources, in a world of increasing numbers of persons condemned to live in poverty, we open ourselves to the spirit of Jesus. We open ourselves to the power of the Word of God. Let us unfurl the scroll again; let us contemplate the scroll and read there in the experience of women religious of the United States.

In an inner-city school in Chicago, Illinois, a woman religious works tirelessly developing the reading skills of third graders. While teaching these children, she evokes abilities of critical thinking; she fosters human dignity; she represents the distinguished tradition of the women religious of the United States who built the Catholic school system, the pride of the Catholic Church in the United States.

In Southern Mississippi, in a cramped dingy space, a woman religious participates with women prisoners as they produce beautiful multicolored quilts. Through her relationship with these women, she learns about vulnerability, oppression, and redemption. Her mission is not only to bring the gospel to these women, but more importantly, to learn the gospel from them.

In Los Angeles, California, a professionally prepared woman religious administers a large Catholic hospital. Her ministry effectively facilitates the care of the sick, a ministry central to the service of women religious throughout the world for hundreds of years, a ministry sorely in need of the ethical values brought to it by a woman religious. Her service to the sick concretizes the essential value of human dignity.

In rural Iowa, darkness surrounds a chapel where women religious chant the office at 3 o'clock in the morning. This prayer, celebrated morning after morning, testifies to the presence of God in our world. It testifies to the power, beauty, and transcendence of the contemplative life.

In Minneapolis, Minnesota, a woman religious cooperates with other health care personnel in developing programs for AIDS victims. In this ministry she reflects the Church's traditional concern for the most abandoned.

In a small town in Idaho a woman religious, who is a pastoral administrator, works with a lay committee as together they plan a parish renewal program. Their common efforts are a realization of the imperative of the Vatican document, *Lumen Gentium*, which insisted that all Christians are called to "the fullness of Christian life and to the perfection of charity."[1]

In Washington, D.C., a woman religious testifies at a Senate Hearing about legislation affecting the poor. In her well-researched and relentless efforts, she promotes the systemic change essential to enhancing human dignity.

In a poor neighborhood in New Mexico, a woman religious welcomes an abused woman into a shelter for battered women. Her ministry reaches out to those persons concretely affected by the impoverishment of women.

In a classroom at a Catholic college in Boston, Massachusetts, a woman religious, a full professor of English, explores the interpretation of a Shakespearean play with a small group of English majors. This woman religious exemplifies the extraordinary leadership of religious congregations in the field of college/university education. Her ministry, like that of her predecessors, probes the deepest meaning of the human spirit in its quest for knowledge, truth, and beauty.

In a barrio in Recife, Brazil, a woman religious from the United States reflects on the gospel as a member of a base community. Her presence in Latin America symbolizes the ministry of U.S. missionary congregations throughout the world; the response of U.S. Catholics to Pope John XXIII's call to service in Latin America; the interdependence of all persons on this planet.

The ministries described here are merely illustrative of the complete picture of the ministries of women religious in the United States. These ministries are exercised in a context of faith and in a context of lack of faith. They are exercised in a world thirsting for holiness, thirsting for God. These ministries, sustained and nourished by the prayer and suffering of retired sisters, are a priceless gift to the Church, the nation and the world.

We women who minister in these diverse ways are women who prize our identity as women of God and as women of the Church. We responded eagerly to the call for renewal issued by the Second Vatican Council when the Council directed us to renew the life of our congregations in the light of the gospel, the founding spirit and the signs of the times.

This renewal, as well as the universal call to holiness emphasized by the Council, opened religious life to a rebirth of the spirit. This rebirth of the spirit is a continuing action, an action which invites us to ongoing, faithful, loving response. Through this response women religious:

- experience a revitalized prayer-life based on the gospel;

---

1. See *Documents of Vatican II*, "Lumen Gentium." Chapter 5. New Revised Edition. A.P. Flannery, ed. (Grand Rapids: Eerdmans, 1984).

- create a community life characterized by profound respect for persons;

- develop different governmental structures which foster participation in decision making;

- initiate new ministries addressing unmet needs;

- expand our awareness of global relationships and responsibilities;

- and work for peace and justice through systemic change.

In our work for peace and justice, we answer the plea of Pope Paul VI who insisted "religious must hear the cry of the poor, rising up more pressing than ever."[2] In working for peace and justice, we reflect your own call, Pope John Paul II, "that the Church consecrate herself to the poor, the suffering, those without influence, resources, and assistance with a love that is neither exclusive nor excluding, but rather preferential."[3]

Our response to the needs of the poor, as well as our response to the fundamental call of the spirit for ongoing conversion, is characterized by struggle. We women religious struggle with our own personal sinfulness, our tendency to selfishness, to isolation. We struggle with our congregational sinfulness, our preoccupation with internal issues at the expense of mission.

At the same time we recognize that our experience is a place where God speaks and where God reveals God's self. We desire for ourselves, and for all believing women, complete incorporation in the Church. In its critical decision-making responsibility, the Church needs the fullness of women's gifts and the strength of women's commitments.

Women, in the company of all God's people who experience the blessings of our Church, nation, and world, also contend with sinfulness in our Church, nation, and world. Acknowledging the essential holiness of the Church, nevertheless we contend with the reality of sin in the Church when we encounter the inability to dialogue with an openness born of love. We contend with national sinfulness, materialism, militarism, and the stockpiling of nuclear weapons which threatens the very future of creation.

We contend with international sinfulness, the disregard for the value and dignity of human life evidenced in widespread abuse of human rights, disinterest in the plight of the poor, the abuse of women, racism, and abortion. We confront what is not of God, in ourselves, and in our congregation, in the nation, in the Church and in the world.

In the midst of this struggle, we experience a profound sense of

---

2. Pope Paul VI. *Evangelica Testificatio*, 7.
3. Pope John Paul II. *Address to Bishops of Brazil*, May 22, 1986.

thanksgiving, thanksgiving for the loving-kindness and fidelity of our God who brings new life to our religious congregations; thanksgiving for the "greatest grace of our century, the Second Vatican Council;"[4] thanksgiving for the leadership of the United States bishops in proclaiming the historic pastorals on peace and the economy; thanksgiving for this great country, the United States of America, for its blessings of freedom, of due process, of respect for individual rights; thanksgiving for your own great love for the poor and oppressed, Pope John Paul II, your challenge to give of our substance; thanksgiving for the prophets among us urging us to a deeper commitment to peace and justice; thanksgiving to the people of God who share with us the mystery of the death and resurrection of Jesus; thanksgiving for the believers of other faiths who work with us for the advancement of human dignity everywhere. Ultimately, we experience a profound sense of thanksgiving for the spirit of God whose love is poured out in our hearts through the Holy Spirit who has been given to us.

The Spirit calls us to deeper communion, to the intimate communion of the people of God in Jesus Christ which is the Church. We yearn for this intimate communion within the Church and with all of our brothers and sisters on this planet. We yearn for the complete communion given us in Jesus. We yearn for this communion while experiencing divisions among us. These divisions reflect some of the critical questions of our time.

How can the nations of the world develop a genuine global community of peace?

How can the resources of the earth be put at the service of the entire human family?

How can the full rich fabric of human life be reverenced and brought to plenitude?

How can the wonders of science and technology be directed by the force of moral values?

How can each person in the Church realize the fullness of baptismal grace?

How can women participate completely in the life of the Church and in the life of society? How can their rich, generous, loving spirit influence the great issues of our time, the great mission of our Church?

These questions require genuine dialogue, the dialogue which Pope Paul VI eloquently described as clear, meek, trusting, and prudent.[5] Such a dialogue finds its source, its strength, and its meaning in the Word of God named Jesus, Jesus who announced his mission in Nazareth over two thousand years ago. May his spirit be present with us today, opening us to dialogue, to communion, to mission. May his spirit be upon us bringing good tidings to the poor, proclaiming liberty, announcing the favor of God.

---

4. Synod of Bishops. *Final Report.* 1985.
5. Pope Paul VI. *Ecclesiam Suam* (National Catholic Welfare Conference, Washington, D.C., 1964) p. 34.

Presentation by Reverend Stephen Tutas

Introduction

In the name of the men religious, 850 brothers and 22 thousand priest religious, I want to thank you for scheduling this time to speak to religious in the United States as well as to the American religious serving the Church in other lands.

In meeting with us, you also honor those who have gone before us. Religious women and men, most of them missionaries from Europe, were instrumental in founding the dioceses and parishes, seminaries and schools, colleges and hospitals, movements and ministries, which have developed so abundantly in the history of our country. And with new members from the United States, our religious communities were enabled not only to help build up the Church here, but also to reach out in service to the building up of God's reign around the world.

At this moment in our history as religious communities, and as the Church in the United States, we find ourselves in the midst of a profound transition. In this transition many of us have found direction for our life and action in the words of Pope Paul VI who said that the work of the Second Vatican Council can be summed up in a single objective: "to make the Church of the twentieth century ever better fitted for proclaiming the gospel to the people of the twentieth century." We are trying to realize this objective in our own religious communities and to cooperate with others in the building of a Church that calls forth the gifts entrusted to each and every member of the Body of Christ.

As our participation in the living out of the theme of your visit, "Unity in the Work of Service: Building up the Body of Christ," the men religious selected "Collaboration" as the theme for our 1987 National Assembly held last month in Duquesne. Collaboration with women religious, the diocesan clergy, and the laity has been intensified in recent years as a result of the ongoing dialogue between bishops and religious in this country. The Pontifical Commission on Religious Life chaired by Archbishop John Quinn has helped us come to a better appreciation of the ecclesial dimension of our vocation. As a consequence of the better mutual relations between bishops and religious in the United States, it is our hope that we can develop structures for even better collaboration in the future.

Our concern for collaboration is not limited to the local scene. By written communications and regular meetings, we have experienced an ever greater mutual understanding between ourselves and the Congregation for Religious and Secular Institutes. We are grateful for the efforts that the Congregation is making to understand our hopes and concerns in giving us an opportunity to discuss an issue that

190

affects us before a decision is made. It is important to us that the regular channels of communication are used, namely the Unions of Superiors General and the National Conference of Religious.

As religious we are committed to the renewal of our own communities and to collaborating with others for the renewal of the Church.

Renewal of Our Communities

Within our own communities, our attempt to become ever better fitted for proclaiming the gospel to the people of the twentieth century is effecting a profound renewal. In examining our founding charisms in the light of the needs of the world today, we have formulated a new vision of religious life that finds expression in our revised Constitutions and Rules of Life approved by the Holy See. But the process of renewing our lives individually and as communities has just begun.

Our renewal as religious begins with our appreciation of the value of religious life in itself. For that reason, your address to the *Plenaria* of the Congregation for Religious and Secular Institutes on the role of the brother in the Church was especially encouraging for us men religious. It is our conviction that the vocation of the brother expresses in a particularly evident way the authentic nature of religious life as such. And in our United States context, which highlights equality of rights, opportunities, and duties for all, we believe that effective promotion of the vocation of the brother is best realized when brothers have the possibility of equal access to positions of governance. We believe that in a religious community, all members, whether priest or lay, should be accorded participation in the internal life of each Institute to the fullest extent compatible with its charism. Your words to the *Plenaria* have helped to give full recognition to the brothers and have reminded the priest religious of their specific identity as members of religious communities. Among the elements of renewal, one of the most challenging is the communitarian dimension of our lives. Those who feel called by God to religious life in the United States today invariably tell us about their hopes for community. In striving to renew our religious communities, we want to make them places where all love and are loved, where all strive to bring out the best in others, where we call forth the gifts God has given each of us, where we recognize Christ as the central person in our lives. And we want our communities to be open to the larger community around us so that we can participate effectively in the renewal of the Church open to the world.

Renewal of the Church

In our commitment to evangelization in the modern world, the agenda of the Church is our agenda as religious. We want to collaborate with others in working for the radical transformation of the world according to the principles of the gospel. We want to do our part to help make human life more fully human.

We are energized when you and the bishops of the Church in the United States call all Christians to be prophetic, as you have done through your repeated insistence on the importance of evangelizing culture, and as the American bishops have done in the pastoral letters *The Challenge of Peace* and *Economic Justice for All*. As members of a democratic society, in union with others who share the same ideals, we realize the great opportunity and responsibility we have to help fashion the economic and political structures of life in the United States of America.

While we feel called to oppose many currents in our culture, we also recognize values and gifts in American culture which we find especially rich for the Church today. We see the need to help build the Church in the United States in a way that responds to the needs of the American people and in a style that is appropriate to our culture which values equality, freedom, openness, and participation in decision making that effects our lives. We esteem initiative and creativity, imagination and the pioneering spirit; we believe in dialogue, collaboration, participation and communication. Through prayerful reflection and community discussion, province assemblies, and general chapters, we religious try to discern what God is calling us to be and to do at this time in history. We believe that our best experience of community discernment is one of the gifts we can offer the local churches where we are engaged. We want to join with others in a common discernment to see how we can help make the Church in the United States ever better fitted for proclaiming the gospel to the American people.

As members of international communities, we are heartened by the developing global awareness in the Church in the United States. We have close bonds with our fellow religious in Canada and in Latin America. Through our missionaries we experience the vitality of the Church in other cultures. All of us have much to learn from each other.

Here in the United States we are excited about the developing role of the laity in the Church. Many of our communities have programs to support the laity in their response to the call of the Church in our time. We are confident that the coming Synod will help us move forward toward a realization of the vision of Church stated in the Second Vatican Council documents, especially in terms of shared responsibility. Likewise, we are especially hopeful about recognizing the rightful role of women—religious or lay, married or single—in the Church in the United States.

Our experience is that the Church in the United States is enriched by an atmosphere which enables everyone—bishops, diocesan clergy, religious women and men, lay people, married and single—to participate fully in making the Church ever better fitted for proclaiming the gospel to the American people.

Conclusion

In summary, as we religious strive to help each other in this period of transition, listening together to the ways God speaks to us, we recognize our mission not only to renew our communities, but also to collaborate with others in the Church in responding to the call to profound change given us by the Second Vatican Council. Through our own experience of renewal, we see our mission as religious to be messengers of hope in a time of transition.

In the months preceding this historic meeting with you, we have been united with you in thought and prayer in the hope that our time together here in San Francisco would mark a significantly new moment not only for ourselves as religious, but also for the entire Church in the United States.

Now in this solemn time of prayer and reflection with you, we know we are not alone. Many here in the United States and throughout the world are united with us in prayer for the success of this meeting. And we are confident this is a moment of great grace. For when men and women, open to the Spirit, are gathered together, great things happen. And when the community of faith is united in person with the Vicar of Christ, the power of the Spirit is tangibly present. It is with this faith that we are gathered here this evening.

John Paul II's Response

Dear Sisters and Brothers in Christ, Dear Religious of the
United States of America,

In their deepest spiritual significance, the Vespers that we are praying together are the voice of the bride addressing the bridegroom (cf. *Sacrosanctum Concilium*, 54). They are also the voice of the bridegroom, "the very prayer which Christ himself, together with his body, addresses to the Father" (ibid.). With one and the same voice the bride and the bridegroom praise the Father in the unity of the Holy Spirit.

In this liturgical song of praise we give expression to "the real nature of the true Church"—"both human and divine, visible and yet invisibly endowed, eager to act and yet devoted to contemplation, present in the world and yet not at home in it" (ibid., 2). It is precisely the presence of God in human life and human affairs that you proclaim

193

through your religious consecration and the practice of the evangelical counsels. It is to the reality of God's love in the world that you bear witness by means of the many forms of your loving service to God's people.

Dear religious sisters and religious priests and brothers, for me, this is one of the most important moments of my visit. Here, with all of you, men and women religious of the United States, and in the spiritual presence of all the members of your congregations spread throughout this land or serving in other countries, I give heartfelt thanks to God for each and every one of you. He who is mighty has done great things for you, holy is his name! (cf. Lk 1:49).

I greet each one of you with love and gratitude. I thank you for the warm welcome you have given me and I thank Sister Helen Garvey and Father Stephen Tutas, who have presented a picture of your dedicated lives. I rejoice because of your deep love of the Church and your generous service to God's people. Every place I have visited in this vast country bears the marks of the diligent labor and immense spiritual energies of religious of both contemplative and active congregations in the Church. The extensive Catholic educational and health care systems, the highly developed network of social services in the Church—none were it not for your highly motivated dedication and the dedication of those who have gone before you. The spiritual vigor of so many Catholic people testifies to the efforts of generations of religious in this land. The history of the Church in this country is in large measure your history at the service of God's people.

As we remember your glorious past, let us be filled with hope that your future will be no less beneficial for the Church in the United States, and no less a prophetic witness of God's Kingdom to each new generation of Americans.

The single most extraordinary event that has affected the Church in every aspect of her life and mission during the second half of the twentieth century has been the Second Vatican Council. The Council called the whole Church to conversion, to "newness of life," to renewal—to a renewal that consists essentially in an ever increasing fidelity to Jesus Christ her divine Founder. As "men and women who more closely follow and more clearly demonstrate the Savior's self-giving" (Lumen Gentium, 42), it is only natural that religious should have experienced the call to renewal in a radical way. Thousands of religious in the United States have generously responded to this call, and continue to live it, with profound commitment. The results, the good fruits of this response are evident in the Church: we see a gospel-inspired spirituality, which has led to a deepening of personal and liturgical prayer; a clearer sense of the Church as a communion of faith and love in which the grace and responsibility entrusted to each member are to be respected and encouraged; a new appreciation of the legacy of your founders and foundresses, so that the specific charism of each congregation stands out more clearly; a heightened awareness of the urgent needs of the modern world where religious,

194

in close union with the bishops and in close collaboration with the whole Church, seek to carry on the work of the Good Shepherd, the Good Samaritan, and the Good Teacher.

It would be unrealistic to think that such a deep and overall process of renewal could take place without risks and errors, without undue impatience on the part of some and undue fears on the part of others. Whatever the tension and polarization occasioned by change, whatever the mistakes made in the past, I am sure that all of you are convinced that the time has come to reach out once again to one another in a spirit of love and reconciliation, both within and beyond your congregations.

During the past two decades, there have also been profound insights into the meaning and value of religious life. Many of these insights, conceived in the experience of prayer and penance and authenticated by the teaching charism of the Church, have contributed greatly to ecclesial life. These insights have borne witness to the enduring identity of religious consecration and mission in the life of the Church. At the same time they have testified to the need for religious to adapt their activity to the needs of the people of our times.

Fundamental to the Council's teaching on religious life is an emphasis on the ecclesial nature of the vocation to observe the evangelical counsels. Religious consecration "belongs inseparably to the life and holiness of the Church" (*Lumen Gentium*, 44). "The counsels are a divine gift, which the Church has received from her Lord and which she ever preserves with the help of his grace" (ibid., 43). It was precisely within this ecclesial context that in 1983 I asked the bishops of the United States to render a pastoral service by offering to those of you whose institutes are engaged in apostolic works special encouragement and support in living your ecclesial vocation to the full. I now wish to thank the bishops and all of you for your very generous collaboration in this important endeavor. In particular I thank the Pontifical Commission headed by Archbishop John Quinn. By God's grace there now exists a fresh cooperative spirit between your religious institutes and the local churches.

Your continuing participation in the mission of the Church at the diocesan and parish levels is of inestimable value to the well-being of the local churches. Your communion with the local bishops and collaboration with the pastoral ministry of the diocesan clergy contributes to a strong and effective spiritual growth among the faithful. Your creative initiatives in favor of the poor and all marginalized persons and groups, whose needs might otherwise be neglected, are deeply appreciated. Your evangelizing and missionary work both at home and in other parts of the world is one of the great strengths of the Church in the United States. Alongside your traditional apostolates—which are as important now as ever before and which I encourage you to appreciate in their full significance—you are engaged in almost every area of defending human rights and of building a more just and equitable society. This is a record of unselfish response to the gospel of Jesus Christ. Yes, the entire Church in the United States benefits from the dedication of American religious to their ecclesial mission.

At the same time you are concerned about certain weaknesses affecting the structure of your institutes. The decline in vocations and the aging of your membership are serious challenges for each one of your institutes and for the corporate reality of religious life, and yet these are not new phenomena in the long experience of the Church. History teaches us that in ways generally unpredictable the radical "newness" of the gospel message is always able to inspire successive generations to do what you have done, to renounce all for the sake of the Kingdom of God, in order to possess the pearl of great price (cf. Mt 13:44-45).

You are called at this hour to fresh courage and trust. Your joyful witness to consecrated love—in chastity, poverty, and obedience— will be the greatest human attraction for young people to religious life in the future. When they sense the authenticity of renewal in you and your communities, they too will be disposed to come and see! The invitation is directly from Christ but they will want to hear it from you too. Your own essential contribution to vocations will come through fidelity; penance and prayer, and through confidence in the power of Christ's Paschal Mystery to make all things new.

In the best traditions of Christian love, you will know how to show your special appreciation for the aged and infirm members of your communities, whose contribution of prayer and penance, suffering and faithful love is of immense value to your apostolates. May they always be comforted in knowing that they are respected and loved within their own religious families.

Your vocation is, of its very nature, a radical response to the call which Jesus extends to all believers in their baptismal consecration: "Seek first his kingship over you, his way of holiness" (Mt 6:33). Your response is expressed by your vowed commitment to embrace and live in community the evangelical counsels. Through chastity, poverty, and obedience you live in expectation of an eschatological kingdom where "they neither marry nor are given in marriage" (Mt 22:30). And so, even now, "where your treasure is there your heart is also" (Mt 6:21).

Through your religious profession, the consecration which the Holy Spirit worked in you at baptism is powerfully directed anew to the perfection of charity. By practicing the vows, you constantly die with Christ in order to rise to new life with him (cf. Rom 6:8). In fidelity to your vow of chastity you are empowered to love with the love of Christ and to know that deep encounter with his love which inspires and sustains your apostolic love for your neighbor. Treading the path of poverty you find yourselves truly open to God and aligned with the poor and suffering in whom you see the image of the poor and suffering Christ (cf. Mt 25:31 ff.). And through obedience you are intimately united with Jesus in seeking always to fulfill the Father's will. Through such obedience there is unlocked in you the full measure of Christian freedom which enables you to serve God's people with selfless and unfailing devotion. The Catholic people, and indeed the vast majority of your fellow-citizens, have the highest respect for your religious consecration and they look to you for the "proof" of the transcendent Christian hope that is in you (cf. 1 Pt 3:15).

The disciple, though, is not above the Master. It is only right for you to expect, as has always been the Church's understanding, that if you follow the laws of Christ's Kingdom—in essence, the new commandment of love and the new values proclaimed in the Beatitudes—you will be in conflict with the "wisdom of this age" (cf. 1 Cor 2:6). In a particularly personal and courageous way, religious have always been in the front line of this never ending struggle.

Today, the encounter between the saving message of the gospel and the forces that shape our human culture calls for a profound and prayerful discernment of Christ's will for his Church at this moment of her life. In this regard the Second Vatican Council remains the necessary point of reference and the guiding light. This discernment is the work of the whole Church. No person or group of people can claim to possess sufficient insights so as to monopolize it. All members of the Church, according to the ministry received for the good of the whole Body, must be humbly attuned to the Holy Spirit who guides the Church into the fullness of truth (cf. Jn 16:13; *Lumen Gentium*, 4), and produces in her the fruits of his action, which Saint Paul lists as "love, joy, peace, patient endurance, kindness, generosity, faith, mildness, and chastity" (Gal 5:22-23). And since the Holy Spirit has placed in the Church the special pastoral charism of the Magisterium, we know that adherence to the Magisterium is an indispensable condition for a correct reading of "the signs of the times" and hence a condition for the supernatural fruitfulness of all ministries in the Church.

You indeed have an important role in the Church's dialogue with the complex and varied cultural environment of the United States. The first law of this dialogue is fidelity to Christ and to his Church. And in this fundamental act of faith and trust you already show the world the basis of your special position within the community of God's people. Also required for this dialogue is a true understanding of the values involved in America's historical experience. At the same time the Christian concepts of the common good, of virtue and conscience, of liberty and justice, must be distinguished from what is sometimes inadequately presented as the expression of these realities.

As religious, you are especially sensitive to the implications of this dialogue with the world in which you are called to live and work. As men and women consecrated to God, you are aware of having a special responsibility to be a sign, an authentic prophetic sign, that will speak to the Church and to the world, not in terms of easy condemnation, but humbly showing forth the power of God's word to heal and uplift, to unite and bind with love.

At this important moment of the history of the human family it is essential for the Church to proclaim the full truth about God—Father, Son and Holy Spirit—and the full truth about our human condition

197

and destiny as revealed in Christ and authentically transmitted through the teaching of the Church. The faithful have the right to receive the true teaching of the Church in its purity and integrity, with all its demands and power. When people are looking for a sure point of reference for their own values and their ethical choices, they turn to the special witnesses of holiness and justice—to you religious. They expect and want to be convinced by the example of your acceptance of God's word.

Dear sisters and brothers, the life we now live is not our own; Christ is living in us. We still live our human life, but it is a life of faith in the Son of God, who loved us and gave himself for us (cf. Gal 2:20). In these words Saint Paul sums up the core of our Christian experience, and even more so the heart of religious life. The validity and fruitfulness of religious life depends upon union with Jesus Christ.

Union with Christ demands a true interior life of prayer, a life of closeness to him. At the same time it enables you to be effective witnesses before the world of the healing and liberating power of the Paschal Mystery. It means that above all in your own lives and in your own communities the Paschal Mystery is first being celebrated and experienced through the Eucharist and the Sacrament of Penance. In this way your works of charity and justice, of mercy and compassion will be true signs of Christ's presence in the world.

The challenges which you faced yesterday you will face again tomorrow. The thousand tasks that now draw upon your courage and your energies will hardly disappear next week, next month, next year. What then is the meaning of our meeting? What "word of the Lord" is addressed to us here? As the one who for the time being has been given the place of the Fisherman from Galilee, as the one who occupies the Chair of Peter for this fleeting hour in the Church's life, allow me to make my own the sentiments of the reading from our Evening Prayer: "Be examples to the flock" (1 Pt 5:3)—examples of faith and charity, of hope and joy, of obedience, sacrifice, and humble service. And "when the Chief Shepherd appears, you will win for yourselves the unfading crown of glory" (1 Pt 5:4).

To the contemplative religious of the United States, whose lives are hidden with Christ in God, I wish to say a word of profound thanks for reminding us that "here we have no lasting city" (Heb 13:14), and that all life must be lived in the heart of the living God. May the whole Church in this land recognize the primacy and efficacy of the spiritual values which you represent. The Second Vatican Council deliberately chose to call you "the glory of the Church" (*Perfectae Caritatis,* 7).

Brothers and sisters, men and women religious of the United States, your country needs the witness of your deep spirituality and your commitment to the life-giving power of the gospel. America needs to see all the power of love in your hearts expressed in evangelizing zeal. The whole world needs to discover in you "the kindness and love of God our Savior" (Ti 3:4). Go forward, therefore, in the mystery of the dying and rising of Jesus. Go forward in faith, hope, and charity, expending yourselves in the Church's mission of evangelization and service. Always be examples to the flock. And know that "when the Chief Shepherd appears, you will win for yourselves the unfading crown of glory" (1 Pt 5:4).

In this Marian Year of grace may you find joy and strength in an ever greater devotion to Mary, the Virgin Mother of the Redeemer. As "the model and protectress of all consecrated life" (Can 663, 4) may she lead each one of you to perfect union with her Son, our Lord Jesus Christ, and to ever closer collaboration in his redemptive mission. And may the example of Mary's discipleship confirm you all in generosity and love.

Meeting with the Laity from throughout the United States
Saint Mary's Cathedral

Presentation by Mrs. Donna Hanson

We, the American Catholic laity, 98 percent of the Catholic Church in the United States, welcome you, to our land of rich diversity. I speak to you this morning from my own perspective: woman, wife, mother of two sons, social minister in Catholic Charities, and volunteer chairperson of the National Advisory Council of the National Conference of Catholic Bishops. In preparation for today, I have spent much time in consultation with my lay sisters and brothers. They were pleased to be asked their opinions; it is now my hope to give voice to their dreams and desires.

The microcosm of church represented here today gives you some perspective of my difficult challenge. In this assembly of three thousand are people from virtually every profession, culture and ethnic diversity in the United States. To this assembly we bring differing political perspectives and varied experiences of church. We are young and old, rich and poor; we are unique yet unified in our love of Christ and His Church. Although our loyalty to the Church is deep, we are committed to call her to even deeper gospel faithfulness. Unity, not division, is our goal; service, not power, is our mission.

The Native Americans, the original inhabitants of our land, provide me with a central theme for today. Their wise counsel is "Never judge another's life until you have walked in their shoes for a day." It is my hope that today we may walk together.

On our journey I would like to tell you about our unique American culture. I would like for you to know how our experience and tradition have helped to form us in our faith and continue to impact us in our families and in our parishes.

Your Holiness, the United States *Declaration of Independence* expresses the country's founding belief that all men, women, and children are created equal. The reason that my great-grandparents immigrated to this country was to escape the famine in Ireland and persecution in Germany. Yet as I grew up in the southern United States, I watched my father and his compatriots build a church so that Black Catholics in our community could have a separate place of worship. In 1960 I saw billboards that proclaimed why bible-reading Christians could not in conscience vote for John F. Kennedy for president.

200

From these early life experiences I, like so many others, learned to question immigration practices, civil injustices, religious persecution. Today, my culture compels me to keep questioning those in leadership positions. I question them about public policies related to abortion, development of nuclear arms, the exploitation of our environment. Not to question, not to challenge, not to seek understanding is to be less than a mature, educated, and committed citizen.

When I come to my Church, I cannot discard my cultural experiences. Though I know the Church is not a democracy ruled by popular vote, I expect to be treated as a mature, educated, and responsible adult. Not to question, not to challenge, not to have authorities involve me in a process of understanding is to deny my dignity as a person and the rights granted to me both by church and society.

Your Holiness, within my circle of friends, there are those who are ranchers and those who are city dwellers, those who are politically conservative, and avant-garde liberals, some who are traditional and some who are progressive Catholics. I rejoice that within my culture there is room for this incredible diversity. The challenge before the Church in the United States is to be welcoming of these same diversities. Can we be as inclusive as Christ who reached out to the woman at the well, who invited a tax collector to be an apostle, who brought the centurian's daughter back to life? Can we reach out and be more inclusive of women, our inactive clergy, homosexuals, the divorced, and all people of color?

Your Holiness, the diversity in our culture is mirrored in our families. We are traditional families, extended families, single parents, widowed, and divorced. In our families, we often struggle with the tensions between gospel values and the excesses of our society. For many newly formed families, there is the challenge of being a loving spouse while at the same time making responsible decisions about parenthood. In our young families, we often juggle the demands of homemaking with the need for employment. In our growing families, there is the challenge of helping our young adult children understand their sexuality as well as appreciate the dangers of drugs and alcohol. In our maturing families, there is the balance of nurturing our grandchildren while caring for our frail, elderly parents.

Your Holiness, in our parish communities, we are also experiencing significant change. The lay members of our church are now among the best educated and the most highly theologically trained in the world. Yet we hunger for spiritual education and formation. We long for structures in which to truly share responsibility. As the pastors in our immigrant churches worked along side us to build labor unions and the most comprehensive Catholic school network in the world, we were building both church and society from the ground up.

Today our parishes are in transition. Many parishes do not have a resident pastor. Eucharistic celebrations are limited and our people cannot regularly receive the Sacrament of Reconciliation. Lay ministers are involved as never before, but full acceptance by both clergy and the people of God has not been fully realized.

At the same time, in other parishes, the pastors, deacons, men and women religious, and professional and volunteer lay ministers work side by side. They experience the needs of the people, and together they respond: with housing for the elderly, with shelters for the homeless, with immigration counseling for the undocumented. They reach out in love: in peer ministry to the engaged, married, widowed, divorced. They reach out in hope: in bringing the Eucharistic Christ to the homebound. They create small communities of faith; they take Christ into the marketplace; they are the Church in the world.

But how does all of this come together for those of us here today? I began by suggesting a walk. My request now is that you permit me to walk with you.

Let me walk with you so that I can understand the challenge of being Peter's successor. Let me share the burdens you carry as you reflect on the pain of your people: persecution in your beloved Poland, starvation in Ethiopia, consumerism in the United States.

Let me walk with you as you seek to preserve orthodox teachings and challenge the world with gospel values. Let me also be at your side as you plead for peace on every continent.

Let me walk with you as you prepare for the Synod on the Laity. I know that we in the United States are not representative of the majority of people in the world. At the same time, I know that our concerns are universal: family, spirituality, and collaboration.

Your Holiness, please let me know that you are also willing to walk with me. Accustomed as I am to dialogue, consultation, and collaboration, I do not always feel that I am heard. In my cultural experience, questioning is neither rebellion nor dissent. Rather it is a desire to participate and is a sign of both love and maturity.

Walk with me. My family experiences continually remind me that examples speak louder than words. To become the family of God it is imperative that both we parents and the church witness the gospel we preach. Above all, we must be just, compassionate and forgiving.

Your Holiness, please walk with each one of us. As you, we gladly give our lives in service to the Church. As you, we seek forgiveness 70 times seven. Yet we know that we are a pilgrim people, that we are individually gifted and that the Holy Spirit speaks uniquely to each of us. We are all children of God: may we continue to walk and talk together?

Presentation by Dr. Patrick S. Hughes

Your Holiness,

I speak to you as a lay person who shares the vision, commitment, and competence that are characteristic of so many American lay Catholics today. As a professional who works for the Church of the Archdiocese of San Francisco, I also represent the tens of thousands of men and women who have dedicated their lives to serve the People of God throughout the United States as professional lay ministers.

Lay Professionals Increasing

Our numbers are increasing. In the Archdiocese of San Francisco, for example, two of the four members of the archbishop's immediate staff are lay persons. Half of our archdiocesan agencies are headed by lay persons, and two thirds of our departments and divisions have lay persons in the top administrative positions. Statistics from our parishes, schools, and other institutions mirror the same reality. The Archdiocese of San Francisco is a microcosm of what is happening in the United States and the world. Because of their commitment to the gospel and the discernment of their own vocation, more lay people are working within ecclesial structures. Their ministry contributes tremendous time, energy, and talent to the church. The entire Church benefits greatly because of this contribution.

Identity of Lay Professionals

This increase of lay professionals in ecclesial settings often causes some misunderstanding of who we are. There are those who too readily divide life and ministry into two distinct realities: "the world" for lay people and "the church" for priests and vowed religious. Because our work does not readily fit into these categories, we are at times perceived with some ambiguity. This lack of clarity is in many ways a result of the present transitional state of our Church. Sometimes too, we must clarify our own identities. Often the first ones hired for a new ministry, we must create job descriptions which have no precedent. If we are the first lay person to occupy a role traditionally held by a priest or vowed religious, we struggle with the communities we serve to find new understandings and expectations for that role. Enthusiastic about our work, we often find ourselves striving to balance our commitments to both our families and our ministries.

Our certainty of vocation, however, comes from the personal discernment of our baptismal call and of our particular gifts. The declining numbers of priests and members of religious communities is not the cause of our response to the Church's needs. For many of us, the Second Vatican Council was a significant personal turning point. We began to see ourselves as active adult participants in the life of the Church. This new awareness came to some of us through an adult conversion experience. For many of us this new consciousness of ourselves as church came as a gradual awakening to the reality of our being called and being sent.[1] However it occurred, as a result of that "rebirth of Christ"[2] we wanted to give our lives more explicitly to serve within the Church.

Our Solidarity with All People

We firmly believe that the joy and hope, the grief and anguish of all people, "especially of those who are poor or afflicted in any way,"[3] are ours as well. Our ministries bring us a great deal of personal satisfaction. We experience the joy promised by Christ to all who identify themselves with their brothers and sisters. We are grateful for the opportunities to serve and to respond, to be present with others on their sacred journeys through time.

Special Concerns

Now however, Your Holiness, we wish to address five areas of special concern. While these concerns are related specifically to lay professionals, they are shared by many others with whom we collaborate in ministry as well as by many lay people in the Church.

Vocational Awareness

Our first area of concern is in regard to vocational awareness. More laity are becoming aware, as you have said, that their Christian vocation corresponds to the evangelical call.[4] In many ways the responsibility for deciding how to live out our baptismal commitment is personal. It is rooted in our individual lives of prayer and our participation in the sacramental life of the Church. This discernment is aided by our prayerful dialogue with others, ordained and lay.

Lay persons working with the Church and those considering this vocational option need the help of the Church.

We would benefit greatly if more dioceses would provide educational and employment information for lay people. It is important that diocesan vocation offices promote the universal call to ministry including the call to full-time lay ministry as a vocation and value to the Church. It is important that we publicly and ceremonially celebrate

---

1. See Edward C. Sellner. "Discernment of Vocation for Pastoral Ministry," *Spirituality Today.* Spring, 1985: 47-58; Emilie Griffin. *Turning: Reflections on the Experience of Conversion* (Garden City, NY: Doubleday, 1980), describes a pattern in many people's experience of adult conversion.

2. *Dogmatic Constitution on the Church*, 32.

3. *Pastoral Constitution on the Church in the Modern World*, 1.

4. See John Paul II. *To the Youth of the World.* (Washington, D.C.: USCC Office of Publishing and Promotion Services, 1985) pp. 32-33.

the ministry provided by lay persons. The ongoing spiritual life of lay ministers must also be respected and supported. Let us witness the unity of service we proclaim.

Ministerial Formation

A second area of concern has to do with the ministerial formation of lay people. There are now over 200 programs in 120 dioceses which prepare laity for church ministry.[5] The laity in these programs bring a new perspective to the study of theology and the vital work of ministry. We believe that these formation programs must take seriously the diversity of lay experiences. Lay persons need to be involved in the formation, administration, and evaluation of these programs. We also believe that greater cooperative efforts in the formation of church professionals—clerical, religious and lay—would have advantages for all.

Theological and ministerial formation transforms those involved in it, and is a source of the ongoing transformation of both the Church and society. The Church's mission demands that formation be available for all members. Financial assistance should be provided by the Church to those laity who are unable to participate because of cost.[6]

Women in Ministry

A third area of concern has to do specifically with women in ministry. We acknowledge the great diversity of opinions among women themselves regarding their participation in church life. We also acknowledge that there has been some progress in the Church as more women have moved into significant ministerial positions. Still, "sexism" remains a major issue among those who work for the Church. One woman's words of pain regarding her lay ministry are representative of so many: "I have spent a lot of time, hours, love and money to prepare myself for a ministry that could reach out and touch the lives of our Christian communities, only to realize that my Church does not want me, not because I am unqualified to do the job, but because I am a woman."[7]

---

5. See Suzanne Elsesser and Rev. Eugene Hemrick. *Preparing Laity for Ministry: A Report on Programs in Catholic Dioceses throughout the United States,* unpublished paper, 1986, which explains and explores the data from Elsesser, ed., *Preparing Laity for Ministry: A Directory of Programs in Catholic Dioceses Throughout the United States* (Washington, D.C.: USCC Office of Publishing and Promotion Services, 1986). The data is a result of a recent survey developed by the National Conference of Catholic Bishops' Committee on the Laity in conjunction with the National Association for Lay Ministry. The programs in this study do not include the thousands of lay women and men presently enrolled in Stephen Ministries, Befrienders, and other forms of volunteer ministry formation.

6. See especially "Ministries," *Segundo Encuentro* (Washington, D.C.: Committee on Evangelization) pp. 357-59.

7. See Marian Schwab. *Career Lay Ministers: Who Are They and What Do They Care About?,* unpublished. 1986 paper summarizing research conducted by the National Association for Lay Ministry on the concerns of lay professionals in the United States.

Bishop James Malone stated his own concern when he addressed his fellow bishops last November: "Increasingly voices are raised, insisting that more needs to be done to effect this equality (of women) . . . The years given to remedy it are not limitless."[8] We agree.

Personnel Issues

As lay professionals, we are also concerned about personnel issues associated with our work. We believe that our work helps us achieve fulfillment as human beings and that, as you have said, it "constitutes a foundation for the formation of family life."[9] Many of us serve the Church with lower salaries than we would enjoy if we were employed at commensurate positions within other institutions. This is not a statement of complaint, but a simple recognition of our special commitment to serve the Church in an explicit way. We hope, however, that the Church will continue to commit itself to the establishment of equal and just salaries for men and women in church jobs. Established procedures of accountability for hiring, promotion, or firing as well as clear grievance procedures and methods of due process,[10] need to continue to be developed.

Availability of the Eucharist

Finally, we too are concerned about the declining numbers of the ordained. As laity, we cannot overlook the closing of parishes and the declining availability of full participation in the Eucharist, the heart of our Christian faith and community. Again, as Bishop Malone cautioned us: "If trends continue, by the year 2000 we will have half the number of active priests serving the Church in this country."[11] We are concerned not only about this decrease, but also about its effects upon the ordained, many of whom are already confronted with unrealistic role expectations. We affirm the dignity and worth of all ministries and encourage the ongoing discernment of what is the nature of ordained ministry and who should be called to it. We are convinced that ordained ministry is intimately related to the ministries of all, and when one form of ministry is impoverished, all suffer.

Commitment to Collaboration

In the name of the thousands of lay professionals who are working within the Church, I want to thank you, Your Holiness, for listening to these concerns. While we are a new phenomenon in the Church,

---

8. James W. Malone. *Presidential Address to the General Meeting of the NCCB/USCC.* November 10, 1986, p. 5.

9. Pope John Paul II. *On Human Work* (Washington, D.C.: USCC Office of Publishing and Promotion Services, 1981) pp. 20ff.

10. See NACPA. *Just Treatment for Those Who Work for the Church* (Cincinnati, Ohio: NACPA National Office, 1986), for recommendations regarding personnel issues.

11. Malone. *Presidential Address*, pp. 5-6.

we also believe that we are heirs before we are pioneers. We bring not only competence and enthusiasm to our ministries, but also a commitment to collaboration: to cooperate in whatever ways we can for the building up of the Kingdom of God. We affirm the lay vocation and the growth of lay ministries wherever they may occur, for they truly are a sign of hope in today's Church.

John Paul II's Response

To him whose power now at work in us
can do immeasurably more than we ask or imagine
to him be glory in the Church and in Christ Jesus
through all generations . . . (Eph 3:20-21).

Dear Brothers and Sisters, Dear Catholic Lay People of America,

I am grateful to you for your kind welcome and pleased to be with you this morning in glorifying the Father, "in the Church and in Christ Jesus," through the working of the Holy Spirit. I also wish to thank you for the informative presentations which have been made in the name of the Catholic laity of the United States.

The reading from the Letter of Saint Paul to the Ephesians which we heard a few moments ago has a deep meaning for the life of each one of us. The text movingly describes our relationship with God as he reveals himself to us in the mystery of the Most Holy Trinity. Saint Paul reminds us of two fundamental truths: first, that our ultimate vocation is to glorify the God who created and redeemed us; and secondly, that our eternal and highest good is to "attain to the fullness of God himself"—to participate in the loving communion of the Father and the Son and the Holy Spirit for all eternity. God's glory and our good are perfectly attained in the Kingdom of heaven.

The apostle Paul also reminds us that salvation, which comes as a free gift of divine love in Christ, is not offered to us on a purely individual basis. It comes to us through and in the Church. Through our communion with Christ and with one another on earth, we are given a foretaste of that perfect communion reserved for heaven. Our communion is also meant to be a sign or sacrament which draws other people to Christ, so that all might be saved.

This gift of the redemption, which originates with the Father and is accomplished by the Son, is brought to fruition in our individual lives and in the life of the world by the Holy Spirit. Thus we speak of the gifts of the Spirit at work within the Church—gifts which include the hierarchical office of shepherding the flock, and gifts given to the laity so that they may live the gospel and make their specific contribution to the Church's mission.

The Council tells us that "everyone in the Church does not proceed by the same path, nevertheless all are called to sanctity and have received an equal privilege of faith through the justice of God (cf. 2 Pt 1:1). And if by the will of Christ some are made teachers, dispensers of mysteries, and shepherds on behalf of others, yet all share a true equality with regard to the dignity common to all the faithful for the building up of the Body of Christ" (*Lumen Gentium*, 32). Through a great diversity of graces, and works, the children of God bear witness to that wonderful unity which is the work of one and the same Spirit.

Dear brothers and sisters, it is in the context of these mysteries of faith that I wish to reflect with you on your role as laity in the Church today. What is most fundamental in your lives is that by your baptism and confirmation you have been commissioned by our Lord Jesus Christ himself to share in the saving mission of his Church (cf. *Lumen Gentium*, 33). To speak of the laity is to speak of hundreds of millions of people, like yourselves, of every race, nation and walk of life, who each day seek, with the help of God, to live a good Christian life. To speak of the laity is to speak of the many of you who draw from your parish the strength and inspiration to live your vocation in the world. It is to speak also of those of you who have become part of national and international ecclesial associations and movements that support you in your vocation and mission.

Your struggles and temptations may differ according to your various situations, but all of you cherish the same basic hope to be faithful to Christ and to put his message into practice. You all cherish the same basic hope for a decent life for yourselves and an even better life for your children. All of you must toil and work and bear the sufferings and disappointments common to humanity, but as believers you are endowed with faith, hope, and charity. And often your charity reaches heroic dimensions within your families or among your neighbors and co-workers. To the extent that your resources and duties in life permit, you are called to support and actively to participate in Church activities.

It is within the everyday world that you the laity must bear witness to God's Kingdom; through you the Church's mission is fulfilled by the power of the Holy Spirit. The Council taught that the specific task of the laity is precisely this: to "seek the Kingdom of God by engaging in temporal affairs and by ordering them according to the plan of God" (*Lumen Gentium*, 31). You are called to live in the world, to engage in secular professions and occupations, to live in those ordinary circumstances of family life and life in society from which is woven the very web of your existence. You are called by God himself to exercise your proper functions according to the spirit of the gospel and to work for the sanctification of the world from within, in the manner of leaven. In this way you can make Christ known to others, especially by the witness of your lives. It is for you as lay people to direct all temporal affairs to the praise of the Creator and Redeemer (cf. ibid.).

The temporal order of which the Council speaks is vast. It encompasses the social, cultural, intellectual, political, and economic life in which all of you rightly participate. As lay men and women actively engaged in this temporal order, you are being called by Christ to sanctify the world and to transform it. This is true of all work, however exalted or humble, but it is especially urgent for those whom circumstances and special talent have placed in positions of leadership or influence: men and women in public service, education, business, science, social communications, and the arts. As Catholic lay people you have an important moral and cultural contribution of service to make to the life of your country. "Much will be required of the person entrusted with much" (Lk 12:48). These words of Christ apply not only to the sharing of material wealth or personal talents, but also to the sharing of one's faith.

Of supreme importance in the mission of the Church is the role that the laity fulfill in the Christian family. This role is above all a service of love and a service of life.

The love of husband and wife, which is blessed and sealed in the Sacrament of Marriage, constitutes the first way that couples exercise their mission. They serve by being true to themselves, to their vocation of married love. This love, which embraces all the members of the family, is aimed at forming a community of persons united in heart and soul, an indissoluble communion where the love of spouses for each other is a sign of Christ's love for the Church.

The service of life rests on the fact that husband and wife cooperate with God in transmitting the gift of human life, in the procreation of children. In this most sacred responsibility, the service of life is intimately united to the service of love in the one conjugal act, which must always be open to bringing forth new life. In his encyclical *Humanae Vitae*, Pope Paul VI explained that in the task of transmitting life, husband and wife are called to "conform their activity to the creative intention of God, expressed in the very nature of marriage and of its acts, and manifested by the constant teaching of the Church" (10).

While "love and life constitute the nucleus of the saving mission of the Christian family in the Church and for the Church" (*Familiaris Consortio*, 50), the family also performs a service of education, particularly within the home, where the parents have the original and primary role of educating their children. The family is likewise an evangelizing community, where the gospel is received and put into practice, where prayer is learned and shared, where all the members, by word and deed and by the love they have for one another, bear witness to the Good News of salvation.

At the same time we must recognize the difficult situation of so many people with regard to family living. There are many with special burdens of one kind or another. There are the single-parent families and those who have no natural family; there are the elderly and the widowed. And there are those separated and divorced Catholics who, despite their loneliness and pain, are striving to preserve their fidelity and to face their responsibilities with loving generosity. All of these people share deeply in the Church's mission by faith, hope and charity, and by all their many efforts to be faithful to God's will. The Church assures them not only of her prayers and spiritual nourishment, but also of her love, pastoral concern and practical help.

Although, in fidelity to Christ and to his teaching on Christian marriage, the Church reaffirms her practice of not admitting to Eucharistic Communion those divorced persons who have remarried outside the Church, nevertheless, she assures these Catholics too of her deep love. She prays for them and encourages them to persevere in prayer, to listen to the word of God and to attend the Eucharistic Sacrifice, hoping that they will "undertake a way of life that is no longer in contradiction to the indissolubility of marriage" (*Familiaris Consortio*, 84). At the same time the Church remains their mother, and they are part of her life.

I wish to express the deep gratitude of the Church for all the contributions made by women over the centuries to the life of the Church and of society. In speaking of the role of women special mention must of course be made of their contribution, in partnership with their husbands, in begetting life and in educating their children. "The true advancement of women requires that clear recognition be given to the value of their maternal and family role, by comparison with all other public roles and all other professions" (*Familiaris Consortio*, 23). The Church is convinced, however, that all the special gifts of women are needed in an ever-increasing measure in her life, and for this reason hopes for their fuller participation in her activities. Precisely because of their equal dignity and responsibility, the access of women to public functions must be ensured. Regardless of the role they perform, the Church proclaims the dignity of women as women, a dignity equal to men's dignity and revealed as such in the account of creation contained in the word of God.

The renewal of the Church since the Council has also been an occasion for increasing lay participation in all areas of ecclesial life. More and more, people are joining with their pastors in collaboration and consultation for the good of their diocese and parish. An increasing number of lay men and women are devoting their professional skills on a full-time basis to the Church's efforts in education, social services, and other areas, or to the exercise of administrative responsibilities. Still others build up the Body of Christ by direct collaboration with the Church's pastoral ministry, especially in bringing Christ's love to those in the parish or community who have special needs. I rejoice with you at this great flowering of gifts in the service of the Church's mission.

At the same time we must ensure both in theory and in practice that these positive developments are always rooted in the sound Catholic ecclesiology taught by the Council. Otherwise we run the risk of "clericalizing" the laity or "laicizing" the clergy, and thus robbing both the clerical and lay states of their specific meaning and their complementarity. Both are indispensable to the "perfection of love," which is the common goal of all the faithful. We must therefore recognize and respect in these states of life a diversity that builds up the Body of Christ in unity.

As lay men and women you can fulfill this great mission authentically and effectively only to the extent that you hold fast to your faith, in communion with the Body of Christ. You must therefore live in the conviction that there can be no separation between your faith and your life, and that apart from Christ you can do nothing (cf. Jn 15:5). Since union with God in Christ is the goal of all Christian living, the laity are called to prayer: personal prayer, family prayer, liturgical prayer. Generations of devout lay people have found great strength and joy in invoking the Blessed Virgin Mary, especially through her rosary, and in invoking the saints.

In particular, the laity must realize that they are a people of worship called to service. In the past I had occasion to emphasize this aspect of the life of the laity in the United States: "All the striving of the laity to consecrate the secular field of activity to God finds inspiration and magnificent confirmation in the Eucharistic Sacrifice. Participating in the Eucharist is only a small portion of the laity's week, but the total effectiveness of their lives and all Christian renewal depends on it: the primary and indispensable source of the true Christian spirit!" (*Ad Limina Discourse*, July 9, 1983).

Every age poses new challenges and new temptations for the People of God on their pilgrimage, and our own is no exception. We face a growing secularism that tries to exclude God and religious truth from human affairs. We face an insidious relativism that undermines the absolute truth of Christ and the truths of faith, and tempts believers to think of them as merely one set of beliefs or opinions among others. We face a materialistic consumerism that offers superficially attractive but empty promises conferring material comfort at the price of inner emptiness. We face an alluring hedonism that offers a whole series of pleasures that will never satisfy the human heart. All these attitudes can influence our sense of good and evil at the very moment when social and scientific progress requires strong ethical guidance. Once alienated from Christian faith and practice by these and other deceptions, people often commit themselves to passing fads, or to bizarre beliefs that are either shallow or fanatical.

We have all seen how these attitudes have a profound influence on the way people think and act. It is precisely in this society that lay men and women like yourselves, all the Catholic laity, are called to live the Beatitudes, to become leaven, salt, and light for the world, and sometimes a "sign of contradiction" that challenges and transforms that world according to the mind of Christ. No one is called to impose religious beliefs on others, but to give the strong example of a life of justice and service, resplendent with the virtues of faith, hope, and charity.

On moral issues of fundamental importance, however, it is at times

211

necessary to challenge publicly the conscience of society. Through her moral teaching the Church seeks to defend, for the benefit of all people, those basic human values that uphold the good which humanity seeks for itself and that protect the most fundamental human rights and spiritual aspirations of every person.

The greatest challenge to the conscience of society comes from your fidelity to your own Christian vocation. It is up to you the Catholic laity to incarnate without ceasing the gospel in society, in American society. You are in the forefront of the struggle to protect authentic Christian values from the onslaught of secularization. Your great contribution to the evangelization of your own society is made through your lives. Christ's message must live in you and in the way you live and in the way you refuse to live. At the same time, because your nation plays a role in the world far beyond its borders, you must be conscious of the impact of your Christian lives on others. Your lives must spread the fragrance of Christ's gospel throughout the world.

Saint Paul launched a great challenge to the Christians of his time and today I repeat it to all the laity of America: "Conduct yourselves, then, in a way worthy of the gospel of Christ, so that, whether I come and see you or am absent, I may hear news of you, that you are standing firm in one spirit, with one mind, struggling together for the faith of the gospel, not intimidated in any way . . . " (Phil 1:27-28).

Dear brothers and sisters, representatives of the millions of faithful and dedicated Catholic laity of the United States, in bringing my reflections to a conclusion I cannot fail to mention the Blessed Virgin Mary who reveals the Church's mission in an unparalleled manner. She, more than any other creature, shows us that the perfection of love is the only goal that matters, that it alone is the measure of holiness and the way to perfect communion with the Father, the Son, and the Holy Spirit. Her state in life was that of a laywoman, and she is at the same time the Mother of God, the Mother of the Church, and our Mother in the order of grace.

The Council concluded the *Dogmatic Constitution on the Church* with an exhortation on the Blessed Virgin. In doing so, the Council expressed the Church's ancient sentiments of love and devotion for Mary. Let us especially during this Marian Year, make our own these sentiments, imploring her to intercede for us with her Son, for the glory of the Most Holy and Undivided Trinity (cf. *Lumen Gentium*, 69).

Homily at San Francisco Eucharist
Candlestick Park

Go . . . and make disciples of all nations (Mt 28:19).

It was in Antioch that the disciples were called Christians
for the first time (Acts 11:26).

Dear Fellow Christians, Dear Brothers and Sisters,

Today, here on the west coast of America, in San Francisco, we hear
once again the words with which Jesus sends the Apostles into the
world after his resurrection. He hands on to them a mission. He sends
them forth as he himself had been sent by the Father.

These words of Christ come at the end of his earthly Messianic
mission. In his cross and resurrection are found the basis for his
"authority both in heaven and on earth" (Mt 28:18). This is the authority of the redeemer, who through the blood of his cross has
ransomed the nations. In them he has established the beginning of
a new creation, a new life in the Holy Spirit; in them he has planted
the seed of the Kingdom of God. In the power of his authority, as he
is leaving the earth and going to the Father, Christ says to his apostles:
"Go . . . and make disciples of all nations. Baptize them in the name
of the Father, and of the Son, and of the Holy Spirit. Teach them to
carry out everything I have commanded you. And know that I am
with you always, until the end of time" (Mt 28:19-20).

The Acts of the Apostles describe the beginning of this mission.
The point of departure was the upper room in Jerusalem. From Jerusalem the travels of the apostles and of their first collaborators led
them first to the neighboring countries and to the people who lived
there. In today's second reading, we hear that the witnesses of the
Crucified and Risen Christ reached Phoenicia, Cyprus, and Antioch
(cf. Acts 11:19).

This occurred also as a result of the dispersion which began with
the death of the deacon Stephen and with the persecution of the
disciples of Jesus. We know that, at the stoning of Stephen, Saul of
Tarsus was present as a persecutor. But the Acts of the Apostles later
present him as Paul, after his conversion on the road to Damascus.
Together with Barnabas, Paul worked for a whole year in Antioch,
and there "they instructed many people." And it was precisely "in
Antioch that the disciples were called Christians for the first time"
(Acts 11:26).

What does it mean to be a Christian?

It means accepting the testimony of the apostles concerning the
Crucified and Risen Christ. Indeed, it means accepting Christ himself
who works in the power of the Holy Spirit. This acceptance is ex-

213

pressed in baptism, the sacrament in which we are born again of water and the Holy Spirit (cf. Jn 3:5). In this sacrament, Christ comes to meet us spiritually. As Saint Paul teaches, we are baptized into Christ's death. Together with him we die to sin, in order to rise with him, to pass from the death of sin to life in God, to the life of sanctifying grace. To new life!

Christians then are those who have been baptized. We are those to whom Christ has come with the salvific power of his Paschal Mystery, those whose lives have been totally shaped by this salvific power. Indeed, baptism gives us an indelible sign—called a character—with which we are marked throughout all our earthly life and beyond. This sign is with us when we die and when we find ourselves before the judgment of God. Even if in practice our lives are not Christian, this indelible sacramental sign of baptism remains with us for all eternity.

The readings of today's liturgy permit us to respond still more fully to the question: What does it mean to be a Christian?

In the book of the prophet Isaiah we read about "the mountain of the Lord's house" (Is 2:2), raised above all things. The prophet says: "All nations shall stream toward it; many peoples shall come and say: 'Come, let us climb the Lord's mountain, to the house of the God of Jacob, that he may instruct us in his ways, and we may walk in his paths.' For from Zion shall go forth instruction, and the word of the Lord from Jerusalem" (Is 2:2-3). Yes, the word of the Lord did go forth from Jerusalem. This word is the word of the gospel. The word of the cross and resurrection. Christ charged his apostles to go forth with this word to all the nations—to proclaim it and to baptize.

Through baptism Christ comes to every person with the power of his Paschal Mystery. To accept Christ through baptism, to receive new life in the Holy Spirit—this is what it means to become a Christian. In this way, through the centuries, individuals and entire nations have become Christian.

To be a Christian means to go up to the mountain to which Christ leads us. To enter into the temple of the living God that is formed in us and in our midst by the Holy Spirit. To be Christian means to continue to become Christian, learning from Christ the ways of the Lord so as to be able "to walk in his paths" (cf. Is 2:3). To be a Christian means to become one every day, ascending spiritually toward Christ and following him. In fact, as we recall, when Christ first called those who were to become his disciples, he said to them: "Follow me."

"It was in Antioch that the disciples were called Christians for the first time." And it was more than 200 hundred years ago that people in the San Francisco area were called Christians for the first time. Since the arrival of the first settlers and the missionary efforts of Father Palou and his companions, there have always been Christians in San Francisco—people of the most varied cultural backgrounds who have believed God's word, been baptized, and followed in the footsteps of the Lord.

Here is a city built on hopes: the hopes of Father Serra's Franciscan missionaries who came to preach the Good News, the hopes of pioneers who came to make their fortunes, the hopes of people who came here to seek peace, the hopes of those who still come to find refuge from violence, persecution or dire poverty. It is the city in which, some 40 years ago, statesmen met to establish the United Nations Organization, an expression of our common hopes for a world without war, a world committed to justice and governed by fair laws.

But this city was built also with hard work and effort. Here the Church advanced from the little Mission Dolores to the establishment of the Archdiocese of San Francisco in 1853. It took effort and determination for the city and the Church to recover from the devastating effects of the severe earthquake and terrible fire in the spring of 1906. Yes, it takes great effort to move from initial enthusiasm to something that will really last. "There are in the end," Saint Paul tells us, "three things that last: faith, hope and love, and the greatest of these is love" (1 Cor 13:13). It is precisely these virtues—faith and hope and love—that have directed and sustained all the efforts of the Church in San Francisco in the past, and that will sustain her well into the future.

"It was in Antioch that the disciples were called Christians for the first time." Here in San Francisco, and in every city and place, it is necessary for the followers of Jesus to deepen their communion with him so that they are not just Christians in name. The primary means the Church has always employed for this task is a systematic catechesis.

When Jesus sent his disciples forth on mission, he told them to baptize and to teach. Baptism alone is not sufficient. The initial faith and the new life in the Holy Spirit, which are received in baptism, need to advance to fullness. After having begun to experience the mystery of Christ, his followers must develop their understanding of it. They must come to know better Jesus himself and the Kingdom which he proclaimed; they must discover God's promises in the Scriptures, and learn the requirements and demands of the gospel.

In the Acts of the Apostles we are told that the members of the first Christian community in Jerusalem "devoted themselves to the apostles' instruction and the communal life, to the breaking of bread and the prayers" (Acts 2: 42). Here we have a model of the Church that can serve as a goal of all catechesis. For the Church needs continually to feed on God's word which comes to us from the apostles, and she needs to celebrate the Eucharist, to be faithful to regular prayer and bear witness to Christ in the ordinary life of the community.

The experience of history has proved the importance of a carefully programmed study of the whole of the Christian mystery. "Teach them to carry out everything I have commanded you," Jesus tells the apostles (cf. Mt 28:20). There is no substitute for a systematic presentation of all the essentials of our Catholic faith, a presentation which can provide the basis for sound judgments about the problems of life and society, and which can prepare people to stand up for what they believe with both humility and courage. As I stated in my apostolic exhortation on catechesis: "Firm and well thought out convictions lead to courageous and upright action. . . . Authentic catechesis is

215

always an orderly and systematic initiation into the revelation that God has given of himself to humanity in Christ Jesus, a revelation stored in the depths of the Church's memory and in Sacred Scripture, and constantly communicated from one generation to the next by a living, active *traditio*" (*Catechesi Tradendae*, 22).

What is the purpose of catechesis? What does it mean, not only to be called Christians, but truly to be Christians? It means being identified with Christ, not only at Mass on Sunday—which is extremely important—but also in all the other activities of life. In speaking about our relationship to him, Jesus himself said: "Remember what I told you: no slave is greater than his master. If they persecuted me, they will also persecute you. If they kept my word, they will also keep yours" (Jn 15:20).

To be identified with Christ means that we must live according to God's word. As the Lord told his first disciples: "You will live in my love if you keep my commandments, even as I have kept my Father's commandments and live in his love" (Jn 15:10). For this reason the Church never ceases to proclaim the whole of the gospel message, whether it is popular or unpopular, convenient or inconvenient. And the Church is ever mindful of her great task to call people to conversion of mind and heart, just as Jesus did. The first words spoken by Jesus in the gospel are these: "This is the time of fulfillment. The reign of God is at hand! Reform your lives and believe in the gospel" (Mk 1:15).

Those who accept the grace of conversion and who live according to God's word find that, with God's grace, they begin to put on the mind and heart of Christ. They become increasingly identified with Christ, who is a sign of contradiction. It was Simeon who first foretold that the newborn Son of Mary would be for his own people a sign of contradiction. He tells the Virgin Mother: "This child is destined to be the downfall and the rise of many in Israel, a sign that will be opposed" (Lk 2:34). And so it happened. Jesus met with opposition in the message that he preached, and in the all-embracing love that he offered to everyone. Almost from the beginning of his public ministry, he was in fact "a sign that people opposed."

Simeon's words hold true for every generation. Christ remains today a sign of contradiction—a sign of contradiction in his Body, the Church. Therefore, it should not surprise us if, in our efforts to be faithful to Christ's teachings, we meet with criticism, ridicule or rejection. "If you find that the world hates you," the Lord told the Twelve, "know that it has hated me before you. If you belonged to the world, it would love you as its own; the reason it hates you is that you do not belong to the world. But I chose you out of the world" (Jn 15:18-19).

These words of our loving Savior are true for us not only as individuals but also as a community. In fact, the witness to Christ of the entire Christian community has a greater impact than that of a single individual. How important, then, is the gospel witness of every Christian community, but especially that most fundamental of them all, the Christian family. In the face of many common evils, the Christian family that truly lives the truth of the gospel in love is most certainly a sign of contradiction; and at the same time it is a source of great hope for those who are eager to do good. Parishes, too, and dioceses, and all other Christian communities which "do not belong to the world," find themselves meeting opposition precisely because they are faithful to Christ. The mystery of the cross of Christ is renewed in every generation of Christians.

When Jesus Christ sent his apostles throughout all the world, he ordered them to "teach all the nations" (cf. Mt 28.19-20).

The gospel, and together with it the salvific power of Christ's redemption, is addressed to every person in every nation. It is also addressed to entire nations and peoples. In his vision, the prophet Isaiah sees the peoples who go up to the mountain of the house of the Lord, asking to be instructed in his ways and to walk in his paths (cf. Is 2:2-3). We too ask to walk in the paths of the living God, the Creator and Redeemer, the one God who lives in inscrutable unity as Father, Son, and Holy Spirit.

Continuing to describe his vision, Isaiah says:

> He shall judge between the nations,
> and impose terms on many peoples.
> They shall beat their swords into plowshares
> and their spears into pruning hooks;
> One nation shall not raise the sword against another,
> nor shall they train for war again (Is 2:4).

How greatly we desire to see the future of humanity in the light of these prophetic words: How greatly we desire a world in which justice and peace prevail! Can the Church, which has come forth from such a prophecy, the Church of the gospel, ever cease to proclaim the message of peace on earth? Can she ever cease to work for the true progress of peoples? Can she ever cease to work for the true dignity of every human person?

To be Christian also means to proclaim this message untiringly in every generation, in our generation, at the end of the second millennium and at the threshold of the third!

> O house of Jacob, come,
> let us walk in the light of the Lord! Amen.

DETROIT, MICHIGAN

Saturday, September 19, 1987

Meeting with Polish Americans
Hamtramck

You are to be my witnesses . . . to the ends of the earth (Acts 1:8).

Dear Polish Brothers and Sisters of America,

In the course of my lengthy pilgrimage to the Church in the United States, God has led me to Detroit, the largest community of people of Polish origin after Chicago.

Right from the beginning I wish to tell you two things: first, as Saint Paul would say, I have longed to come to you. I have greatly desired to be with you in this important moment, to give prominence to the solicitude of the Church, and my own personal apostolic solicitude for you, and to manifest publicly the natural bonds, the bonds of blood, origin, faith, culture, and, to a certain extent also, of language and of love for our common mother, the homeland: your homeland or that of your parents or forebears.

And I wish also to extend our meeting today, which is necessarily limited by time and place, to all the United States, and in a certain sense to all of America. I see it as a meeting with the entire American Polonia, with every American man and woman whose origin is drawn from the old country on the Vistula, with every Pole whose destiny it is to live in this land.

I wish then to meet both those whose roots have been deeply set here for generations and those who, while their hearts are still filled with the scenery of the land of their birth, are seeking a new beginning, certainly not without difficulty. In saying this, I am well aware that I find myself before the largest part of the Polish emigration in the world, which constitutes a large part of the Church in the United States. Even today there are more than 800 Polish parishes.

You are to be my witnesses . . . to the ends of the earth.

How can we not thank God then for this meeting and for our prayer

219

together? How can we not thank those who have made it possible and those who have prepared this encounter? The American authorities and those of the American Polonia, the bishops, priests, sisters, lay people, the various organizations.

Together with the host of this encounter, Archbishop Edmund Szoka, I wish to greet most cordially and to welcome all of you who are gathered here and all the guests who honor us with their presence. I cordially greet all those who are spiritually united with us.

I extend a word of cordial greetings to all our brothers and sisters from other Slavic nations, and in particular from the kindred Ukrainian community, who are present here in large number.

In Ukrainian:

I cordially greet the entire Ukrainian community of Detroit. You are close to my heart. As you solemnly celebrate the Millennium of Christianity in the Rus of Kiev and in the Ukraine, from the depths of my Slavic heart I bless all the sons and daughters of Saint Vladimir and Saint Olga, as well as all the faithful of the Church in the Ukraine and in the diaspora.

Meanwhile today, we wish to be closely united with the sons and daughters of Poland who live on this continent, with all who share or should share in the historical heritage of the same homeland and the same Church. In this way we find ourselves together before the homeland and the whole nation, before its history, its heritage, before its "yesterday" and its "today." And at the same time we find ourselves before all the heritage of Polonia in this vast and rich country which has received and continues to receive so many people from all continents, nations, races, and languages; the country that became the homeland for your forebears is also yours.

If we recall the past, if we look attentively at our "today," we do so above all with thought and concern for the future. For, as it has been said: "the nation which lets itself be cut off from its tradition descends to the level of a tribe" (A. Slominski).

We recall briefly the first Poles who, according to the chronicles, came to North America in 1608 and settled in Jamestown, Virginia. And then those who in the second half of the eighteenth century gave the beginning to Polonia in Michigan.

The greatest wave of emigration took place, as is known, at the end of the last century and at the beginning of the present century. It was an economic emigration. There were enterprising, hard-working people, worthy people who in the homeland were unable to find food. They left a Poland which had been torn apart by partitions, and, as the latest arrivals, they were viewed in different ways. Most often they were uneducated. They brought with them no material riches, but they possessed two great values: an innate love of the faith and of the Polish spirit. Besides, many of them had left with the thought of returning after a time. They did not think that their descendants would put down stable roots in a new country and would collaborate fruitfully in its construction at the end of the second and beginning of the third millennium after Christ.

Their tears, suffering, difficulties, humiliations, wanderings, and nostalgia are known and described. Yet it was they who built all that is until now, and will remain in the future, the glory and the patrimony of Polonia in North America.

First of all they created a whole network of parishes with monumental churches, schools, hospitals, houses of assistance, organizational structures, the press, publications. We recall here Father Leopold Moczygemba and his nearly hundred parishioners who on Christmas Eve 1854 founded the first Polish parish and gave rise to the village of Panna Maria (the Virgin Mary) in Texas. And also those who in 1872 founded the first Polish parish in Detroit, dedicated to Saint Albertus. With great emotion I journey spiritually as a pilgrim to these two places.

Moreover, these immigrants have produced a great number of priestly and religious vocations, and thousands of vocations of women religious, both to Polish Congregations and to others. There arose also the various new Polish congregations of women. All this served to make the contribution of the immigrants to the development of religious life and to ecclesiastical structures a great and irreplaceable treasure for the Church in America.

The same spirit was deepened and developed by the different Catholic organizations—both by the older ones which have been more than one hundred years in existence, as well as by those which were established more recently. It is not possible to mention all of them here. However, I came to know of them in the course of earlier visits to the United States as Archbishop of Cracow and through their letters to me in Rome on different occasions.

This faithful dedication to the Church is closely tied to a love for Poland and everything associated with it. One has only to think of the volunteers for General Haller's army during the First World War; the financial support for independence activities before the year 1918, and in particular for the support of the Polish Committee in Paris; the enormous gifts and loans to Poland after it regained its independence and began to rise from destruction and ruin. Nor may we forget that this same generation of immigrants, by hard work and sacrifice, also secured a better life for their children and grandchildren.

Another page in the history of Polonia was written by Saints Cyril and Methodius Seminary, established in Detroit and later transferred to Orchard Lake, which not long ago celebrated its centenary. This seminary grew out of a true love of the Church and out of an attachment to the Polish spirit. Using the language of the Second Vatican Council, we may say that it sought to read "the signs of the times" and to meet the needs of Polish immigration. It developed into a complete scientific and educational complex, from which more than three thousand priests for the service of Polish immigrants and approximately 15 thousand immigrant leaders have come forth. It disseminates Polish culture and the liturgy in the Polish language, and contributes to the preservation of awareness concerning the Polish origins of so many Americans. To the representatives of Orchard Lake who are here today I express gratitude for all that has been accomplished in the past; my hope is for a constant fidelity and a new responsiveness to the needs of today's Church and of Polonia as it exists in the world today.

Later history witnessed new events, new trials, and a new wave of emigrants.

As a result of the Second World War and its aftermath, many more Poles came to the United States. These emigrants were different than the first group in that they came with a higher level of culture, and with a different national and political consciousness that retained a strong solidarity with the homeland and the nation. A word of acknowledgment is due to the Polish American Congress for its many activities on behalf of the nation, and also to the Catholic League which provided great material aid to the Church in Poland after the war, and continues to provide that aid today. For this I wish to express the heartfelt gratitude of the Church in Poland as well as my own personal gratitude.

The most recent great undertaking of Polonia throughout the world, but especially of Polonia in the United States and of some American friends, is the Foundation in the Vatican and the Pilgrim House, the Center for Polish Christian Culture and the Documentation Center in Rome which that foundation operates.

I know that efforts continue; for example, the establishment of associations of friends of the foundation to ensure the continued activity and development of these institutions. God will surely reward them.

And so, having touched only briefly on past history, we arrive at the present, and the tasks the present creates for Polonia and the Church.

The last wave of emigration, like those that preceded it, also becomes a "sign of the times" for today and a challenge. It calls us to reflection and action. Each emigration has brought with it a new richness as well as new problems. There have been and there continue to be cases of harmful divisions, even splits, which have impeded Polonia in the United States from playing the full role of which it is capable in both the religious and spiritual spheres and the social and political spheres.

Thus there remains, always alive and very real, a process of integration that is twofold. It is integration in the sense of a growth in awareness and maturity in Polonia itself, and integration within the country which is now your home.

Dear brothers and sisters, the more you are aware of your identity, your spirituality, your history, and the Christian culture out of which your ancestors and parents grew, and you yourselves have grown, the more you will be able to serve your country, the more capable will you be of contributing to the common good of the United States.

Precisely out of concern for the common good, this country—in the face of a diversity of peoples, races and cultures unknown elsewhere—has sought integration in various ways. Theories include "nativism," the "melting pot" and others that proved incapable of giving results. Today there is talk of the ethnic principle, of "roots," since from these roots the full personality of the individual, the community and the nation arises.

The Church wishes to be at the service of such personal and social integration. I have spoken of this on numerous occasions and many documents of the Church address this issue. It is necessary to study them and put them into practice.

Today I wish to repeat once again the words of the poet: "There are so many strengths in the nation", and I wish to pray with him: "Make us feel the strength" (S. Wyspianski, *Liberation*).

Our strength comes from faith, from God himself, and from our millenary heritage in which there resounds, in such a vibrant way, the Paschal Mystery of Christ: his passion and resurrection. This richness has been manifested and continues to be manifested in the love of ideals, of truth, of freedom—"ours and yours," in the love of peace, and in respect for the dignity of individuals and of nations.

In our own day there have been moments when these values have shone before the whole world with special brightness. Who among us, and not only us, can forget first the beatification and then the canonization of that son of Polish soil and spiritual son of Saint Francis, the humble priest Saint Maximilian Mary Kolbe, who, in the midst of atrocities and the inhumanity of the concentration camp, exhibited once again before all of contemporary humanity that love unto the end!

These values, this richness, this inheritance were also manifested in a fuller way and acquired a new light during my three pilgrimages to the homeland. I dwell only on the saints and the blessed because they express most fully that which is partially in each of us individual and in all of us together. At the same time they are the most perfect models on our pilgrimage toward our final destiny in Christ.

There is Blessed Brother Albert Chmielowski, a patriot and artist, who wished to be all kindness in the face of Polish poverty and toward the needy; Blessed Raphael Kalinowski; Blessed Ursula Ledochowska; Blessed Caroline Kozka, a simple country girl who gave her life in defense of her dignity; finally, the last in order of time, Blessed Michael Koza, bishop and martyr of Dachau.

But this inheritance, as a testimony of the Polish soul, has also been manifested in recent years in another form, when the millennial Christian nation reclaimed its own dignity and legitimate rights.

Among other things, I spoke of this on the Polish sea-coast, and much of what I said refers to the whole world, including the United States. There, on the Baltic, "the word 'solidarity' was spoken . . . in a new way that at the same time confirms its eternal content . . . In the name of man's future and the future of humanity, it was necessary to say that word, 'solidarity'. Today it rolls like a wide wave over the face of the world, which realizes that we cannot live according to the principle of 'all against all,' but only according to another principle 'all with all,' 'all for all.' Solidarity must take precedence over conflict. Only then can humanity survive, can each nation survive and develop within the great human family . . . Solidarity means a way of existing, for example, of a nation, in its human variety, in unity, with respect for differences, for all the diversity that exists among people, and so, unity in variety, in plurality. All this is contained in the concept 'solidarity' " (*Address in Gdynia*, 11 June 1987).

With justifiable pride and gratitude we may turn to the great authors of our culture: to writers, poets, artists, politicians, to religious and spiritual guides, to all those who also in this land have pointed out new ways to the human spirit.

Tadeusz Kosciuszko, Kazimierz Puraski, Wrodzimierz Krzyzanowski, Ignacy Paderewski, Helena Modrzejewska, Artur Rubinstein, and the already mentioned Father Leopold Moczygemba, Father Jozef Dabrowski, founder of the Polish seminary, Father Theodore Gieryk and Jan Barzynski, Father Witold Buhaczewski, and so many others without forgetting the authors and leaders alive today.

But along with them we remember too the unknown multitudes of mothers and fathers of families who, guided by their force of temperament and sense of faith; living an authentic Christian life and in fidelity to God and their human ideals, were able to mold those lofty ideas into the values that model and determine everyday living. In their daily lives they themselves lived those values, forged down through the centuries, and they succeeded in transmitting them in their families to each new generation. How many priests are there today who bear witness that they owe their priestly vocation in the first place to their saintly mothers.

Perhaps the most threatened institution in today's world is precisely the family. For that reason, the Church "wishes to offer guidance and support to those Christians and others who are trying to keep sacred and to foster the natural dignity of the married state and its superlative value" (*Gaudium et Spes*, 47).

The fundamental task of the family is to serve life, "transmitting by procreation the divine image from person to person" (*Familiaris Consortio*, 28).

Faithfulness to the family extends also to education. The Second Vatican Council teaches that "since parents have conferred life on their children, they have a most solemn obligation to educate their offspring. Hence, parents must be acknowledged as the first and foremost educators of their children" (*Gravissimum Educationis*, 3).

Family—the domestic Church. . .

You are to be my witnesses . . .

I now wish to address you, "servants of Christ and administrators of the mysteries of God" (1 Cor 4:1); you the priests, the pastors of Polonia. I have spoken at length about the priesthood during this present visit to the United States. In the context of the present meeting I wish to thank you for all the good that the American Polonia has received and continues to receive from your ministry. Remember that the Polish emigration is important for Poland, just as Poland is important for the emigration. From your awareness of and relationship to our common Christian heritage will depend, in great part, the bonds between your faithful and the Nation of which they are sons and daughters, bonds of faith, culture and language. Respect for and preservation of this heritage should constitute one of the fundamental principles of your pastoral care. How consoling it is that young people throughout the world are experiencing a growing interest in their past. Young people discover themselves as they search for the foundations of their own identity, its sources and roots, the first strata from which it proceeds.

I know that our young people living here are very much a part of this process, and that more and more they are willing to learn the history, the language, and all the richness of the homeland from which their forebears came. They gladly say: "I am proud to be American." But they are no less proud of their origins, especially when they know more about them, because then they feel no complex. Help them in this learning and liberation. Then too, meet the spiritual needs of the most recent emigration. Do not lose heart. Do not be enclosed in the golden tower of prejudice, routine, pastoral minimalism, and ease.

Do not diminish, do not reduce, do not close whatever serves the true well-being of the faithful, strengthens their spiritual relationship with the Savior and leads to genuine growth of the spirit.

Dear brothers and sisters, "You are to be my witnesses . . . to the ends of the earth." This announcement and call was addressed by Christ to the apostles shortly before his ascension. Before that, he said to them: "you will receive power when the Holy Spirit comes down on you" (Acts 1:8). That is, you are to be my witnesses when you receive the power of the Holy Spirit. We are witnesses of Christ in the power of the Holy Spirit.

The Holy Spirit is the beginning, the source, the foundation of Christian life in the new era of the history of salvation, in the time of the Church, in the time of mission, in the time of witness. May his power fill your hearts and minds and wills, to enable you to bear witness to Christ with your own witness and that of your forefathers, with the witness of the millenary Christian heritage of that land that has the right and wishes to call you her sons and daughters.

This heritage is marked in a special way by the presence of the Blessed Virgin, the Mother of God, Mary blessed by God. She who "defends bright Czestochowa, and shines in the morning Gate!" Our poet cried out to her: "carry there my soul full of nostalgia!" Your hearts do not feel nostalgia, because you are already sons and daughters of this land and citizens of this country. Still, may Mary carry your souls toward everything that is good, beautiful, great; toward those values that make life worth living. This we ask of her, especially today. This we ask of her in the Marian Year.

Now I wish to bless all of you present, your families, and dear ones, the children and young people, the sick, the old, those who are alone. I bless the priests, the deacons, the religious families of men and women, the seminarians, the parishes, the places of work and recreation. I bless the whole of Polonia in North America.

Meeting with Permanent Deacons
and Their Wives
Ford Auditorium

Welcome by Deacon Samuel M. Taub

Your Holiness:

It is with great joy and a sense of history that we greet you. We praise God for this day and the milestone which it marks in the growth and development of the permanent diaconate in our country.

Gathered here are representatives of the permanent deacons and wives of deacons in the United States, a group which represents a remarkable and unparalleled flowering of ministry in response to the invitation of the fathers of Vatican Council II and the call of the bishops of the United States.

We represent in a unique way the diversity of the local churches in our country: the celibate and married status, family structures, ethnic richness, the whole range of socio-economic backgrounds, the geographic spread of our country, ages, work experience, neighborhood roots, vocations, ministries of sacrament, word and charity.

We are gathered in a city known as a symbol of industrial achievement and the American dream, yet familiar for all the challenges facing life in an era of change, necessary adjustment and, inevitably, by social change with consequent human cost, a city which knows the faces of human needs. This is a city which had an early Catholic presence which has responded to the needs of a pluralistic, multi-cultured society. It is in such a setting, replicated many times over in our country, that the restoration and the renewal of the permanent diaconate has its origins and development. It is also in this city that the first of four permanent diaconate formation programs was begun in 1969, just a short 18 years ago.

It is in this context that the restoration of the permanent diaconate is an example of the Church reaching into her history and tradition in restoring a ministry which was instituted by the apostles, ordaining men to a lifetime of service, not unto the priesthood but to the ministry of charity.

We are keenly aware that the focal point of the deacon's mission and ministry is the human person who has been created by God with dignity that is unique, sacred, and inviolable. We are coming to appreciate increasingly how the diaconate can be and is a means of strengthening the presence of the Church in the marketplace. We continue to remind ourselves that, as we are a recognized sacramental sign of service, it is expected that we be a catalyst for an expanding notion of church and ministry and that we see the empowerment of the laity as one of our prime responsibilities.

Permanent deacons are assuming increasingly responsible ministries of service and administration. In this we are beginning to have a new appreciation of the fact that we are deacons 24 hours a day and that no matter where we may be we are "heralds of the gospel," giving witness within the community of faith, in our neighborhoods, and at our work places as to who and what we are for the life of the Church.

Assembled with us are wives of deacons who, in a demonstration of mutual sacrificial love, give unstingily in sharing husband and father, their own lives, convenience, and needs with the Church as they encourage, heal and sustain the husband's diaconal commitment.

It is in this context, in the love with which faithful sons and daughters greet their Father, that we ask you to address us.

John Paul II's Response

Dear Brothers in the Service of Our Lord, Dear Wives and Collaborators of These Men Ordained to the Permanent Diaconate,

I greet you in the love of our Lord Jesus Christ, in whom, as Saint Paul tells us, God has chosen us, redeemed us, and adopted us as his children (cf. Eph 1:3ff.). Together with Saint Paul, and together with you today, I praise our heavenly Father for these wonderful gifts of grace.

It is a special joy for me to meet with you because you represent a great and visible sign of the working of the Holy Spirit in the wake of the Second Vatican Council, which provided for the restoration of the permanent diaconate in the Church. The wisdom of that provision is evident in your presence in such numbers today and in the fruitfulness of your ministries. With the whole Church, I give thanks to God for the call you have received and for your generous response. For the majority of you who are married, this response has been made possible by the love and support and collaboration of your wives. It is a great encouragement to know that in the United States over the past two decades almost eight thousand permanent deacons have been ordained for the service of the gospel.

It is above all the call to service that I wish to celebrate with you today. In speaking of deacons, the Vatican Council said that "strengthened by sacramental grace, in communion with the bishop and his presbyterate, they serve the People of God in the service of the liturgy, the word, and charity" (*Lumen Gentium*, 29). Reflecting further on this description, my predecessor Paul VI was in agreement with the Council that "the permanent diaconate should be restored . . . as a driving force for the Church's service (*diakonia*) toward the local Christian communities, and as a sign or sacrament of the Lord Christ himself, who 'came not to be served but to serve' " (*Ad Pascendum*, August 15, 1972, Introduction). These words recall the ancient tradition of the Church as expressed by the early Fathers such as Ignatius of Antioch, who says that deacons are "ministers of the mysteries of Jesus Christ . . . ministers of the Church of God" (*Ad Trallianos*, II, 3). You, dear brothers, belong to the life of the Church that goes back to saintly deacons, like Lawrence, and before him to Stephen and his companions, whom the Acts of the Apostles consider "deeply spiritual and prudent" (Acts 6:3).

This is at the very heart of the diaconate to which you have been called: to be a servant of the mysteries of Christ and, at one and the same time, to be a servant of your brothers and sisters. That these two dimensions are inseparably joined together in one reality shows the important nature of the ministry which is yours by ordination.

How are we to understand the mysteries of Christ of which you are ministers? A profound description is given to us by Saint Paul in the reading we heard a few moments ago. The central mystery is the heavens and on earth into one under the headship of Christ, his beloved Son. It is for this that all the baptized are predestined, chosen, redeemed, and sealed with the Holy Spirit. This plan of God is at the center of our lives and the life of the world.

At the same time, if service to this redemptive plan is the mission of all the baptized, what is the specific dimension of your service as deacons? The Second Vatican Council explains that a sacramental grace conferred through the imposition of hands enables you to carry out your service of the word, the altar, and charity with a special effectiveness (cf. *Ad Gentes*, 16). The service of the deacon is the Church's service sacramentalized. Yours is not just one ministry among others, but it is truly meant to be, as Paul VI described it, a "driving force" for the Church's *diakonia*. By your ordination you are configured to Christ in his servant role. You are also meant to be living signs of the servanthood of his Church.

If we keep in mind the deep spiritual nature of this *diakonia*, then we can better appreciate the interrelation of the three areas of ministry traditionally associated with the diaconate, that is, the ministry of the word, the ministry of the altar, and the ministry of charity. Depending on the circumstances, one or another of these may receive particular emphasis in an individual deacon's work, but these three ministries are inseparably joined together as one in the service of God's redemptive plan. This is so because the word of God inevitably leads us to the Eucharistic worship of God at the altar; in turn, this worship leads us to a new way of living which expresses itself in acts of charity.

This charity is both love of God and love of neighbor. As the First Letter of John teaches us, "One who has no love for the brother he has seen cannot love the God he has not seen . . . whoever loves God must also love his brother" (1 Jn 4:20-21). By the same token, acts of charity which are not rooted in the word of God and in worship cannot bear lasting fruit. "Apart from me," Jesus says, "you can do nothing" (Jn 15:5). The ministry of charity is confirmed on every page of the gospel; it demands a constant and radical conversion of heart. We have a forceful example of this in the Gospel of Matthew proclaimed earlier. We are told: "offer no resistance to injury." We are commanded: "love your enemies and pray for your persecutors." All of this is an essential part of the ministry of charity.

Certainly today's word is not lacking in opportunities for such a ministry, whether in the form of the simplest acts of charity or the most heroic witness to the radical demands of the gospel. All around us many of our brothers and sisters live in either spiritual or material poverty or both. So many of the world's people are oppressed by injustice and the denial of their fundamental human rights. Still others are troubled or suffer from a loss of faith in God, or are tempted to give up hope.

In the midst of the human condition it is a great source of satisfaction to learn that so many permanent deacons in the United States are involved in direct service to the needy: to the ill, the abused and battered, the young and old, the dying and bereaved, the deaf, blind, and disabled, those who have known suffering in their marriages, the homeless, victims of substance abuse, prisoners, refugees, street people, the rural poor, the victims of racial and ethnic discrimination, and many others. As Christ tells us, "as often as you did it for one of my least brothers, you did it for me" (Mt 25:40).

At the same time, the Second Vatican Council reminds us that the ministry of charity at the service of God's redemptive plan also obliges us to be a positive influence for change in the world in which we live, that is, to be a leaven—to be the soul of human society—so that society may be renewed by Christ and transformed into the family of God (cf. *Gaudium et Spes*, 40). The "temporal order" includes marriage and the family, the world of culture, economic, and social life, the trades and professions, political institutions, the solidarity of peoples, and issues of justice and peace (cf. *Apostolicam Actuositatem*, 7; *Gaudium et Spes*, 46ff.). The task is seldom an easy one. The truth about ourselves and the world, revealed in the gospel, is not always what the world wants to hear. Gospel truth often contradicts commonly accepted thinking, as we see so clearly today with regard to evils such as racism, contraception, abortion, and euthanasia—to name just a few.

Taking an active part in society belongs to the baptismal mission of every Christian in accordance with his or her state in life, but the permanent deacon has a special witness to give. The sacramental grace of his ordination is meant to strengthen him and to make his efforts fruitful, even as his secular occupation gives him entry into the temporal sphere in a way that is normally not appropriate for other members of the clergy. At the same time, the fact that he is an ordained minister of the Church brings a special dimension to his efforts in the eyes of those with whom he lives and works.

Equally important is the contribution that a married deacon makes to the transformation of family life. He and his wife, having entered into a communion of life, are called to help and serve each other (cf. *Gaudium et Spes*, 48). So intimate is their partnership and unity in the sacrament of marriage, that the Church fittingly requires the wife's consent before her husband can be ordained a permanent deacon (Can. 1031, 2). As the current guidelines for the permanent diaconate in the United States point out, the nurturing and deepening of mutual, sacrificial love between husband and wife constitute perhaps the most significant involvement of a deacon's wife in her husband's public ministry in the Church (*Guidelines*, NCCB, p. 110). Today especially, this is no small service.

In particular, the deacon and his wife must be a living example of fidelity and indissolubility in Christian marriage before a world which is in dire need of such signs. By facing in a spirit of faith the challenges of married life and the demands of daily living, they strengthen the family life not only of the Church community but of the whole of society. They also show how the obligations of family, work and ministry can be harmonized in the service of the Church's mission. Deacons and their wives and children can be a great encouragement to all others who are working to promote family life.

Mention must also be made of another kind of family, namely the parish, which is the usual setting in which the vast majority of deacons fulfill the mandate of their ordination "to help the bishop and his presbyterate." The parish provides an ecclesial context for your ministry and serves as a reminder that your labors are not carried out in isolation, but in communion with the bishop, his priests and all those who in varying degrees share in the public ministry of the Church. Permanent deacons have an obligation to respect the office of the priest and to cooperate conscientiously and generously with him and with the parish staff. The deacon also has a right to be accepted and fully recognized by them and by all for what he is: an ordained minister of the word, the altar, and charity.

Given the dignity and importance of the permanent diaconate, what is expected of you? As Christians we must not be ashamed to speak of the qualities of a servant to which all believers must aspire, and especially deacons, whose ordination rite describes them as "servants of all." A deacon must be known for fidelity, integrity, and obedience, and so it is that fidelity to Christ, moral integrity and obedience to the bishop must mark your lives, as the ordination rite makes clear (cf. also *Ad Pascendum*, Introduction). In that rite the Church also expresses her hopes and expectations for you when she prays:

> Lord, may they excel in every virtue: in love . . . concern . . . unassuming authority . . . self-discipline and in holiness of life. May their conduct exemplify your commandments and lead your people to imitate their purity of life. May they remain strong and steadfast in Christ, giving to the world the witness of a pure conscience. May they . . . imitate your Son, who came, not to be served but to serve.

Dear brothers, this prayer commits you to lifelong spiritual formation so that you may grow and persevere in rendering a service that is truly edifying to the People of God. You who are wives of permanent deacons, being close collaborators in their ministry, are likewise challenged with them to grow in the knowledge and love of Jesus Christ. And this of course means growth in prayer—personal prayer, family prayer, liturgical prayer.

Since deacons are ministers of the word, the Second Vatican Council invites you to constant reading and diligent study of the Sacred Scriptures, lest—if you are a preacher—you become an empty one for failing to hear the word in your own heart (cf. *Dei Verbum*, 25). In your lives as deacons you are called to hear and guard and do the word of God, in order to be able to proclaim it worthily. To preach to God's people is an honor that entails a serious preparation and a real commitment to holiness of life.

As ministers of the altar you must be steeped in the spirit of the liturgy, and be convinced above all that it is "the summit toward which the activity of the Church is directed and at the same time the source from which all her power flows" (cf.*Sacrosanctum Concilium*, 10) You are called to discharge your office with the dignity and reverence befitting the liturgy, which the Council powerfully describes as being "above all the worship of the divine majesty" (ibid., 33). I join you in thanking all those who devote themselves to your training, both before and after your ordination, through programs of spiritual, theological, and liturgical formation.

"Sing a new song unto the Lord! Let your song be sung from mountains high!" Sing to him as servants, but also sing as friends of Christ, who has made known to you all that he has heard from the Father. It was not you who chose him, but he who chose you, to go forth and bear fruit—fruit that will last. This you do by loving one another (cf. Jn 15:15ff.). By the standards of this world, servanthood is despised, but in the wisdom and providence of God it is the mystery through which Christ redeems the world. And you are ministers of that mystery, heralds of that gospel. You can be sure that one day you will hear the Lord saying to each of you: "Well done, good and faithful servant, enter into the joy of your Lord" (cf. Mt 25:21).

Dear brothers and sisters, as one who strives to be "the servant of the servants of God," I cannot take leave of you until, together, we turn to Mary, as she continues to proclaim: "I am the servant of the Lord" (Lk 1:38). And in the example of her servanthood we see the perfect model of our own call to the discipleship of our Lord Jesus Christ and to the service of his Church.

Address on Social Justice Issues
Hart Plaza

Dear Friends,

I am happy that, almost at the end of my second pastoral visit to the United States, I am able to address such a large number of people in this well-known industrial city of Detroit. I greet all of you most cordially: Christian leaders and leaders of other religions; civic leaders from the federal, state, and municipal governments; people of various races and ethic backgrounds; fellow Catholics; Christian and non-Christian brothers and sisters; men and women of good will!

I feel that I must thank the Lord our God for this wonderful occasion. Detroit is a place where work, hard daily work, that privilege, duty, and vocation of the human person (*Laborem Exercens,* 9), is truly a distinctive characteristic of urban life. This is indeed a city of workers, and very many of you here—men and women, younger people and older people, immigrants and native-born Americans—earn your living and that of your families in and around Detroit through the work of your hands, your mind, indeed your whole person. And many of you suffer from the problems that not infrequently characterize the work situation in an industrial urban setting.

This is why I would like to make reference to a subject which, as you are well aware, is close to my heart. This subject is social progress and human development in relation to the requirements of justice and to the building of a lasting peace, both in the United States and throughout the world.

Of course, dear friends, dear people of Detroit and this whole area, it is you I have primarily in mind in dealing with such a subject, you have been created in the image and likeness of God, you who have been redeemed by the blood of the Savior, you who are children of

God and brothers and sisters of Christ, you who for all of these reasons possess an incomparable dignity. But in looking at you assembled here in Hart Plaza, I see beyond all the people of this country and the peoples of the whole world. I see all the men and women who, like you, are confronted every day anew with the obligation and challenge to provide for their livelihood and for the livelihood of their family through their own work. Work means any activity, whether manual or intellectual, whatever its nature or whatever its circumstances, by which a human person earns his or her daily bread and contributes to science and progress, civilization and culture (cf. *Laborem Exercens*, 1). Human work is such a fundamental dimension of human existence, that one cannot speak about it without touching upon all its aspects.

Social progress and human development are the concern of all. They are of particular concern to the Church. From the very beginning of her existence in time, the Church has endeavored to fathom the total richness of the message which Jesus Christ proclaimed both by his words and his actions. Sent by the Father to assume our humanity and bring salvation to all, the Lord Jesus Christ provided us with the key to understanding our humanity. He taught us about our origin and destiny, which are in God. He taught us the transcendent value of all human life and the supreme dignity of the human person, created in the image and likeness of God (cf. Gn 1:27). He taught us that human life is fulfilled in knowing and loving God, and in loving our neighbor according to the measure of God's love for us. He invited us to follow him, to become his disciples. He summoned us to be converted in our hearts by entering into the mystery of his passion, death, and resurrection. He revealed that we are God's partners in bringing creation to fulfillment. And now he fashions us into a chosen people, a communion of faith with a commitment to his Kingdom.

In fidelity to Christ, the Church has endeavored to bring his message to bear on all aspects of life, throughout the changing circumstances in the course of the centuries, bringing out from the heritage of the gospel "both the new and the old" (Mt 13:52). New challenges affecting the life of every person individually and of society as a whole have presented themselves at every turn on the path of humanity through history. In trying to meet those challenges, the People of God have always turned to the message of Jesus, in order to discover the principles and the values that would ensure solutions in consonance with the dignity and the destiny of the human person. Throughout her history, the Church has listened to the words of Scripture and has sought to put them into practice, in the midst of different political, economic, and social circumstances. This has been truly a common effort. Individual Christians have struggled to be faithful to the gospel inspiration in their daily lives; centers of learning have contributed their specialized studies; groups and associations have addressed issues of particular concern; communities have developed practical initiatives; individual bishops and episcopal conferences have provided guidance; and the Magisterium of the Church has made pronouncements and issued documents. In a continuous interaction the Church has thus developed a tradition of thought and practical guidelines that are called the social teaching of the Church. This social teaching has been expressed in the documents of the Second Vatican Council and in the writings of the popes, who have systematically addressed the rapid changes in contemporary society.

Also today, the various categories of the People of God, according to their respective calling, continue to address the social problems in their various historical and cultural sayings.

Today, dear friends, on the last day of my second extended visit to the United States of America, I would urge you to continue your personal involvement in that never-ending quest for justice and peace. Under the guidance and inspiration of the Church's Magisterium, which is that of the pope and the bishops in union with him, each one of you is called to make a contribution. Each one of you must be instrumental in promoting a social order that respects the dignity of the human person and serves the common good. Each one of you has an irreplaceable contribution to make to secure a social order of justice in peace. In your country today, participation at different levels of economic, social, and political life has greatly intensified the awareness of the unique dignity of every human person and at the same time reinforced your sense of responsibility to yourselves and to others. As Christians you find in your faith a deep motivation for your social responsibility and involvement. Do not let this hour pass without renewing your commitment to action for social justice and peace. Turn to the gospel of Jesus Christ to strengthen your resolve to become instruments for the common good! Learn from the gospel that you have been entrusted with the justice and peace of God! We are not merely builders of justice according to the standards of this world, but we are bearers of the life of God, who is himself justice and peace! Let your endeavors to achieve justice and peace in all the spheres of your lives be a manifestation of God's love.

In a setting similar to this one some eight years ago in New York's Yankee Stadium, I proclaimed the gospel challenge contained in the parable of the rich man and Lazarus. You are all familiar with this marvelous lesson in social responsibility which Jesus left us. Knowing your faith and your openness to challenge, I now ask you today: What have you done with this parable? How many times in the past eight years have you turned to that parable to find inspiration for your Christian lives? Or have you put it aside thinking that it was no longer relevant to you or to the situations in your country?

In any modern society, no matter how advanced, there will always be situations, some old and some new, that summon your Christian sense of justice to action. Our Lord has said, "The poor you will always have with you (Mt 26:11)." You must therefore discover the poor in your midst. There is poverty among you when the old and the weak are neglected and their standard of living constantly declines. There is poverty when illness takes away the wage earner from a family. There are material need and suffering in those areas or groups where unemployment risks becoming endemic. There is poverty in the future of those who cannot enjoy the benefits of basic education.

Some modern technological developments contain the potential for new hardships and injustice and must therefore be part of our concern. The introduction of robotics, the rapid development of communications, the necessary adaptation of industrial plants, the need to introduce skills in management—these are but some of the factors that, if not analyzed carefully or tested as to their social cost, may produce undue hardship for many, either temporarily or more permanently.

These are just a few areas where our social responsibility is challenged. Others include the situation of marriage and family life and the factors that threaten their underlying values; the respect for the sacredness of unborn human life; the situation of newly arrived immigrants; open or disguised expressions of discrimination based on "race, origin, color, culture, sex, or religion" (*Octogesima Adveniens*, 16). To the degree that its social conscience is sensitive, every community will discover where instances of injustice or threats to peace still exist or are potentially present.

But the very attempt to look at some of the challenges in the domestic scene, brings us to another important consideration regarding progress and human development. I am referring to the international dimension.

Without implying in any way that domestic or national problems do not exist any more—and they most certainly do—it becomes ever more evident that such local or national problems, and their solutions, are fundamentally linked with realities that transcend the boundaries of countries. Not only do decisions taken by one nation affect other regions of the world, but the solution to many domestic problems can no longer be found except on an international, and even, a worldwide level. All major problems that concern the life of the human person in society have become world problems. Any decision that is envisaged in the political, economic, or social sphere must be considered in the context of its worldwide repercussions. What now most deeply affects any debate on social progress and human development is the fact of worldwide interdependence.

Already 20 years ago in 1967, Pope Paul VI wrote at the very beginning of his encyclical letter *On the Development of Peoples* (*Populorum Progressio*): "Today the principle fact that we must all recognize is that the social question has become worldwide" (3). In following years, this affirmation of Paul VI was further vindicated by a succession of events. There was the emergence on the political scene of peoples who, after centuries of colonial domination and dependence, demanded ever more forcefully their rightful place among nations and in the international decision making. A worldwide economic crisis brought home the fact that there exists an increasingly interdependent economy. The continuing existence of millions of people who suffer hunger or malnutrition and the growing realization that the natural resources are limited make clear that humanity forms a single whole. Pollution of air and water threatens more and more the delicate balance of the biosphere on which present and future generations depend and makes us realize that we all share a common ecological environment. Instant communication has linked finance and trade in worldwide dependence.

The poorer nations of the world are inclined to view this interdependence as a continuing pattern of economic domination by the more developed countries, while the latter sometimes view interdependence as the opening up of new opportunities for commerce and export. Interdependence clearly demands that the relations between nations be seen in this new context and that the social question needs an appropriate ethic. Nobody can say anymore: "Let others be concerned with the rest of the world!" The world is each one of us!

When I addressed the participants of the Sixty-eighth Session of the International Labor Organization on June 15, 1982, I was able to state: "There is a common good which can no longer be confined to a more or less satisfactory compromise between sectional demands or between purely economic requirements. New ethical choices are necessary; a new world conscience must be created; each of us without denying his origin and roots of his family, his people and his nation, or the obligations arising therefrom, must regard himself as a member of this great family, the world community. . . . This means that the worldwide common good requires a new solidarity without frontiers" (10).

The Church's social teaching sees this new solidarity as a consequence of our faith. It is the attitude, in the international reality, of those who heed the Lord's commandment: "Love one another as I have loved you" (Jn 15: 12). It is the consequence of our faith in the mystery of creation that God has created every human person in his own image and likeness. Every human being is endowed with the same fundamental and inalienable dignity. Every individual is called to acknowledge this fundamental equality within the unity of the human family. Everyone is invited to respect the common destiny of everyone else in God. Everyone is asked to accept that the goods of the earth are given by God to all for the benefit of all.

For the disciple of Christ, solidarity is a moral duty stemming from the spiritual union of all human beings, who share a common origin, a common dignity, and a common destiny. In creating us to live in society, in a close network of relations with each other, and in calling us through redemption to share the life of the Savior not merely as individuals but as members of the pilgrim people, God himself has created our basic interdependence and called us to solidarity with all. This teaching is formulated in an incomparably effective manner in the parable of the good Samaritan, who took care of the man who was left half dead along the road to Jerusalem to Jericho. We all travel that road and are tempted to pass by on the other side. Referring to the Samaritan, who was moved by compassion, Jesus told his listeners: "Go, and do the same." Today, Jesus repeats to all of us when we travel the road of common humanity "Go, and do the same" (cf. Lk 10:37).

In speaking to you about social progress and human development, I feel, impelled to stress the international dimension because of the objective need to promote a new worldwide solidarity.

There is also another reason why I am especially mindful today of the larger international scene. You well know that the Bishop of Rome and the Holy See follow closely international activities and therefore have a special interest in the work of the United Nations Organization in New York. I would have liked very much to visit once again its headquarters, as I did in 1979, and as Pope Paul VI did in 1965. I regret that I am not able to accept at this time the kind invitation which the secretary general of the United Nations has extended for a new visit. The interest of the Catholic Church in this international organization is linked to the importance of the issues that it treats and to the reasons for which it was founded. The work for the establishment and maintenance of a just and lasting peace is a goal that deserves support and collaboration. This is in fact why the United Nations Organization was created in the first place, in the bright daylight which followed the long drawn-out night of the Second World War. I pray that despite its inevitable shortcomings it will be able to fulfill ever more effectively its unique role of service to the world, a service that the world truly needs.

The United Nations deals with disarmament and arms control—the control of nuclear weapons in the first place, but, also biological, chemical, and conventional weapons. Its patient, painstaking, and sometimes even frustrating dedication to this cause of paramount importance for all the world and all its people is recognized and appreciated as being an incentive and support for the bilateral negotiations by the superpowers for arms reduction. Here it is indeed a question that must be addressed with unfailing commitment, extreme lucidity, and a clear sense of the value of human life and the integrity of creation.

The United Nations is also concerned with many of the other conditions for true peace. It is fitting here to reflect on some of them in relation to the international dimension of the social question.

In the first place, I would like to single out the concern for human rights. You remember, I am sure, that the United Nations adopted, more than 40 years ago, the Universal Declaration of Human Rights. The basic inspiration of this important document was the recognition that the way toward a peaceful and just world must necessarily pass through the respect for each human being, through the definition and recognition of the basic human rights, and through the respect for the inalienable rights of individuals and of communities of peoples. The adoption of the Universal Declaration was followed over the years by many declarations and conventions on extremely important aspects of human rights, in favor of women, of children, of handicapped persons, of equality between races, and especially the two international covenants on economic, social, and cultural rights, and on civil and political rights, together with an optional protocol. In 1981, the General Assembly also adopted a solemn declaration against every

237

form of religious intolerance. The United Nations must also be given proper credit for having set up the Commission for Human Rights as a monitoring organ to follow carefully the positive and negative developments in this important field. The commitment of the United Nations to human rights goes hand in hand with its commitment to peace. Experience has taught that disrespect or lack of respect for human rights, oppression of the weak, discrimination because of sex, color, origin, race, or religion create conflict and jeopardize peace. Here again, what concerns human beings in any one place affects human beings everywhere.

Through the different specialized institutions and programs, the United Nations develops its commitment to a more just and equitable international society. This work and commitment include the struggle against disease and illiteracy; action undertaken for the advancement of women; protecting the rights of children and the handicapped; the development of international law; the peaceful use of atomic energy; the protection and the preservation of famous monuments which belong to the cultural patrimony of humanity; the defense of the environment; the struggle against hunger, malnutrition, and underdevelopment; and the defense of the homeless.

The existence and the activities of the United Nations Organization, its achievements and also its failures, underline in a dramatic way the need for reinforcing international authority at the service of the global common good. It is already a sign of great progress that the importance of global social issues and the need for effectively promoting peace are becoming more universally recognized. It is also a sign of hope that an international organization, formed by the great majority of states, tries, within the limited means at its disposal, and not withstanding internal and external difficulties to increase the awareness of worldwide problems and their appropriate solutions.

It is also a marvelous challenge for all the peoples and nations of the world—now that every day we become more aware of our interdependence—to be called upon by the urgent demands of a new solidarity that knows no frontiers. Now that we move toward the threshold of the millennium of Christianity, we are given the unique chance, for the first time in human history, to make a decisive contribution to the building up of a true world community. The awareness that we are linked in common destiny is becoming stronger; the efforts to reach that goal are being multiplied by men and women of good will in a diversity of activities—political as well as economic, cultural as well as social. People in all walks of life and nations and governments alike are being challenged in the name of our common humanity, in the name of the rights of every human being and in the name of the rights of every nation.

In order to succeed and give the correct answer to the many demands that the *de facto* interdependence of all nations makes upon the sense of solidarity of all, we must create a just balance between the constraints put by interdependence upon the nations and the call for effective solidarity addressed to all the nations. In the life of every nation, social progress and human development are ensured by the respect given to the rights of the human person. The human person's very existence in dignity and his or her rightful participation in the life of the community are safeguarded by the deep respect that every person entertains for the dignity and the rights of every fellow human being. In the same way, respect for the rights of peoples and nations must safeguard the existence in liberty of every nation and thus make possible its rightful and effective participation in all aspects of international life. Without this, it would be impossible to speak about solidarity. In order to be capable of global solidarity nations must first of all respect the rights of their citizens and in turn be recognized by their people as the expression of their sovereignty; secondly nations must respect the full rights of their fellow nations and know that also their rights as a nation will not be disavowed.

Dear friends, America is a very powerful country. The amount and quality of your achievements are staggering. By virtue of your unique position, as citizens of this nation, you are placed before a choice and you must choose. You may choose to close in on yourselves, to enjoy the fruits of your own form of progress and to try to forget about the rest of the world. Or, as you become more and more aware of your gifts and your capacity to serve, you may choose to live up to the responsibilities that your own history and accomplishments place on your shoulders. By choosing this latter course, you acknowledge interdependence, and opt for solidarity. This, dear friends, is truly a human vocation, a Christian vocation, and for you as Americans it is a worthy national vocation.

In drawing attention to the need for an ever greater social consciousness in our day, I also with to draw attention to the need for prayer. Prayer is the deepest inspiration and dynamism of all social consciousness. In speaking to the Bishops of America in 1983 I stated: "It is indeed in prayer that a social consciousness is nurtured and at the same time evaluated. It is in prayer that the bishop, together with his people, ponders the need and exigencies of Christian service. . . . Through prayer the Church realizes the full import of Christ's words: 'This is how all will know you for my disciples: your love for one another' (Jn 13:35). It is in prayer that the Church understands the many implications of the fact that justice and mercy are among 'the weightier matters of the law' (Mt 23:23). Through prayer, the struggle for justice finds its proper motivation and encouragement, and discovers and maintains truly effective means" (*Ad Limina Address*, December 3, 1983).

Finally, to you the Catholic people of Detroit and all this area I repeat the words with which Paul VI concluded his message to the Call to Action Conference that was held 11 years ago in this very City of Detroit: "In the tradition of the Church, any call to action is first of all a call to prayer. And so you are summoned to prayer, and above all to a greater sharing in Christ's Eucharistic Sacrifice. . . . It is in the Eucharist that you find the true Christian spirit that will enable you to go out and act in Christ's name." And for all of you dear friends, people of every religion, race and ethnic group, I ask God's help so that you may be ever more aware of global interdependence and ever more sensitive to human solidarity.

Homily at Detroit Eucharist
Pontiac Silverdome

Conduct yourselves in a way worthy of the gospel of Christ (Phil 1:27).

Dear Brothers and Sisters in Christ,

The apostle Paul addresses this appeal to the Christians of Philippi. And today the Church's liturgy repeats this appeal to all who believe in Christ. As my visit to your country comes to an end, it is my special joy this evening to reflect on those words with you, the people of the Church in Detroit, as well as visitors from elsewhere in Michigan, from nearby Canada, and from other areas.

From the humble beginnings of the foundation of Detroit in the year 1701, the proclamation of God's word in this region has continued unbroken despite hardships and setbacks and has reached a level of maturity and a fruitfulness unimagined by the early missionaries. Many years separate us from the first celebration of the Eucharist by the priests who accompanied Cadillac, the founder of Detroit, and yet we know that our communion this evening in the Body and Blood of Christ also links us with them and with all who have gone before us in faith.

With you, I give thanks to God for the courage, dedication, and perseverance of the many clergy, religious, and laity who worked so hard during all these years, first to share their faith with the Native Americans of this area, and then to preserve and spread the faith among those of almost every race and nation who settled here. I also give thanks with you for the intrepid Catholic faith of so many of your parents and grandparents who came to Michigan in order to find liberty and in order to build a better life for themselves and especially for you, their children, and grandchildren. Whatever may be the path by which you have received the gift of your Catholic faith, it is due in some measure to those who have gone before you here. Their voices are joined to that of Saint Paul when he says to us: "Conduct yourselves in a way worthy of the gospel of Christ."

We read this exhortation this evening in the light of the gospel parable of the workers sent by the owner of an estate into his vineyard, after he has agreed with them on the daily wage. Our Lord often taught through parables like this one. By using images from daily life, he led his hearers to insights about the Kingdom or Reign of God. Using parables, he was able to raise their minds and hearts from what is seen to what is unseen. When we remember that the things of this world already bear the imprint of God's Kingdom, it is not surprising that the imagery of the parables is so well suited to the gospel message.

On the one hand, the vineyard of which Jesus speaks is an earthly reality, as is the work to be done in it. On the other hand, the vineyard is an image of the Kingdom of God. This Kingdom is described in the gospels as "the vineyard of the Lord."

Let us reflect for a moment on the first of these realities—the earthly vineyard—as a workplace, as the place where you and I must earn our daily bread. As I said in the encyclical *Laborem Exercens*: "Man must work, both because the Creator has commanded it and because of his own humanity, which requires work in order to be maintained and developed. Man must work out of regard for others, especially his own family, but also for the society he belongs to, the country of which he is a child, and the whole human family of which he is a member, since he is the heir to the work of generations and at the same time a sharer in building the future of those who will come after him in the succession of history" (16).

Accordingly, the Church considers it her task to focus attention on the dignity and rights of workers, to condemn violations of that dignity and those rights, and to provide guidance for authentic human progress (cf. *Laborem Exercens*, 1). The Church's goal is to uplift ever more the family of mankind in the light of Christ's word and by its power.

Central to the Church's teaching is the conviction that people are more important than things; that work is "for man" and not man "for work"; that the person is both the subject and purpose of all work and cannot be reduced to a mere instrument of production; that the person is to be valued for what he or she is rather than for what he or she owns (cf. *Laborem Exercens*, 6,12; *Gaudium et Spes*, 35). This last truth in particular reminds us that the only gift we can offer God that is truly worthy of him is the gift of ourselves, as we discover in the message of today's gospel parable.

That message, as I mentioned, has to do with a spiritual reality, the Kingdom of God, toward which Jesus seeks to raise the minds and hearts of his listeners. He begins today's parable with the words: "The reign of God is like the case of the owner of an estate who went out at dawn to hire workmen for his vineyard" (Mt 20:1). That our Lord is speaking about more than just human work and wages should be clear from the owner's actions and the ensuing conflict between him and some of the workers. It is not that the owner refuses to honor the agreement about wages. The dispute arises because he gives the same pay to everybody, whether the person worked all day or only part of the day. Each receives the sum which had been agreed upon. Thus the owner of the estate shows generosity to the latecomers, to the indignation of those who had worked all day. To them this generosity seems to be an injustice. And what response does the owner give? "I am free," he says, "to do as I please with my money, am I not? Or are you envious because I am generous?" (Mt 20:15).

In this parable we find one of those seeming contradictions, those paradoxes, that appear in the gospel. It arises from the fact that the parable is describing two different standards. One is the standard by which justice is measured by things. The other standard belongs to the Kingdom of God, in which the way of measuring is not the just distribution of things but the giving of a gift, and, ultimately, the greatest gift of all—the gift of self.

The owner of the estate pays the workers according to the value of their work, that is, the sum of one denarius. But in the Kingdom of God the pay or wages is God himself. This is what Jesus is trying to teach. When it comes to salvation in the Kingdom of God, it is not a question of just wages but of the undeserved generosity of God, who gives himself as the supreme gift to each and every person who shares in divine life through Sanctifying Grace.

Such a recompense or reward cannot be measured in material terms. When a person gives the gift of self, even in human relations, the gift cannot be measured in quantity. The gift is one and undivided because the giver is one and undivided.

How can we receive such a gift? We look to Saint Paul for an answer. His words in the Letter to the Philippians are fascinating: "I firmly trust and anticipate that I shall never be put to shame for my hopes. . . . Christ will be exalted through me, whether I live or die. For, to me, 'life' means Christ; hence dying is so much gain" (Phil 1:20-21).

With these words of Saint Paul we find ourselves at the very heart of that standard of measurement which belongs to the kingdom of heaven. When we receive a gift, we must respond with a gift. We can only respond to the gift of God in Jesus Christ, his cross and resurrection, in the way that Paul responded with the gift of ourselves. All that Paul is, is contained in this gift of self: both his life and his death. The gift of a person's life cannot be valued merely in terms of the number of hours spent in an earthly vineyard.

Saint Paul, and everyone like him, realizes that one can never match or equal the value of God's gift of himself to us. The only measure that applies is the measure of love. And love's measure, as Saint Bernard says, is to love without measure (De Diligendo Deo, I,1). This makes it possible for the last to be first, and the first last (cf. Mt 20:16).

There is another episode in the gospel of Luke when Jesus says to one of the pharisees who is scandalized at the behavior of a woman known to be a sinner: "her many sins are forgiven . . . because of her great love" (Lk 7:47). We do well to reflect upon the love in the heart of this woman, who washed the Lord's feet with her tears and wiped them with her hair. We can imagine the bitter sorrow that led her to such an extravagant gesture. Yet by giving herself humbly to God, she discovered the far greater and undeserved gift of which we have spoken, namely, God's gift of himself to her. Through this exchange of gifts, the woman found herself once again, only now she

242

was healed and restored. "Your sins are forgiven," Jesus says to her, " . . . go in peace" (Lk 7: 48,50).

For us too, sinners that we are, it is all too easy to squander our love, to use it in the wrong way. And like the pharisees, we do not easily understand the power of love to transform. Only in the life, death, and resurrection of Christ do we come to see that love is the measure of all things in the Kingdom of God, because "God is love" (1 Jn 4:8). We can fully experience love in this life only through faith and repentance.

"Conduct yourselves in a way worthy of the gospel of Christ." As Christians we live and work in this world, which is symbolized by the vineyard, but at the same time we are called to work in the vineyard of the Lord. We live this visible earthly life and at the same time the life of the Kingdom of God, which is the ultimate destiny and vocation of every person. How then are we to conduct ourselves worthily in regard to these two realities?

In the Credo of the People of God proclaimed by my predecessor Paul VI, we find an answer to that question—an answer that reflects the faith of the Church in the light of the Second Vatican Council, particularly the *Pastoral Constitution on the Church in the Modern World*:

> We confess that the Kingdom of God . . . is not of this world . . . and that its growth cannot be confused with the progress of civilization, science or technology. The true growth of the Kingdom of God consists in an ever deeper knowledge of the unfathomable riches of Christ; in an ever stronger hope in eternal blessings, in an ever more fervent response to the love of God. . . . But this same love also leads the Church to show constant concern for the true temporal welfare of people. . . . Although the Church does not cease to remind her children that here they have no lasting city, she also urges them to contribute—according to their vocation and means—to the welfare of this their earthly home . . . and to devote themselves to helping the poorest and neediest of their brothers and sisters. This intense solicitude of the Church . . . for the needs of people, their joys and hopes, their griefs and labors, is nothing other than her great desire to be present with them in order to illuminate them with the light of Christ and gather them into one in him who alone is their Savior (*Credo of the People of God*, June 30, 1968).

Dear brothers and sisters, these words tell us what is meant by conduct worthy of the gospel of Christ—that gospel which we have heard and believed, and are called to live every day. And today in this Eucharistic Sacrifice we offer our work, our activities, our whole lives to the Father through his Son, Jesus Christ. We call upon God to accept the gift of ourselves.

> The Lord is just in all his ways
> and holy in all his works.

The Lord is near to all who call upon him,
to all who call upon him in truth" (Ps 145:17-18).

In the first reading, the prophet Isaiah speaks in the name of the Lord, who in the gospel parable is symbolized by the owner of the vineyard. The Lord says: "my thoughts are not your thoughts, nor are your ways my ways. . . . As high as the heavens are above the earth, so high are my ways above your ways and my thoughts above your thoughts" (Is 55:8-9).

And so, my brothers and sisters, "Conduct yourselves in a way worthy of the gospel of Christ," that is to say, measure the things of this world by the standard of the Kingdom of God.

Not the other way around!
Not the other way around!

Seek the Lord while he may be found,
call to him while he is near (Is 55:6).

He is near! The Lord is near!
The Kingdom of God is within us. Amen.

Departure from Detroit Metropolitan Airport

Mr. Vice-President, Dear Friends, Dear People of America,

Once again God has given me the joy of making a pastoral visit to your country, the United States of America. I am filled with gratitude to him and to you. I thank the vice-president for his presence here today, and I thank all of you from my heart for the kindness and warm hospitality that I have received everywhere.

I cannot leave without expressing my thanks to all those who worked so hard to make this visit possible. In particular I thank my brother bishops and all their collaborators, who for many months have planned and organized all the details of the last ten days. My gratitude goes to all those who provided security and ensured such excellent public order. I thank all those who have worked to make this visit above all a time of fruitful evangelization and prayerful celebration of our unity in faith and love.

I am also grateful to the people of other churches and creeds and to all Americans of good will who have accompanied me, in person or through the media, as I traveled from city to city. A particular word of thanks goes to the men and women of the media for their constant and diligent assistance in bringing my message to the people, and in helping me to reach millions of those with whom otherwise I would have had no contact. Most importantly, I am grateful to all those who supported me by their prayers, and the sick, who are so dear to the heart of Jesus Christ.

As I leave, I express my gratitude to God also for what he is accomplishing in your midst. With the words of Saint Paul, I too can say with confident assurance "that he who has begun the good work in you will carry it through to completion, right up to the day of Christ Jesus" (Phil 1:6-7). And so I am confident too that America will be ever more conscious of her responsibility for justice and peace in the world. As a nation that has received so much, she is called to continued generosity and service toward others.

As I go, I take with me vivid memories of a dynamic nation, a warm and welcoming people, a Church abundantly blessed with a rich blend of cultural traditions. I depart with admiration for the ecumenical spirit that breathes strongly throughout this land, for the genuine enthusiasm of your young people, and for the hopeful aspirations of your most recent immigrants. I take with me an unforgettable memory of a country that God has richly blessed from the beginning until now.

America the beautiful! So you sing in one of your national songs. Yes, America, you are beautiful indeed, and blessed in so many ways:

> In your majestic mountains and fertile plains;
> In the goodness and sacrifice hidden in your teeming cities and
> expanding suburbs;
> In your genius for invention and for splendid progress;
> In the power that you use for service and in the wealth that you
> share with others;
> In what you give to your own, and in what you do for others
> beyond your borders;
> In how you serve, and in how you keep alive the flame of hope
> in many hearts;
> In your quest for excellence and in your desire to right all
> wrongs.

Yes, America, all this belongs to you. But your greatest beauty and your richest blessing is found in the human person: in each man, woman, and child, in every immigrant, in every native-born son and daughter.

For this reason, America, your deepest identity and truest character as a nation is revealed in the position you take toward the human person. The ultimate test of your greatness is the way you treat every human being, but especially the weakest and most defenseless ones.

The best traditions of your land presume respect for those who cannot defend themselves. If you want equal justice for all, and true freedom and lasting peace, then, America, defend life! All the great causes that are yours today will have meaning only to the extent that you guarantee the right to life and protect the human person.

> Feeding the poor and welcoming refugees;
> Reinforcing the social fabric of this nation;

245

Promoting the true advancement of women;
Securing the rights of minorities;
Pursuing disarmament, while guaranteeing legitimate defense: all this will succeed only if respect for life and its protection by the law is granted to every human being from conception until natural death.

Every human person—no matter how vulnerable or helpless, no matter how young or how old, no matter how healthy, handicapped or sick, no matter how useful or productive for society—is a being of inestimable worth created in the image and likeness of God. This is the dignity of America, the reason she exists, the condition for her survival—yes, the ultimate test of her greatness: to respect every human person, especially the weakest and most defenseless ones, those as yet unborn.

With these sentiments of love and hope for America, I now say goodbye in words that I spoke once before: "Today, therefore, my final prayer is this: that God will bless America, so that she may increasingly become—and truly be—and long remain—'One country with liberty and justice for all' " (October 7, 1979).

May God bless you all.

God bless America!

The Office of Publishing and Promotion Services wishes to thank the following presenters for consenting to have their talks included in this publication.

Mrs. Alfretta M. Antone, Vice-President
Salt River Pima-Maricopa Indian Community, Arizona, with grateful thanks
   to the Tekakwitha Conference, Fr. Michael Galvin, Fr. Gilmore Hemauer

Sister Helen Maher Garvey, BVM, President
Leadership Conference of Women Religious

Mrs. Donna Hanson, Chairperson
United States Bishops' National Advisory Council

Dr. Maher M. Hathout, M.D., Spokesman
Islamic Center of Southern California

Dr. Patrick S. Hughes, Director
Pastoral Ministries
Archdiocese of San Francisco

Rev. Frank J. McNulty, Pastor
Blessed Sacrament Church, Roseland, New Jersey

Venerable Dr. Havanapola Ratanasara

Swami Swahananda, Minister
Vedanta Society of Southern California

Rev. Stephen Tutas

Rabbi Mordecai Waxman, Honorary President
Synagogue Council of America

Rabbi Alfred Wolf, Director
Skirball Insititute on American Values of the American Jewish Committee
Rabbi Emeritus; Wilshire Boulevard Temple

Columbia Dialogue Group:

The Reverend James E. Andrews, Stated Clerk
Presbyterian Church (U.S.A.)

Rev. Dr. Harold C. Bennett, President, Treasurer
Executive Committee
Southern Baptist Convention

The Reverend Dr. Ralph A. Bohlman, President
The Lutheran Church—Missouri Synod

The Most Reverend Edmond Lee Browning, Presiding Bishop
The Episcopal Church

The Reverend Dr. Arie R. Brouwer, General Secretary
National Council of the Churches of Christ in the U.S.A.

The Reverend Robert C. Campbell, General Secretary
American Baptist Churches in the U.S.A.

Herbert W. Chilstrom, Bishop
Evangelical Lutheran Church in America

Bishop Philip R. Cousin, Secretary
Council of Bishops
African Methodist Episcopal Church

Dr. Paul A. Crow, Jr., President
Council on Christian Unity
Christian Church (Disciples of Christ)

The Reverend James R. Crumley, Jr., D.D., Bishop
Lutheran Church in America

Bishop J. Clinton Hoggard
Fourth Episcopal Area
African Methodist Episcopal Zion Church

The Reverend John O. Humbert, General Minister, President
Christian Church (Disciples of Christ)

Bishop Earl G. Hunt, Jr., President
Council of Bishops
United Methodist Church

Archbishop Iakovos, Primate
Greek Orthodox Archdiocese
North and South America

Dr. T. J. Jemison, President
National Baptist Convention, U.S.A., Inc.

The Reverend C. J. Malloy, General Secretary
Progressive National Baptist Convention, Inc.

The Most Reverend Archbishop Torkom Manoogian
Primate, Eastern Diocese
Armenian Apostolic Church of America

The Reverend Dr. Gerald F. Moede, General Secretary
Consultation on Church Union

The Reverend Avery D. Post, President
United Church of Christ

The Reverend Dr. David W. Preus, Presiding Bishop
The American Lutheran Church

The Most Reverend Metropolitan Philip Saliba
Antiochian Orthodox Christian Archdiocese of New York and
All North America

The Most Reverend John F. Swantek, Prime Bishop
Polish National Catholic Church of America

Dr. Sylvia Talbot

The Most Blessed Theodosius, Primate
Archbishop of Washington
Metropolitan of All America and Canada
The Orthodox Church in America

Ms. Carolyn Weatherford, Executive Director
Woman's Missionary Union

Dr. George Hunston Williams
Hollis Professor of Divinity Emeritus
Harvard Divinity School

Dr. Thomas Zimmerman
International Lausanne Conference